CW01067326

Towards Corporeal Cosmopolitanism

Towards Corporeal Cosmopolitanism

Performing Decolonial Solidarities

Anjana Raghavan

ROWMAN &
LITTLEFIELD
INTERNATIONAL

London • New York

Published by Rowman & Littlefield International Ltd
Unit A, Whitacre Mews, 26–34 Stannary Street, London SE11 4AB
www.rowmaninternational.com

Rowman & Littlefield International Ltd.is an affiliate of Rowman & Littlefield
4501 Forbes Boulevard, Suite 200, Lanham, Maryland 20706, USA
With additional offices in Boulder, New York, Toronto (Canada), and Plymouth (UK)
www.rowman.com

British Library Cataloguing-in-Publication Data
A catalogue record for this book is available from the British Library

ISBN: HB 978-1-78348-795-0

Library of Congress Cataloging-in-Publication Data Available

ISBN: 978-1-78348-795-0 (cloth : alk. paper)
ISBN: 978-1-78348-796-7 (electronic)

♾™ The paper used in this publication meets the minimum requirements of American
National Standard for Information Sciences – Permanence of Paper for Printed Library
Materials, ANSI/NISO Z39.48–1992.

Printed in the United States of America

For my *Amma* and *Appa*: your love makes everything possible.

Contents

viii Contents

Acknowledgements

Remembering and expressing gratitude is a profound privilege. It is also a reminder of the tremendous support and love that have been given so freely and generously to me. I am almost certain that I will not be able to thank everyone I want to, so my first debt of gratitude is to the people I am unable to name here, and to every one of my extraordinary teachers. Thank you all.

To my editors, Dhara Patel, Mike Watson and Anna Reeve (who was with me at the beginning), thank you for being so patient with my anxiety and my never-ending stream of questions. You have been remarkable bearers of gentleness, patience and guidance.

My special thanks to Anisha Verghese, my dear friend and wonderful artist who designed the cover image. You *saw* the book I wrote.

I do not know who you are, but to the person who read and reviewed my final manuscript, thank you for your time, your attention to detail and your faith in my work. It means the world to me. Many thanks to Dr. Jimmy Casas Clausen for your generous solidarity, and also to my other anonymous reviewer, both of whose support and discerning comments were invaluable.

To friends and colleagues who read and responded to chapters, ideas and pieces of work, my enormous gratitude (in mostly chronological order): Veronique Pin-Fat, for saying yes the first time; Andy Price, for setting me on the path to this book; Pavithra Prasad, for believing and always knowing what I needed; Padma Govindan, for navigating minefields with me; Mathangi Krishnamurthy, for your attentiveness and ready laughter; Desirée Reynolds, for your insights and love; and L. Ramakrishnan, for combining intellectual incisiveness with such kindness.

I also owe much gratitude to my colleagues and friends at work who gave me greatly needed emotional, intellectual and material support as I completed this mammoth task: Julia 'academic fairy godmother' Hirst, Jon Dean, Cinnamon Bennett and Ian Woolsey.

To my dearest friends, who have listened to endless reams of my thoughts, panics and ramblings, no thanks will suffice: Sharanya Manivannan, for a timeless bond; Aniruddhan Vasudevan, for sharing in my fears and hopes; Bob Jeffery, for your steadfastness and presence; Niveditha Subramaniam, for your wisdom and sweetness; Beth Kamunge, for your incredible kindness; Carissa Honeywell, for your generosity and affection; and Mark Pendleton, for always renewing my spirits.

And, this final debt of enormous love and gratitude to the people who have been my keepers: my parents, grandparents and brother, for your infinite love, patience and support; and Robert Davies, for your deliberate love, quiet strength and superior editing skills.

Note from the Author

Double quotation marks have been used to indicate terms which may have multiple, ironic, or particularly contentious meanings and/or implications.

Introduction

Incanting the Body into the Political

The dictionary meanings of the word "introduce" indicate dual purposes – one, to bring something *new* into the world; and, two, to make *known* by *name*, or, put another way, to render *visible*. In a way, all naming is a kind of making; sometimes generative and beautiful, and at others, deeply violent. A thing *known* is always a thing named. The complex necessities and mysteries of naming are wonderfully captured in Walter Benjamin's (1979) writing, where he delicately teases out the intricacies of naming the self through the naming of "others". For Benjamin, the naming of the "other" is really a communication of the self (Benjamin 1979, 110). The politics of naming, of rendering visible, are of central importance to this book, the beginnings of which lie in my doctoral research. To introduce this book, then, I must recount some stories, and, in the simplest sense, this is also what fuels the core questions that I grapple with in, and through, my work: the task of storytelling, the place of storytellers and the myriad ways in which stories travel.

It would not be an exaggeration to say that my meeting with cosmopolitanism was completely unplanned and somewhat strange. Having resided squarely in the disciplinary spaces of cultural studies, feminist and postcolonial theory, I remain wary of spaces that advocate ideals of universalism and lofty solidarities of "humanity". My work has always been interested in questions of multiplicities and the exploration of otherness, often stemming from my own experiences as a South Asian, Tamil woman occupying multiple positions across vectors of privilege, as well as vicious exclusions. Cosmopolitanism, both as politics and idea, was therefore not really within my orbit of work, or if it was, I did not call it by that name. When I began my doctoral programme, I had been teaching in India for some time, following the completion of a master's degree in cultural studies in Britain, as well as a few years spent working in the nonprofit sector in India – specifically in the areas of gender, sexuality and advocacy – trying to help build communities of support, communication and information, mostly among vulnerable women and children. My first teaching stint was a zealous attempt to teach critical social theory and feminism at an all-women's college in India. My new-found, radical, privileged, poststructural language and enthusiasm, combined with my still-developing skills in critique and translation, as well as extant social, cultural and moral rules, brought me up against the crushing, deafening silences of exclusions through gender, sexuality, class, colour, religion, age, caste, appearance and speech. I also became increasingly aware of my own limitations in speaking, as well as listening. Of all the silences that I encountered – and in this, I include my experiences with everyday living, as well as in the worlds of theory making, and the enormous spaces in-between, where we are always theorising practice and practising theory, and making extraordinary strides and messes – the silence of bodies was the loudest. Hearing silences is also a function of positionality, of course, and I wholly acknowledge and claim the influences and elisions of being woman, being non-white and being victim to un-numbered and un-named abuses, in my own sensitivity to some silences over others. Bodies have so many stories to tell, but they are bound, gagged the tightest, bludgeoned, disciplined the hardest and reminded of their own inadequacy and inferiority, by discourses of science, culture, religion and societal structures at large. I began to consider the absurd, difficult and painful contradictions of my own positionality, in India, as an academic, a committed feminist, a nonbinarist, and a woman of privilege and of marginalisation. My racialised experiences in Britain underscored my exclusions in particular, often violent ways, but my cultural and economic privileges protected me in other ways. The cacophonous mess of contradictions I was left with brought me back to Gayatri Chakraborty Spivak's (1988) question, 'Can the Subaltern Speak?', and I found myself unable to understand it, let alone answer it, with the certainty I used to possess. It came to me that perhaps the question is not so much whether the subaltern *can* speak – they do, all the time – but whether there exist spaces for listening. Spaces where privilege names itself and opens up to comprehension, accountability and love.[1] I began, then, slowly and clumsily to dismantle the dictionary of names that I had catalogued. I began to recognise that my treatment of "otherness" had foreclosed itself, in some important ways, to the possibilities of conversation.

It was roughly during this time that I took a break from teaching, to begin my doctoral study, and found myself eyeballs-deep in a week-long workshop on contemporary understandings and applications of cosmopolitanism, run by Indian and European academics. We read Immanuel Kant, Jürgen Habermas, David Held, Kwame Anthony Appiah, Seyla Benhabib and Martha Nussbaum. We debated the possibilities of global/local communities and an ethos that could encompass both universalisms and particularisms that could not only support a common "humanness" but also "celebrate differences". Almost everything we discussed and deliberated was around the possibility of dialogue. Almost everything we discussed and deliberated was rooted in the Enlightenment and Europe, in hetero-maleness, liberal Western democracy and whiteness. I came away not only feeling a little unsettled and curious but also very saddened, because it seemed to me that this kind of cosmopolitanism did not really have enough room to actually listen to all the stories it claimed to want to include. I also perceived some of these exclusions as being fundamentally marked upon the body as differences of the flesh. Humanness becomes a gradient of sorts here, increasing with the presence of an able, white (ostensibly performed), heterosexual masculinity and decreasing steadily with deviations from it. Thus, we witness the silencing of female bodies, non-white bodies, poor bodies, disabled bodies, *Dalit* bodies, queer bodies, "insane" bodies and many "other" bodies, who, for very particular reasons, could never be *cosmopolitan* humans in quite the same way. The reason I code these exclusions of "bodies" rather than selves, or identities, is that these identities are marked, performed and rendered (in)visible by and through the body. Furthermore, these so-called differences were often identified, inferiorised and *justified* using discourses of medical, psychoanalytical and biological "science" and employing the rhetoric of reason and empirical proof, making the understanding of cosmopolitan notions of humanness highly contested and precarious. Needless to say, this is not an attempt to debunk the discourse of science as a whole but simply to point out, à la Foucault, that all of these "rational", "empirical" systems of thought and knowledge were as susceptible to hierarchies and hegemonies of power as were any other systems of thought and knowledge. It was at this point that I began to conceive of mapping the exclusions of cosmopolitanisms as exclusions of bodies.

I must admit that at first I began in anger. Anger at the silences and elisions within these strands of cosmopolitanism that I had encountered and read. As I worked my way through parts of the enormous amounts of writing on cosmopolitanism, my initial anger was, as Audre Lorde (1984) writes, helpful in clarifying my thoughts. But, it is impossible to build a generative, compassionate political engagement, with only anger for a foundation, and the anger trapped me and hurt me after a while. So I looked for other voices and other stories, which spoke in productive, resistant ways, and had found some direction, from the anger. I found resonance in the works of Walter Mignolo, Pnina Werbner (2008), Gloria Anzaldúa, Breckenridge et al (2002), Boaventura DeSousa Santos and many "other" voices telling different stories of cosmopolitanism (See also Delanty 2012, Bose and Manjapra 2010 and Mehta 2000). Tales from many cultures and spaces about coloniality, indigenous resistances and subaltern solidarities that traversed the world. I slowly began to comprehend cosmopolitanism not only as a space of both tension and openness – a space that was inherently exclusive because of the ways in which its intellectual/historical legacy was co-opted by Europe and liberal political thought – but also as a space committed to dialogue and exchange. I began to think about the possibilities of articulating the silences of bodies here. With its formidable scope, depth and breadth, and the constant flow of new scholarship, cosmopolitanism emerged as the intellectual and political space to which I wanted to bring this work of naming, and make visible, these (Srinivasan, 1993). I write from many places: at the interstices of political philosophy, feminism, queer, social theory, literature and performance studies. Bodies are forever at the margins, within cracks and between boundaries, and so I write from these spaces of elision.

Thinking about a methodology to render visible, or to speak the abject, is a difficult task, especially when the very problem of invisibility is closely tied to the historical linearity of research methods, particularly in the social sciences. My work is almost entirely informed by feminist and decolonial undertakings of research as storytelling (see Anzaldúa 1987; Mignolo 2002a., 2002b.; Chamberlain 2003; Nagar 2014; Connolly-Shaffer 2010). In her powerful introduction to *Muddying the Waters: Coauthoring Feminisms across Scholarships and Activism*, Richa Nagar writes about the importance of 'radical vulnerability' (Nagar 2014, 13) in her own work, and, following Mignolo's (2000a) conception of conversation as an important research method, she argues for the importance of a 'politics without guarantees' (Nagar 2014, 14) which is open as well as radically vulnerable, allowing for both stories and their tellers to be multiplicitous and fluid to allow for returns and iterations. Stories are not really about endings, morals or singularity. They are, as Nagar observes, discursive narratives about relationality, power plays and social/institutional structures about saying and about not saying. Gaps and silences are an integral part of stories. It is in this sense that I use the phrase 'incanting the body', both in relation to Benjamin and his understanding of naming, as well as to Gloria Anzaldúa, who, in her writing, reveals the importance of speaking, chanting and storytelling as reclamation of indigenous spiritual identities and practices. In the feminist ways of resistance and reclamation, I want this book to be a space of naming and reclaiming emotional and bodily practices. To incant is also to repeat and to iterate, and repetition is about remembering, and it is in this sense that I want to incant bodies and feelings, to name and reclaim them into the realm of the political. Theoretically speaking, I do this work of reclamation through a critical and dialogic engagement, with selected political/philosophical/ideological renderings of contemporary visions of cosmopolitanism, and liberal, Euromerican and Kant-inspired strains, as well as radical, decolonial strains. Part of the explanation for choosing an arguably contentious phrase, 'liberal conceptions of cosmopolitanism' has largely to do with the way in which liberalism deals with what Mignolo terms 'colonial difference' (Mignolo 2000a, 2002b.). While this is by no means an accusation against liberal thought in general, it is an epistemological critique shared by a number of scholars.[2] Of course, cosmopolitanism has its own classifications into sociological, normative, legal, cultural and so on, and my nonadherence to these is motivated by two factors. The first is a larger critique of certain kinds of narrow classifications per se and the restrictions they place on conceiving a genuinely dialogic space. The second is that I have chosen to engage with a multiplicity of cosmopolitan narratives based on their openness to engage with dialogues around embodiment and affect. As David Harvey (2009) points out, there are so many different understandings of cosmopolitanism that identifying common strains of thinking between them is near impossible and 'as so often happens within the academy, these different traditions rarely communicate' (2009, 78). As my relationship with the scholarship around cosmopolitanism grew, the direction of my critique changed, and although the engagement with Euromerican, liberal understandings of cosmopolitanism is certainly critical, my focus is, ultimately, on the capacity for dialogue, and an opening up, rather than a closing off. That is to say, my critique of what I loosely frame as *liberal* strains of cosmopolitanism is by no means absolute and is particularly related to the elision of the body and is rooted in feminist and decolonial ways of resistance and reclamation.

This elaborate explanation of what I mean and do not mean by cosmopolitanism may well raise the question, why use the term *cosmopolitanism* at all, when it is clear that I have no single definition of it? This is an important question and one which I reflect on throughout my work. It would be difficult but possible to create a new term and a new lexicon that does not involve the term *cosmopolitanism* at all but carries over some of its valuable elements into a new space. However, doing so runs the risk of diminishing some of the constitutive violences and silences that form the rubric of the ideas that early understandings of cosmopolitanism were built on, and I believe that the historicity and memories of these violences must be retained, in order for us to conceive of new spaces. When remembrance is built into "knowing", when our knowledge of a place, a nation, a people or a culture is automatically connected with the knowledge of those who were/are silenced, violated and/or annihilated, then, we can find new names and new words. Until then, perhaps the old names will help us to always remember. The cosmopolitanisms I discuss in this book are broadly political, sociological and moral in their orientation. I have tried to craft a contrapuntal discussion of Kant-inspired, Euromerican understandings of cosmopolitanism, humanness and community, with Kant-critical, non-Western, subaltern articulations of cosmopolitanism. It is out of this dialogic firmament that I try to envision a cosmopolitanism of bodies – a corporeal cosmopolitanism.

In order to explore the possibilities of a corporeal cosmopolitanism, it becomes necessary to grapple with the ideological and political arcs of contemporary narratives of cosmopolitanism. Although chronological accounts of the *beginning* of cosmopolitan thought vary, it is generally conceded that one of the earliest articulations comes to us from Diogenes of Sinope (a founder of Cynic philosophy) (Nussbaum 2002, 6; Delanty 2009, 20), who proclaimed himself a 'citizen of the world', recognising identities and affiliations as a series of concentric circles beginning with the self and moving outwards to include the family, community, society and finally, the world. The polis was opened out to the notion of a larger political community (Nussbaum 2002, 9), and Stoicism wedded the ideas of virtue and human emotion to the notions of the polis and political life. Gerard Delanty (2009, 23–25) also notes that it was in the Hellenistic era, with the expansion of the Alexandrian empire, that the distinction between 'Greek' and 'barbarian' began to blur, creating a definitively cosmopolitan moment in European history. Costas Douzinas (2007), in his work, explains that cosmopolitanism in ancient Greece was composed of a well-ordered, hierarchical, closed space: the cosmos. The polis was seen as an earthly means of achieving this order. He also suggests that initially, in the time of the philosopher Zeno, Eros was offered as the god of the republic. With the advent of philosophers like Cicero, however, cosmopolitanism turned increasingly towards universal, 'rational' norms and global law (Douzinas 2007, 151–158) and paved the way for cosmopolitanisms of the European Enlightenment era. This is an important turn in the early history of cosmopolitanism, and as we will see, it is a tendency that has persisted. These liberal, Enlightenment-inspired strands of cosmopolitanisms still hold powerful sway in the articulation of contemporary understandings of cosmopolitan solidarity and world building. While it is certainly not my intention to reduce the "Enlightenment" into a monolithic experience, I am also acutely aware that, as social theorists and interdisciplinary interlocutors, we must deal in generalisations and extrapolations constantly. Thus, when I refer to European Enlightenment-inspired cosmopolitanisms, I refer not to the multiplicitous complexities of the Enlightenment as a political/intellectual period, but more to the ways in, and extents to, which a selection of its discourses (themselves subject to mechanisms of hegemonic power) has influenced our political, social and cultural imaginaries. These include, but are not restricted to, particular kinds of interpretations of the discourses of "rationality" and "reason" as linear, hetero-masculine ideals separate, and superior to, the messy femininity of emotions and "irrationality". Race and the influence of colonial discourses around white superiority are also integral to these discourses of rationality and reason. Many contemporary narratives of cosmopolitanism that draw both from the Enlightenment and the Kantian ideas of universal hospitality and perpetual peace, therefore, possess imbricated political and ideological edges – of liberty, science and equality on the one hand, and racism, misogyny and a violent binarism, on the other. The political, social and cultural constructions of "humanness" and the Enlightenment struggle for various kinds of freedoms must be understood as part of a larger complex of marginalisations and violences including, but not restricted to colonial slavery, similar to Mignolo's (2000a) observation that coloniality *is* the other face of modernity. Similarly, Harvey (2009), in his work, sets up geography and the understanding of space, particularly with reference to colonialism and the liberal collusion with colonial oppression. He identifies two major modes of the justification of colonialism as follows: the first, extreme mode was one that declared indigenous people nonhuman or subhuman, thus erasing their very existence as people, let alone as polity. The second, perhaps less obvious, was (what Harvey terms the *liberal, Kant-inspired justification*) the infantalisation of people who were deemed 'not mature enough' to be politically autonomous (Harvey 2009, 38–39). Harvey writes of liberalism: 'The individualism it contemplates is deracinated, universal, given over, in true Kantian fashion, to a cosmopolitanism of reason and rational action' (2009, 37). Closely related to the discourses of reason, rationality and coloniality is that of Cartesian dualism and the creation of mind/body hierarchies. The "scientific" reconfiguration of body as machine, and the mind as the seat of control, bearing resonances with Christian understandings of the body as a site of sin and excess, radically altered the ways in which humanness was conceived. The attribution of "reason" to the mind and hetero-masculinity, and "unreason" to the body and femininity was simply a subsequent step. Liberal cosmopolitanisms and our political and social lives at large also bear the legacies of these discourses in elaborate, subtle and often insidious ways.

In the collected essays volume on Enlightenment cosmopolitanism (Adams and Tihanov 2011), the editors provide a useful entry point to cosmopolitan thought of the era which included Kant's central work that continues to feature prominently in any discussion of cosmopolitanism today. Reed (2011) comments that the Enlightenment belief in humanness as a common substance is crucial to understanding the cosmopolitanism of that time. The commonality of the human, corporeal body too, is in this sense valid but often irrelevant in the face of conflict. Politics, Reed argues, 'has a cruder reach than culture, in a way deeper, in a way more superficial' (2011, 5). German subjugation under various European powers gave rise to a strange conjunction of strong nationalism and the idea of the world citizen, at this particular point in time. In fact, the 'world citizen' was really an 'internationally minded citizen of Europe' (Reed 2011, 9). Robertson (2011) too, argues that pre-Kantian German thinkers saw German patriotism as perfectly compatible with being a world citizen (Adams and Tihanov 2011, 13–14). As Harvey notes in his work, all universal theories have particularistic origins, and, to that extent, those origins always remain influenced by the 'imperializing moment' (Harvey 2009, 10). The subsequent association of the world citizen with Free Masons and the Illuminati however, damaged its popularity by associating it with radical Enlightenment and religious scepticism (Robertson 2011, 17). Kantian cosmopolitanism arose in this milieu and was fundamentally bound up with the idea of political progress (Reyna 2011, 110–132). As Tihanov remarks, cosmopolitanism in the modern world is primarily concerned with the foundation of a world political order, largely inspired and shaped by Kant's work (2011, 133–152). While the concept of peace was known in Europe through people like St. Paul and St. Pierre, these were primarily Christian notions of peace. It is important to remember, as Delanty notes (2009, 27–29), that this early articulation of morality and universal brotherhood within the Christian church imbued itself in the European imaginary of morality, peace and political community. To that extent, Christianity is philosophically inseparable from these ideas, however subtly, and this in turn affects the discourse or the lack of it, around the body as discussed previously. While Voltaire was the first to discuss the idea of 'eternal peace', Tihanov argues that Kant was the first to envision a 'universal peace' (2011, 137), separate from morality as such, and to challenge absolute sovereignty in Europe and promote geographical exploration and travel. The Kantian ideal in perpetual peace (1917) places republicanism and cosmopolitanism as complementary philosophies and lays emphasis on the structure of a universal morality based on reason. It is also worth noting, at this point, that scholars like Engseng Ho (2006), Walter Mignolo (2000a. 2002b.) and others, have pointed to other spaces and places such as India, the Middle East and Southeast Asia where too, the idea of cosmopolitanisms – cultural, linguistic and political – flourished centuries earlier. The "history" of cosmopolitanism is, therefore, not only extremely long and complex but it is also necessarily contested.

It is this contestation that has sustained and permitted numerous returns, including the one in contemporary scholarship, to the ideas of cosmopolitanism and reconfiguring the notions of *human community*. Given such a colossal historical background, my work is only able to deal with very specific and selective elements of contemporary cosmopolitanism, examining its elisions – both Cartesian and cultural – and offer other possibilities of envisioning cosmopolitan solidarities and political identities. Drawing a broad arc from Immanuel Kant's cosmopolitanism, this book will examine particular understandings of contemporary liberal cosmopolitanisms along with a parallel exploration of more marginal and critical/marginal understandings of cosmopolitanism, to provide an idea of existing theoretical rubrics, their potentials, as well as possible limitations. The emphasis on "humanity" as community, inspired by Kant's universal right to hospitality, means that many strains of contemporary liberal cosmopolitanisms draw heavily on Enlightenment ideals of reason and rationality, and are underpinned by Cartesian binaries of mind/body, as previously discussed, thus denying entry to the narratives of bodies. Because bodies as sites of knowledge, experience and legitimacy have been silenced and delegitimised for so long and across so many intellectual and practical traditions, articulating and recentering them is no easy task. It is for this reason that I engage a variety of scholarship on contemporary cosmopolitanism in critical conversations with each other and attempt to map the interstices and potential openings for new spaces, as well as critically identify the smooth, opaque spaces that will not admit bodies or their stories. Race, ethnicity, sexuality, class and gender – all extremely important to the discussion around cosmopolitanism – are profoundly embodied, affective concepts. They cannot be addressed without addressing bodily trauma, violence and the visceral emotionality that marks them. While cosmopolitanism can, and should be, envisioned as a productive space, in terms of its dialogic capacity to open up the impasses created for instance, within postcolonial and postmodern scholarship, its inability to engage with the corporeal and affective dimensions of belonging, identity and selfhood is a considerable obstacle. An articulation of any kind of global understanding of ethics or ways of living requires a constant engagement with vulnerability, especially in a world that is so deeply wounded by subjugations, colonialisms, violences and genocides. If cosmopolitan narratives are unable or unwilling to deal with the affective and corporeal repercussions of these kinds of experiences, they become closed, elite spaces, without the promise of open dialogue that forms the core of cosmopolitan engagement. The theoretical canvasses that I try to weave together are both vast and messy, and do not aim to provide any grand solutions. What I am trying to articulate is a deeper epistemological preclusion; one that is difficult to both locate and include. This preclusion is to do with the vocabulary of the political that feminist and subaltern scholars have long critiqued. My interest in using cosmopolitanism is motivated, in part, not only by the kind of appeal it continues to draw, despite these complicated histories, but also because of its unswerving commitment to dialogue as engagement. While consciously recognising that *dialogue* is a contentious word, often used in violent ways to silence marginalised voices, I am also attempting to reclaim the term in more equal, and generative ways. There is not, I believe, a readymade place for bodies to articulate themselves within many liberal cosmopolitan frameworks, imbued as they are with notions of solidarity that emerge from both theological and Western democratic ideas of community, and "brotherhood"; but one of the core aims of this book is to explore the possibility of mapping the invisibilisation of feeling, experiencing bodies and, ultimately, to find ways to open up into larger, kinder spaces of uncertainty and vulnerability.

Chapters one and two of the book, therefore, try to provide a broad theoretical trajectory, both of cosmopolitanism and of bodyscapes. In order to explore new articulations of cosmopolitanism, embodiment and affect, it is necessary to establish at least a loose theoretical narrative, which will function partially as a selective review of existing scholarship, as well as a critical creation of a theoretical canvas, upon which I base my own ideas. In chapter one, dealing with cosmopolitanism, theoretical explorations take the forms of selective, critical examinations of liberal cosmopolitan ideas around the notion of belonging and the different relationships between belonging and cosmopolitan community. The initial theoretical exploration of contemporary cosmopolitanism in chapter one aims to examine some important premises of liberal strains of cosmopolitanism and highlight their elisions, particularly with relation to corporeal and emotional identification and belonging. The objective is to create a reasonably balanced perspective of current trends in cosmopolitan thought which lays the ground for what will form the main focus of my work: the discourses of the body, affect and exclusions within contemporary cosmopolitanisms. Although new and important work on cosmopolitanism has examined subalternity, colonialism, feminism and so on, my work deals specifically with both the notional and actual absence of the body and affect within cosmopolitanism. This absence stems from larger epistemological and ontological questions around the understanding of exclusion, otherness and abjection. With its major discourses surrounding the ideas of human rights and indeed what constitutes the human itself, there is a telling silence around the corporeal and embodied understanding of the "human" in liberal cosmopolitan narratives. Liberal cosmopolitanisms, inspired by Kantian ideals, bear the broader criticism of subaltern and feminist scholarship of which the exclusion of the body and sexuality is an important part. However, the body also seems only to be marginally or indirectly present in many of the alternative narratives that deal with contemporary cosmopolitan thought.

Chapter two begins with a selective exploration of the body in feminism and queer scholarship, as well as in biopolitics, as it relates to political belonging and community formations. I look at post-Enlightenment conceptions of embodiment, with a view to critically examine their ubiquity and dominance, while simultaneously placing these conceptions in critical dialogue with postcolonial and subaltern conceptions of embodiment, affect and political community. The aim here, like in chapter one, is to create a selective theoretical trajectory within which to contextualise the exclusion of the body vis-à-vis cosmopolitan imaginations. The potential scope of this chapter is vast, and I therefore examine scholarship that productively and critically engages cosmopolitan understandings of identity and solidarity. The discourse of marginalisation is central to the elision of the body. Indeed, exclusion as a practice is almost always connected to the body and the prejudice that surrounds it – pathologising and delegitimising it, relegating it as a category to either medicine/biology or affect/irrationality, thus silencing ways of knowing and belonging that do not fall into public/political/rational/male realms. This chapter reveals the importance of corporealising our political and epistemological stances and creating an ethics of the body. It also considers the politics of exclusion and how they interpellate the creation of political identities and communities. The larger objective is to find conversant spaces where the questions of embodiment and corporeality directly challenge or intersect the ideas of cosmopolitanism and explore what we can do to encourage these conversations and how they might influence basic notions of citizenship, interiority and belonging. This chapter tries to clarify *why* it is important to conceive of an embodied cosmopolitanism.

Chapters three and four examine instances and spaces within which to locate this need for embodying and corporealising cosmopolitanism – what I have chosen to call *sites*. I use the term *site* rather than case study, because the methods of analysis I employ fall outside the traditional organisation of a case study. Place and space are important to the sites I analyse, but they are also sites of performance and affect, politics and resistance, and inequality and violence. The word *site* is also obliquely connected to the visual dynamics and the nuances of looking and being looked at. The sites that I focus on are meant to be intersectional; bringing together ethnicity, gender, sexuality, coloniality, class and performance as necessary elements in the understanding of community, identity and solidarity. There are a vast number of sites that one might explore to this end, but, acknowledging the limited focus of my own interest, I conceive of two such sites and discuss them over the course of these two chapters. One deals with queerness and cosmopolitanism within the Lesbian, Gay, Bisexual, Transgender, Queer, Intersex+(LGBTQI+) movement, with special focus on television and literary narratives of transgender, *thirunangai* communities in southern India. The other, explores, largely through literature, the multiple identity expressions of the diasporic community of Indo-Caribbean women located in the Caribbean. Both these sites speak about solidarities – political, affective, gendered and queer – in very powerful, embodied ways, and possess narratives that could contribute significantly to cosmopolitan notions of community formation. The rallying together of sexual minorities movements world over, in many ways, represents ideals espoused by cosmopolitanism, with specific reference to the liberal defence of "personal choice" in the so-called private realms of sexuality, desire and affect. The fight for individual, personal freedoms as part of liberal cosmopolitan solidarity is an important one. This chapter will explore some of the commonalities, as well as problems, with the Western "individual freedom" model of political solidarity. I also engage scholars like Massad (2002) who made powerful, though controversial arguments around the "Western" discourse around queerness as being potentially detrimental to "non-Western" articulations of queerness. Similarly, diasporic movement, travel, nomadism and even exile are important to understanding popular strains of cosmopolitanism, particularly, the notions of universal hospitality as outlined by Kant. The two sites that I have chosen thus engage directly and intimately with these cosmopolitan concerns, but they do so in radically embodied, affective ways.

The *thirunangai* communities in Tamil Nadu, India, bring a very specific and unique set of challenges to the commonly held notions of sexual plurality being cosmopolitan, as they destabilise and jettison the ideas of modernity, liberalism and Eurocentrism that contemporary narratives of cosmopolitanism often associate with ideas of "global" belonging and citizenship. Theoretically, I draw on the work of contemporary South Asian queer activists, highlighting the complex forms of queer solidarity in India and the differences and oppressions that intersect it. Chief among these are issues of colonialism, language, class, caste and ethnicity, all deeply embodied and affective factors. I place particular emphasis on how the vicissitudes of class, education and access have appropriated a certain liberal-rational language, making it impossible for "other" kinds of speech to be articulated. I also examine some legal and constitutional dimensions of queerness and sexuality in India and consider the relationship between queer-friendly legislation and the liberal cosmopolitan emphasis on constitutional intervention and change. In the final section of chapter three, I discuss television representations, as well as literary, autobiographical narratives of *thirunangais* from Tamil Nadu, where they articulate their visions and identities of themselves as transwomen and the kinds of communities they wish to create and inhabit, vis-à-vis theoretical and legal understandings of queer solidarity, political identity and community. The politics of queerness is an ever-changing, growing space, and my intention here is to try to provide but a glimpse into the complex, hybrid solidarities that have emerged in India. These postcolonial complexes of the West and the anti-West have theorised and articulated democracy and solidarity in new and challenging ways and provide different ways in which to understand the political, affective and corporeal as a contiguous space.

The Indo-Caribbean diasporic community that I write about, through literary narratives in chapter four, is similarly challenging because of its ethnic and national nuances, along with a very different relationship to the "West" and "Whiteness", and internationalism, once again complicating so-called traditional understandings of cosmopolitan ideals. The colonially forced migration from India to the Caribbean islands calls into question the dynamics of geography, as well as race, gender and sexuality, complicating the international quality of this diasporic movement. The focus on women is intended as a feminist inroad into the question of what it means to be a diasporic, coloured female sexual body in a so-called cosmopolitan space of multiplicities. The chapter deals with specific caveats of diasporic and exilic experiences and how they relate to cosmopolitanism in conjunction with chapters two and three. Once again, I use the theoretical work of Indo-Caribbean activist scholars, who write about the Indo-Caribbean immigration and the history of colonial indenture through the work of scholars. I also navigate academic work, alongside literary accounts, both quasi-fictional and nonfictional, written *by* Indo-Caribbean women on Indo-Caribbean women's experiences of identity, community and solidarity building through specific cultural phenomena and performativity. This is an important move, because both Indo-Caribbean women's literature and the academic scholarship go hand in hand, in keeping with the feminist method, where literature and theory are part of the same complex. The Indian and Indo-Caribbean subaltern spaces bring together some important thematic elements of cultural and linguistic colonialism as well as ways of conceiving the body that are very pertinent to non-Euromerican understandings of political/affective solidarities and community building.

Chapter five does not really aim for a conclusion (read: solution), in the traditional sense, since I offer my work as part of a conversation, not a completed narrative. This chapter tries to speak to the challenges and lacunae – both theoretical and performative – that the previous chapters throw up. I examine some key themes in contemporary, decolonial scholarship around cosmopolitanism and begin to build some theoretical articulations of corporeal cosmopolitanism. Here, I focus on the centrality of the erotic, the chthonic and the affective in community creation and political belonging. I use some key decolonial ideas, in combination with accounts of performative solidarities through music, dance, food and spiritual practices, both in *thirunangai* communities and amongst Indo-Caribbean women, to imagine from the borders the new possibilities of corporeal cosmopolitanism. In the course of imagining and arranging these long conversations between the seemingly incongruous realms of cosmopolitanism, body and affect, they have often displayed great resistance to being in dialogue. I constantly had to remind myself, of what Douzinas (2007) has to say about the earliest visions of cosmopolitanism, both European and non-European, that they were always rooted in dialogue – no matter how uncomfortable and jagged. In addition to which, subaltern and feminist scholarship of the past half-century has been proof enough of the increasing necessity for these difficult conversations. Now, more than ever, we have a need to speak, to ourselves, to each other, to the universe, to our ancestors, to our futures and to the larger bonds that hold us together as communities and societies, as ecosystems and planets. This book is only a micro-attempt at such a conversation, while always remembering that dialogue can never be an imposition, nor the only solution. When it *is* a possibility, I imagine such dialogue through these narratives and stories of political bodies, desiring bodies and resisting bodies. I envision them as dialogues of openness and understanding, of articulation and conflictual multiplicities. I write in the hope of newer, more expansive spaces which will nurture affective, corporeal and vulnerable cosmopolitanisms and ways of living that will allow us to speak, listen and inhabit our bodies and our worlds, with a sense of radical compassion and love.

NOTES

1 Thanks to Dr. Veronique Pin-Fat for teasing out this delicate and highly significant specificity in my work.

2 See Chatterjee 2004; Spivak 1999; Bhabha 2001.

Chapter 1

Locating Corporeal Cosmopolitanism
Theoretical Vicissitudes

It is difficult to clarify a single purpose for chapter one, because I want it to do many things at once. I want this chapter to capture some sense of the exciting vastness and divergence in cosmopolitan scholarship and provide a glimpse of the worlds that are imagined within it. I want this chapter to bear witness and chronicle the contributions that contemporary articulations of cosmopolitanism make to the creation of solidarities and communities. I also want it to witness the silences, exclusions and abjections that are contained in these narratives of cosmopolitanism, as well as to explore "other" cosmopolitanisms which respond to these silences and violences. I am unlikely to fully succeed on all counts, but I hope that will not deter me from making a genuine effort. The literature that I explore in this chapter is not only selective but also limited by constraints of space and specificity. The attempt to open up a conversation about corporeal cosmopolitanism requires both space – physical, emotional and intellectual – and people with whom to *have* this conversation. In reading about and around contemporary cosmopolitan literature, there have been some ideas that have struck me as particularly challenging to, or cooperative of (those two things are not always at odds), a space for embodied and affective cosmopolitan articulations. I am trying to provide a contextual, though selective, review of literature, but also create a kind of patchwork quilt of ideas, conceptual frameworks, challenges and contradictions within which to place my own ideas, thoughts and questions about approaching the notion of corporeal cosmopolitanism. By and large, liberal narratives of cosmopolitanism, both more and less conventional varieties, operate on certain understandings of reason and rationality, often derived, in varying degrees, from Enlightenment conceptions of them. This raises a complex set of debates around the participants – that is, who is deemed *capable* of reason and rationality, and in a more extended sense, of autonomy, sovereignty and citizenship, and why certain people are excluded from these spaces. It also raises questions about the *legitimacy* of the realms of unreason and irrationality – emotions, bodies, art – all become illegitimate conceptual frameworks in "serious" political, social and economic spaces governed by particular discourses of reason and rationality. These discourses of reason and rationality that influence so much of liberal cosmopolitan thought, also have specific understandings of, and relationships to, the idea of generality and universal notions of solidarity and community. I offer the suggestion that a binaristic reduction of debates around universalism and particularism is not always productive, but particularly so when thinking about cosmopolitan notions of belonging. In my own work, I try to problematise certain understandings of universalism, and also explore the possibilities of different conceptions and imaginations that match the scale and largeness of universalistic frameworks but are perhaps not restricted and articulated in the same ways.

This chapter, therefore, tries to engage with these sets of questions and ideas in existing cosmopolitan literature – both liberal and decolonial. The questions around participation, and exclusion, particularly in political cosmopolitanisms, often seem to manifest themselves in debates around the ideas of nationhood, patriotism and political and affective significance of the nation state. As Sara Ahmed (2014) so evocatively points out, the nation is the bearer of both bodies and emotions. Exploring the nuances of the expression 'soft touch' (Ahmed 2014, 2) as applied to a nation, she points to the call for nations to be 'harder' and less emotional. It is interesting that these calls to *harden* often come from emotional places that are critical of the liberal nation state model, which, as we know, is more inclined to follow a dispassionate, "objective" discourse of reason. Several cosmopolitan scholars argue for and against the significance of the nation state, while many of them provide hybrid alternatives, arguing that patriotism and cosmopolitanism are not in direct conflict with one another. My focus here is not so much on the structural ramifications of nation and postnation; or polis and cosmos, but rather of the *affective* and *embodied* elements of the same. What are the emotional and bodily implications of nationhood, national identity and statelessness? I explore contemporary cosmopolitan scholarship, both liberal and decolonial, pro- and antination, not with the aim or concluding the debate, but to acknowledge and accept its diversity and depth. Perhaps what is most interesting about the liberal cosmopolitan articulations around patriotic or nation-related bonds, whether they be tolerant or dismissive of the same, is that these arguments all convene around some common understanding of "reason", or a political similitude of some description. Basing the conception of such a large solidarity on a particular discourse of "reason", which has been repeatedly used as a weapon of colonial and neo-liberal exploitation, is both dangerous, and deeply problematic. Although it is not really part of the journey of this work, decolonial efforts to dismantle European hegemony around the discourse of reason are constantly under way. However, liberal cosmopolitan narratives still largely rely upon a very particular derivative of European, Enlightenment-based reason discourse. This is really what corporeal cosmopolitanism, along with other radical and critical reimaginations of cosmopolitan solidarity, attempts to dismantle. I also focus my discussions of liberal cosmopolitan ideas around patriotism and nation bonds to illustrate the ways in which these Kantian, reason-based discourses are unable to engage with any "unreasonable" (read: emotional) dimensions of nation bonds. Any articulation of embodied or affective cosmopolitanism must be keenly aware of different levels and kinds of identifications that are deeply political and passionate, public and private, all at once. Ultimately, corporeal cosmopolitanism is looking for ways to scramble this impasse. It attempts to find ways in which a variety of solidarities, both large and small, can be connected in embodied and emotional relationalities. These may be situated in nations, sexualities, villages, performances, continents and artistic expressions. I therefore conclude chapter one by looking at some examples of radical and affective cosmopolitanisms, from different parts of, and times in, the world.

Cosmopolitan belonging can be experienced in both exile and welcome, in banishment *from* somewhere and adoption *into* elsewhere – the idea of home is always being challenged and expanded; home is everywhere and nowhere. Chapter one, therefore, is really about belonging and inhabitation; not just of spaces but also of nonspaces and margins, and of bodies, ideas and feelings. Cosmopolitan solidarities may be eked out in all kinds of extraordinary ways – there is no singular directive for how these understandings, exchanges and conversations take place. Through this chapter, I hope to map some of these diversities and try to show the differences and relationalities in existing cosmopolitanisms, their contributions and critiques, and how we may read them in order to understand the exclusion of affective and embodied dimensions in these cosmopolitanisms. I also discuss some possibilities of cosmopolitan narratives which challenge these exclusions of affect, embodiment and otherness in unique and wonderful ways, thus paving the way and making room for the articulation of corporeal cosmopolitanism.

KANTIAN RESONANCES

The powerful presence of Immanuel Kant lingers over significant portions of my work. However, it is often not Kant himself, but particular interpretations and *received* versions of his ideas that animate much contemporary writing on liberal cosmopolitanism, and consequently, this book. As such, it is useful to distinguish Kant's cosmopolitanism from cosmopolitanisms that have been derived from, inspired or otherwise influenced by Kant's original works. My own work challenges many of the premises of these liberal cosmopolitanisms and often argues for radically different premises and trajectories, but, it is also true that much of my work would not be necessary or possible without Kant and the cosmopolitanisms he inspired and influenced. They are my interlocutors, and we are engaged in relations of critique and love, of understanding and despair, of anger and compassion. I treat these relations and conversations as a constitutive part of corporeal cosmopolitanism, although our paths, and perhaps even ends, are very different. I therefore begin with some very brief ideas and concepts in Kant's cosmopolitan vision, which, although very differently interpreted, are clearly reflected in contemporary liberal cosmopolitanisms – discussions of which form the major part of this chapter. I present a few key ideas that inform Kant's vision of cosmopolitanism and connect to contemporary work on liberal cosmopolitanism, which comprises the rest of this chapter, rather than an analysis of Kant's work.

Broadly, Kant indicated that every member of society has a right to freedom, common legislation and the legal equality that follows from the right to freedom (Kant 1917). He was vehemently opposed to an undifferentiated notion of popular rule and believed in the very necessary separation of legislative, judiciary and executive powers, causing him to describe democracy as 'a form of despotism' (Kant 2006, 76). For Kant, democracy consisted of an executive power that could make decisions against itself, if necessary, in the form of majority votes and decisions (Kant 2006, 76–77), and for this reason, he advocated a Republican system where executive and legislative powers were clearly separated. This laid several restrictions on subjects who willingly submitted to the rule of law – including the delegitimisation of revolt and rebellion against the state – but Kant's conceptualisation of *right* was based on very clear moral actions, duties and a legal framework, which would ideally prevent the leaders of states from becoming tyrants, thereby negating the need for bloody rebellion (Kant 2006, 55–57). The idea of an unbounded, "wild" freedom was completely unsustainable to Kant's vision of lasting peace and cosmopolitan solidarity. He had very specific guidelines around freedom and equality, and legislative equality of subjects within a state only applied to the structure of relationships. Thus, hereditary privilege, feudal privilege or any form of innate privilege was not acceptable to Kant, unless one was a woman or a person of colour, in which case they were not considered a subject of the state at all, but 'protected compatriots' (Kant 2006, 49). However, hierarchical relations of power were entirely permissible, because they did not breach the general law and constitutional right. This understanding of constitutional right and law, as observed previously, meant that resistance and rebellion against the head of the state are an active breach and violation of contract and law. Kant instead advocated resistance through the 'freedom of the pen' (Kant 2006, 57) and critical philosophy. This discomfort with, and fear of, unfettered resistance is, in so many unsavoury words, the fear of *savagery*, and I use that word as witness to the totality of colonial-imperial decimation. This fear of unfettered and untameable "wild-ness" (which, in many crucial ways, lies at the heart of resistance and libera-tion), is the large ball, attached to the end of the liberal cosmopolitan chain, and one which corporeal cosmopolitanism actively stands against.

Another key element in Kant's conception of cosmopolitanism is the principle of hospitality and an international legal order. The Kantian right to hospitality refers to the right of any person to visit foreign territories without fear of death or hostility. The visitor may be denied entry according to the discretion of the state, but may not be harmed, unless he or she poses a sig-nificant threat to the state. The right to hospitality meant that Kant opposed colonial and imperialist actions by Europe as inhospitable, but his belief in the fundamental inferiority of non-Europeans, women and Others and his endorsement of hierarchical power relations (Kant 2006, 48–50) make this a slippery space. The familiar slippery space of Empire, where being a bad host is considered rude, but being a coloniser is the mark of progress. Hospi-tability, for Kant, is based on the principle of toleration among peoples and a mutual respect and recognition of one another as equals. However, much like with democratic membership, the real violence of exclusion lies in determin-ing who might be considered *worthy* and capable of belonging to this hospi-tality club. Thus, hospitality, combined with the continuous refinements of reason, and critical thought, would eventually ensure the movement *towards perpetual peace*. Kant's vision and path towards perpetual peace and cosmo-politanism are laid out in the greatest, most painstaking detail. His writing is dense and complex, and moves between a definite, enduring hope in human-ity and an almost uncompromising certainty in the supremacy of reason. Kant offers a detailed programme of how to achieve a state of peace, accompanied by a deep, abiding fear that we will fail to do the right thing, as a species; a fear which is combated with a mixture of hope, reason, white superiority, and constitutional right. Kant's vision of cosmopolitanism is invaluable in understanding liberal, modern political community and solidarity. His work continues to participate significantly in contemporary scholarship, both in contributory and critical capacities.

Kant's work has been carefully and thoroughly critiqued by numerous scholars both within and outside Euromerican scholarship, with particular reference to those he considered capable of being moral agents: as mentioned previously, he excluded women, people of colour and children, among oth-ers. The Enlightenment understanding of and dependence on the supremacy of particular discourses of "reason", "rationality", and "objectivity" as gold standards are also widely critiqued ideas. While it is clear that we must understand the Kantian view within its specific context and history, and be aware of the profound implications that his right to hospitality continues to have upon our present understanding of cosmopolitanism, we must also be aware of its legacy. The legacy of cosmopolitanism is rooted in pre-Kantian

Christian thought and ethics, as well as Kantian and post-Kantian interpretations of reason and rationality. This legacy has very particular implications for marginalised people including women, people of colour and queer peoples; as well as the material realities and experiences of embodiment and affect. For instance, Foucault (1978) explains that the Christian view of morality has very specific and exact positions vis-à-vis the body. In his work on sexuality (1985, 1986, 1988), Foucault clearly outlines the discourse around the body as propagated by the church, making it impossible to speak of, precisely by talking *too much* about it. This way of speaking about the body, cast it in a pathologised, medicalised light, which then paved the way for the Enlightenment and a reason-based approach to the body and affect. Thus, from the Christian view of the body as a repository of desire, and therefore sin, danger or "otherness", we see the movement towards categorising bodies through the straitjacket of normalcy and the creation of archetypes – the female body, the insane body, the sexual body, the hysterical body and so on. Kant, along with other thinkers of the Enlightenment era, saw reason as the seat of moral power, as opposed to the church – an indisputably radical challenge for its time. However, from the point of view of the body, both reason as morality and particular forms of religious morality primarily focused on the mind and the spirit, respectively, thereby delegitimising and devaluing the body either by deeming it a machine – an instrument to be controlled by the mind – or a sin that must be absolved in order to attain paradise. The growth of liberal cosmopolitanisms, based on Enlightenment rationality, in cultural milieus deeply influenced and shaped by a religious morality that completely delegitimised the body and its associates – instincts, feelings, desires, and so on, as a site of knowledge or experience – poses a serious challenge in terms of creating new spaces for their reclamation.

A contemporary example of liberal, Kant-derived cosmopolitanism can be found in David Held's work (2005, 10–27).[1] I am not trying here to converse with Held's cosmopolitanism in terms of negotiating a shared space, as Held's cosmopolitan principles do not appear to have space for a dialogue about affect or embodiment. They do, however, point out some inherent forms of exclusions that close off such a cosmopolitanism to questions of affect and embodiment. Held follows the Enlightenment-appropriated concept of the *world citizen* and the Kantian concept of *cosmopolitan right* in framing his ideas on cosmopolitanism: 'Cosmopolitan right meant the capacity to present oneself and be heard within and across political communities; it was the right to enter dialogue without artificial constraint and delimitation' (Held 2005, 11). The call for the removal of 'artificial constraint' seems to overlook the existence of the very *real* constraints of historic violences and marginalisations which already preclude certain 'political communities' from equal status. This is one of the deep exclusions which characterises Euromerican liberal narratives of cosmopolitanism how they conceive "universal" equality. The idea that there is some kind of possibility for a "clean slate" from which we can all begin as equals requires some form of erasure and forgetting, neither of which I consider productive, or, indeed, possible. Corporeal cosmopolitanism is not only about remembering and articulating but also about holding the possibility of deep healing.

Using an interpretation of Kantian cosmopolitan belonging, Held elucidates eight principles that constitute his understanding of cosmopolitanism as follows (Held 2005, 12):

> (1) Equal worth and dignity; (2) active agency; (3) personal responsibility and accountability; (4) consent; (5) collective decision-making about public matters through voting procedures; (6) inclusiveness and subsidiarity; (7) avoidance of serious harm; and (8) sustainability.

Broadly speaking, Held believes in a universal notion of human dignity, to which particularities must ultimately succumb. He also actively advocates the right to self-determination and autonomous choices, and accepting the consequences of those choices. In Held's understanding, affirming Kant's views, cosmopolitanism is governed by two 'metaprinciples' (19): 'the metaprinciple of autonomy' and 'the metaprinciple of impartialist reasoning' (19). He insists that these are not Western or European notions, but rather that they seek to ensure the freedom and equality of all people regardless of where they may be, and also to protect those who do not have access or structural means to achieve the first six cosmopolitan principles. The metaprinciple of impartialist reasoning 'should be thought of as a heuristic device to test candidate principles of moral worth, democracy, and justice and their forms of justification' (Held 2005, 22). It appears to be a slippery combination of insisting on a certain kind of universal, Euromerican-centric democratic membership and the consequent understandings of terms like *equality*, *autonomy* and, indeed, *choice*, while at the same time allowing for some kind of paternalistic protection for those who cannot achieve this version of perfectly reasonable and universally applicable cosmopolitanism.

As David Harvey candidly observes:

> The use of 'reasonably' as well as the 'assent' inserted into the argument here is telling. It produces a powerful echo of Kant's (and Burke's) appeal to 'mature individuals' as the only acceptable participants in discussions. The elitism and potential class discrimination of this form of cosmopolitanism becomes clear. (Harvey 2009, 86)

Harvey also draws attention to a major lacuna in Heldian cosmopolitanism – that is, the assumption of a functioning, stable democracy in all major nation states that simply needs to be extended into all other realms of the political. Aside from the assumption itself being questionable, there is also the bigger question of this presumed democratic absolutism and whether it is in fact the choice of the world, along with a very particular, neo-liberal framing of human rights and the liberal discourse of autonomous choice. Held's principles of inclusion and consent are extremely problematic because of their inability to address marginalised peoples (See also Mouffe, 2005). The notion of consent, for instance, is both fractured and fragile in several cultures and communities, particularly with reference to gender and sexuality. The assumption of consent as a constitutive principle in democratic societies makes Held's principles both elitist and insensitive to gender, affect and corporeality. Held also writes about the 'metaprinciple of autonomy' where he argues:

> If this notion is shared across cultures it is not because they have acquiesced to modern Western political discourse; it is, rather, that they have come to see that there are certain languages which protect and nurture the notion of equal status and worth, and others which have sought to ignore or suppress it. (Held [2005], 21)

On the face of it, as with many articulations of liberal cosmopolitanism, there is nothing objectionable, or even disagreeable about ideas of equality, freedom and the right to live without fear of violence. Held's fundamental suggestions for a cosmopolitan society are not problematic in and of themselves; however, the *ways* in which these ideas are understood and approached reveal important exclusions and Eurocentric assumptions. The colonial hubris inherent in the 'metaprinciple of autonomy', for instance, cannot be ignored. The idea of *certain* languages or ways of thinking that protects and nurture equality, being set up against "barbaric tongues" that threaten it, is all too familiar. That it forms a core tenet of Held's global cosmopolitanism is indicative of the erasure of colonial narratives of violence – a recurring theme in several articulations of liberal cosmopolitanisms. The cursory dismissal of colonial violence and oppression using a kind of "let's move on" linear narrative is something of a recurring theme in liberal cosmopolitanisms, and can perhaps even be traced back to Kant's own views on the matter. Colonialism is not condoned or encouraged in any overt sense, but it is nearly always set aside in view of the "greater solidarity" that we must achieve. This means that black and queer bodies, *Dalit* and female bodies, disabled and working-class bodies – bodies that are constantly marginalised have no choice but to erase and diminish themselves for this greater, "reasonable" good. This view fails to recognise the centrality of imperialism, colonial violence, neo-liberal capitalism and white privilege in the identities, loves and political formations of the dispossessed and the marginalised. In order for us to move towards any practicable cosmopolitan solidarity, these primal wounds must be expressed, acknowledged and (if possible) healed, first.

As far as my own work and corporeal cosmopolitanism are concerned, it seems that I ought to have a clear-cut response to whether it sees Kant and liberal cosmopolitanism as allies or not. In a clear-cut sort of world, I would have simply said, not. But, decolonising memory is a very messy and heart-breaking business. Painful conversations are usually the foundations of vulnerable, open engagement. I do not mean for these acts to take place in the absence of any protection or care for the self or for those of attempting to broach these dialogues. There will be as many dead ends as possibilities and maybe more refusals than affirmations. This type of engagement is neither a quantitative attempt, nor indeed, an imposition. Liberal cosmopolitanism is an abiding voice, but not always a singular one, and, while I disagree with many of its methods, there do remain concerns that have the potential to be shared. In some sense, they also have to be interlocutors because I am not trying to hold these conversations in a Schmidtian space of friends versus foes. I am also trying to reinscribe my own critique as dialogue: we need to *hear* resistance, anger, pain and protest, before we speak so easily and swiftly from places of privilege. Corporeal cosmopolitanism is not meant to be a fortress, and that will mean that it will be as open to attack as it is to conversation. Its vulnerability is a longer-term fortification, not an immediate one. The *large* questions of universalism that liberal cosmopolitanism poses cannot be dismissed out of hand, but just because a question is vast does not mean it has to be answered with particular discourses of sameness, standardization or reason. There are other ways to hold vastness, that is, different ways to approach questions about the *world*, and corporeal cosmopolitanism attempts to do this by tapping other imaginings of largeness – embodiment, love, compassion and resistance. In keeping with the discussion of Kant and Kant-inspired cosmopolitanism and belonging to the world, the next section turns to questions of inhabitation and belonging in the cosmopolitan imaginary.

MAPPING COSMOPOLITAN BELONGINGS

How do we inhabit the world? As people, as refugees, as citizens, as the dispossessed? Liberal understandings of cosmopolitanism have a varied and fraught relationship with the categories of nationhood and patriotic belonging – disliking the theory of them but unable to really erase the deeper boundaries that nations represent. Is a citizen of everywhere really a citizen of everywhere, or, as a prominent politician so bluntly declared, 'a citizen of nowhere'?[2] What are the insecurities that belonging to everywhere bring to peoples who, through the machinations of neo-liberal and colonial warfare and violence, literally and physically belong to nowhere? The sense of political and spiritual agoraphobia that dispossession brings is somewhat at odds with these global belongings of liberal cosmopolitanism. Yet, in a very material and emotional sense, those who belong to nowhere *understand* the blurring between the lines of everywhere and nowhere, but in very different ways to the elite 'citizen of the world'. It is to some of these tensions and discussions that we now turn.

There are many contemporary liberal views of nationhood and patriotism that have challenged classical notions of the nation state and its importance to political order.

I engage with a selection of ideas in relation to different forms of political belonging to provide a broad theoretical context that I hope will signpost the need for affective, corporeal cosmopolitanisms.

Mapping Cosmopolitan Belongings: Is Patriotism a Cosmopolitan Feeling?

Patriotism is an important iteration of belonging for many peoples. It speaks of a particular bond between a nation and its citizen, often cast in parental terms. These nation parents are sometimes described as "biological" and sometimes "adoptive". In any event, people feel bound to the places they inhabit in deep and complex ways. Martha Nussbaum (2002) takes a very definite stance against patriotism, denouncing it as a danger to the very idea of global harmony. Nussbaum's basic claims are that compassion is rooted in the biological heritage of human beings and is something special to humanity, which makes the very distinction between "us" and "them" morally wrong. Drawing from the Stoic model of concentric circles of obligations towards fellow human beings, she stresses the importance of a cosmopolitan education and mourns the paucity in world knowledge among Western, in particular, North American systems of education. The endorsement of compassion as a kind of *large* emotional scaffold, while still rejecting the smaller scale of community bonds such as patriotism, makes Nussbaum's appeal to the 'biological heritage' of human compassion a little tricky to navigate. That is to say, how does one adjudicate the limits of this compassion, such that we ensure the practice of a large compassion, where we always choose world over village?

Nussbaum suggests that the way we learn and what we know might provide part of the solution. She argues that it is important to understand ourselves through the eyes of the "other", to solve international problems together and recognise our moral obligations – as human beings and citizens – to the world at large. In this vein, she suggests a major overhaul of the education system itself and how important it is to educate differently, particularly with reference to North America. Nussbaum's programme involves consciousness-raising and intellectual reform among privileged white people, in the hope that better knowledge and understanding will forge solidarity among us as a human community. These are important critical observations, and while I do not oppose the spirit of these ideas, I am also deeply aware that this discourse is directed towards the privileged, "global north". Liberation has been too recent for too many to expect the kind of disavowal of patriotism that Nussbaum demands. It is also worth noting that postcolonial nations face entirely different sets of challenges with regard to what and how they learn. Sheer volume of numbers and the struggle to bring education to all children, combined with the ways in which "knowledge" is selected, make this an extremely harrowing, often disheartening issue. The ways in which English language is privileged and the powerful influence of industrialization-based technical education indicate that education in the "global south" is just as impacted by forces of colonial modernity and neo-liberal capitalism, as in America. If knowledge and education are to be important factors in effecting a moral cosmopolitan ethos, then we will have to consider more than just the elite, White, west, and its scholarly narcissism. Nussbaum makes some reference to this as she writes of Rabindranath Tagore's *Shantiniketan* in West Bengal, which was imagined as a seat of cosmopolitan learning but is now threatened by Hindu fundamentalists and nationalists. Tagore's own complex politics of privilege and elitism, however, are absent in this narrative[3]. The erasure of histories and local knowledges, subjugation and violence from colonial armies, and subsequent counter-nationalisms mean that what children of postcolonial legacies learn, depending on where they get an education, is already deeply fractured and often vested. We must never forget that the production and dissemination of "authentic knowledge" were and are key weapons in the colonial and imperial arsenal. Opposing jingoistic nationalism alone is not sufficient – the wound travels much deeper than that, and, unfortunately, Nussbaum's solution, that is, knowledge and education, are often the weapons that cause the deep wounding.

While Nussbaum's concerns over the dangers of patriotism are not all unfounded, it must be recognised that affective bonds of patriotism are also particularly important to those who have chosen to or been forced to flee their own homes. Immigrants, refugees and those who have been dispossessed of their lands, often in brutal ways, look to form bonds with their adoptive nations, and these can sometimes be akin to a form of imprinting. Robert Pinsky (2002), in his response to Nussbaum, offers an affective account of patriotism, particularly for American immigrants, and the importance of patriotism in adopting a new home. While the notion may be accused of romanticism, popular culture is filled with evidence to support his claim. Whether it is the fourth of July we think of, or a World Cup victory, where a whole nation explodes into a theoretically mythical but ephemerally real unitary identity, Pinsky's main observation is to do with the importance of passion and *eros* and the absence of them in Nussbaum's cosmopolitanism, although she does include the affective component of compassion in her work. The argument here seems to be that patriotism is considered beautiful and effective, precisely because of its passion. In order to counter its negative effects, however, there must be an *eros* of cosmopolitanism. Pinsky speaks of patriotism as the love of home and cosmopolitanism as a love of the marketplace. The use of the term *marketplace* is telling, even as it points to the very real neo-liberal, capitalist and globalised structures that cosmopolitanism is necessarily enmeshed in; it also evokes images of a vast space of exchange, being a flâneur, at an enormous *souk* in the world. These passions of home and marketplace are in constant conflict, and ultimately, it is the *eros* of cosmopolitanism that can counterbalance the allure of extreme patriotism and ethnocentrism. In its own strange way, this formulation of *eros* recognises the large-scale and small-scale manifestations of love and belonging, arguing that as long as we recognise both bonds as love, they will ultimately balance each other. Pinsky critiques Nussbaum's cosmopolitanism as belonging to the 'village of the liberal, managerial class' (Pinsky 2002, 87) – the village of the United Nations and international policy makers. The idea that the *eros* of home is in some way inferior to the love for humanity at large is problematic to Pinsky. The attention that the author draws to the place that *eros* and affectivity hold among people is of great significance in that he identifies them as political, community-binding factors that have important consequences in political identities. While Pinsky doesn't offer a more detailed idea of *how* to harness these forms of love into forming new kinds of solidarities and communities, he does identify a key problem in many liberal framings of affective cosmopolitanism. The main impasse in the narratives of contemporary liberal cosmopolitanism is that any discussion around affect and *eros* is only possible in a personal, descriptive narrative, rather than as a larger political act of resistance and solidarity. Theorising affect, *eros*, desire and embodiment within the political is usually excluded within liberal cosmopolitanisms, because, often, their reason-dominated, intellectual foundations are constituted by the exclusion of affect and embodiment.

We see in Nussbaum's work a very clear articulation of community building as a human endeavour and the erasure of difference through the recognition of human empathy as the most crucial bond, superseding all other relations of conflict or consensus. Nussbaum's critique of patriotism and call for "human" solidarity are laudable. However, locating the unfeasibility of the "us/them" binaries in moral terms and trying to *right the wrongs* through a programme of critical education make the endeavour somewhat limited in impact and also does not engage with the power politics of the educational marketplace. "Us/them" distinctions are produced in visceral, bodily ways, and while knowledge can, and must, address the histories, invisibilisations and violences of othering, its reach is often not long enough to address the affective and corporeal experiences of othering in an everyday capacity. The work of compassion and love is critical, but it must be far more active, emotive and actively participatory than Nussbaum's methods suggest. Pinsky's critique of Nussbaum's characterisation of patriotism draws out *some* of the complexities of nation bonds and the necessary relationships between nation and people. Here I want to be careful in distinguishing the affective bonds between nation and people from the affective bonds between land (not to be confused with territory) and people. Both Pinsky and Nussbaum are speaking in politico-affective contexts, rather than embodied affective contexts, and I explore the embodied, material bonds between land and peoples in later chapters (see chapters four and five). Patriotism draws heavily on the imagery of territory as a precious possession in need of armed protection, but these are certainly not the only kinds of affective bonds people form with spaces and places. This brings me to yet another critical factor that influences these affective relations and responses to patriotic sentiment, and that is a very particular kind of wounded, hetero-masculinity being called upon to protect the helpless *femination*. Although Nussbaum's (2002) essay makes some allusions to it, it does not form a significant part of either Nussbaum's or Pinsky's perspectives of patriotism. The gendered, misogynistic characterisation of nation as hapless or violated woman and the subsequent performances of protection that patriotism demands are not unfamiliar in Euromerican contexts, with some exceptions of *nations-as-fathers*. These gendered configurations have been used as monarchic and democratic justifications for militarised violence for many centuries now and have become familiar in the global imaginary. The liberal cosmopolitan critique of patriotism and nation, in not paying closer attention to these embodied connections, both loses a powerful critical angle and, perhaps more importantly, underestimates the power of the patriotic narrative. This gendered narrative of *nation-as-woman* needing her protector sons/consorts issues a visceral, embodied call to a very particular form of wounded hetero-masculinity. A powerful summons in any patriarchal context, it is even more deeply felt in postcolonial nation states where liberation is still a fresh memory, and the whole colonial encounter was explicitly framed in terms of emasculation, rape and possession. The argument that I make for an embodied and emotional cosmopolitanism is not a cosmopolitanism of sweetness and light alone. It is to make room for and recognise these feelings, and violences as well. The *eros* (Pinsky 2002) of patriotism is also pain and horror, and for those reasons, it cannot be dismissed as 'empty symbol-mongering' or 'egocentric self-exaltation' (Nussbaum 2002, 15). Indeed, such an elite dismissal fails to make a material-emotional connection and is therefore unable to either comprehend or speak to the elements of pain and fear that underpin the performance of such an aggressive hetero-masculinity. To be clear, I am in complete solidarity with Nussbaum and my queer-feminist kin in critiquing the performance of violent hetero-masculinity in relation to patriotic pride. I am however suggesting that the actors in this performance do not escape unscathed and that the performance itself is a manifestation of important fears and traumas which require attention rather than dismissal. Those of us who are actors in these performances of violent hetero-masculinities (I use hetero-masculinities and hapless femininities as tropes, not as individual or subject genders) are also interpellated and called to action by violent regimes of power. If it is at all possible, a space must be held for these experiences of violence as well.

Mapping Cosmopolitan Belongings: The Case for Cosmopatriotism

Defending the bond of nation, Kwame Anthony Appiah (2006) argues that the sentiments of patriotism and cosmopolitanism are by no means incompatible, reminiscent of Stoic and German Enlightenment views. Appiah's work on cosmopolitanism (2006) draws considerably on his own life experience as a 'citizen of the world' and is very aware of the nuances of multiple identities, mixed ethnicities and the role of rituals and traditions within culture. Appiah argues that identities are formed only in the face of an opposition or threat to any community in keeping with the postcolonial understandings of identity formation. The act of being threatened provides the circumstances for a certain kind of solidarity and identification, which are then extended to a particular way of living. The parameters of the "good" life are thus always understood in accordance with the particular identification of the community/ society. Identity requires ascription and recognition, internalisation by the bearer and a certain set of behaviours towards the bearer by others. When Appiah provides an account of his own experiences of multiple identities, it becomes quite clear that these experiences belong to an elite milieu of an international citizen. This is not to negate Appiah's experiences of marginalisation, or the reality of his cosmopolitan identification, but simply to point out that this kind of reconciliation tends to be possible only in spaces of privilege. Appiah's descriptions of a universally existing cosmopolitanism, from Ghana, to America, to England, in products, music, art and film, are remarkably celebratory. Having inhabited both postcolonial spaces and privileged spaces, I have certainly seen what Appiah describes as cosmopolitan and shared, but I also recognise that they do not fit the mould of commonality that liberal formulations of cosmopolitanism enshrine. In Appiah's work, every place is described as creating 'pockets of homogeneity' (2006, 103) and the effects of global exposure as extending to clean water, better schooling, and so on – *good things* that we all aspire to and desire. In and of themselves, these points are not problematic or even incompatible with a cosmopolitan understanding of the world, but rather incomplete, in the sense that belonging across countries and continents, for many peoples and communities can be viscerally traumatic and often fractured. That is to say, a universal desire for healthy standards of living and the elimination of poverty, hunger and homelessness is not really universal at all, in that the desire is never equal and always determined by need. A vague, abstract, donation-based desire for clean drinking water is a luxury. In a city slum, or a poor council estate, or a *scheduled caste* zone in a village, the same desire is a life-wish, a prayer to be spared an agonising death. Privilege cleaves these universal desires, and this is something that both Appiah's own narrative, along with other liberal narratives of cosmopolitan commonality, seems to elide.

With all its problems, it is worth remembering that Appiah's point is also made in aid of people's agency and their ability to choose and decide what is good for them. He denounces the notion of 'cultural imperialism' (Appiah 2006, 108), which might translate into either Western impositions upon passive "third world" people, or of so-called authentic traditional impositions aimed at some sort of cultural preservation. Appiah juxtaposes what he calls 'cultural contamination' (2006, 111) against the oppressions of cultural imperialism and preservation. 'Cultural contamination', he argues, might threaten the identities of some people, just as much as it excites others with the possibility of new identities. Appiah uses the provocative term *contamination*, presumably to challenge any pre-existing notion of stability, "purity", or origin. There is, however, little examination of the more insidious relationships of power between states, economies, religions, genders and ethnicities in these processes of *contamination*. That is to say, the notions of "purity and pollution" have been used as organising principles for a variety of cultures and communities, ancient and contemporary. The ways in which these principles have acted as gatekeepers and agents of exclusion make *contamination* a heavy word, particularly in terms of ethnicity, class, gender and sexuality. While 'contamination' functions in a broad, poststructural capacity as a disruption of sorts, it still carries powerful and violent connotations in many parts of the world (say in relation to caste, or menstruation), and I am wary of its use in a liberatory capacity. There is also a broader liberal, and even functionalist, implication that cultural contamination might cause upheavals and painful changes for some, but that these will ultimately result in the possibility of a shared cosmopolitan future. What it tacitly suggests is that, whatever the price, the sacrifice will ultimately be worthwhile, echoing the Kantian assertion that what is morally right is always paramount and supersedes all else. Popularly articulated, it sounds too much like the "hard decisions" that those in power *always* feel they *must* make for the betterment of the world.

Thus, Appiah does not see the allegiance to one's cultural roots or patriotism as in any way antithetical to cosmopolitan belonging. The mandate of cultural contamination allows for these messy affiliations, after all. However, he does not seem to favour too much mess in practice and calls on the state to provide some much-needed order. Appiah recruits the state as part of the cosmopolitan vision, as some kind of benevolent, moral and economic presence. You will recall from earlier in this chapter that Kant himself was very clear about the absolute moral duty of the state and those who held that power. Similarly, Appiah (2002) too believes the state is both intrinsically and morally significant to people because it regulates their lives. In *The Ethics of Identity* (2005), Appiah chalks out a practicable kind of state intervention. He sets out a working model of cosmopolitanism where he suggests that we must all engage in the project of 'soul making' (2005, 208), which refers to the individual crafting of identities and the relationship between individual citizens' identities and political governance. The state is meant to aid this endeavour both through policies and laws. Appiah suggests, for instance, that the government should issue self-management cards to restrict "unreasonable" behaviour such as the abuse of drugs and alcohol. Appiah refers to the human capacity for weakness and temptation, and, in a similar vein to Kant, is quick to point out that, though humans are capable of rational and reasonable behaviour, they do not always engage in it. The 'self-management cards' provided by the state would allow people to "manage" their consumption patterns by entering data into a centralised data base that will then enable stores to refuse sale of certain things, based on people's self-chosen restrictions. For Appiah, this is one way in which the state can help citizens deal with irrational and potentially self-harming behaviour. Appiah's strategy for implementing his vision of cosmopolitanism seems genuinely bewildering. He says little about dynamics of power, and the whole narrative is heavily based on a certain kind of discourse of reason, which implicitly suggests that an "unreasonable" behaviour or group can and *should* be curtailed or "managed" by the state. Awash as we are in bloody histories of continued state violence, it is not clear why Appiah does not choose a radical reframing of the political apparatus and instead wants a reformation of the state. The emphasis placed on choice – this idea that people can *choose* healthy options – also presumes an unbiased, universally accepted and verified discourse around issues of health, good living, eating habits, food, nutrition, weight, beauty and so on. Such an objective discourse is not only absent, but we are in fact deeply influenced by ideas about health and "good living" that derive from Western capitalism, imperialism and rampant consumerism, all of which constantly use the language of science and reason to circulate their harmful agendas. These discourses also tend to be highly gendered, and thus, the 'self-management' choices that people make could very easily be self-surveillance methods. The "common-sense" approach that marks much of Appiah's writing on how cosmopolitanism can be achieved masks a whole host of real dangers.

In addition to these strategies, Appiah argues that the state must provide people with detailed information, that people may develop 'informed desires' (Appiah 2005, 172), not dissimilar to Nussbaum's programme involving education. But, once again, it assumes that providing the right information will suffice and that the deep, and often violent, marginalisations – which have ossified over centuries and play themselves out in bodily psychic practices – can be addressed solely through the offices of democracy and reason. While Appiah's argument is clearly an attempt to make his version of cosmopolitanism practicable, the notion of a state-sponsored surveillance mechanism and the idea of controlling and manipulating what qualifies as "good" and "bad" desire are simply frightening. Investing the state with some kind of inherent moral rightness ignores the vast matrices of power and violence producing and produced by the state. The crux of Appiah's argument, with respect to change, and, by extension, conflict, is that people eventually get used to change and new ideas – slowly but surely (2006). This brings us back to an earlier comparison between Appiah, Kant and functionalism – that is, that initial suffering, conflict is the price we pay for eventual understanding and acceptance. Appiah's formulation ostensibly sets out with the aim of mediating patriotic sentiments with cosmopolitan ones, but it might be more accurate to say that the mediation is really a conflation. The conflation of these two identifications here appears to result in the retention of the state, banishment of *eros* and in the invocation of multiplicities, all of which must be born from a shared understanding of "reason".

There is one particular aspect of Appiah's work that I wish to tackle in greater detail, and that is his critique of identity politics as a form of 'cultural imperialism' (2006, 108). Liberal narratives of cosmopolitanism often argue against identity politics and the dangers of ossifying people's identities on the basis of cultural specificity or difference. Similar to the critique of patriotism, the critique of identity politics seems to take insufficient note of the historical processes, violences and traumas that underlie these forms of identifications. The relevance of abject and marginalised subjectivities is something that Appiah and other liberal cosmopolitans simply do not address. In fact, following his dismissal of identity-based movements, Appiah identifies LGBTQI+, *Dalit* and other such movements not as identity preserving movements but as 'movements for social change' (Appiah 2005, 210). This is a curious kind of distinction in the sense that, for Appiah, 'identity preservation' (2005, 208) easily becomes synonymous with cultural imperialism and, in some spaces, this conflation could well be the case. However, in other spaces, the struggle for identity recognition rather than preservation is still a matter of life and death. The equation of identity preservation to cultural imperialism does not hold in a context where recognition of humanity has yet to take place. Whether it is caste based, or gender based, or sexuality based, the discrimination faced by people is often violent, and here, identity recognition followed by preservation are vital to their selfhood, their bodily integrity and their safety. In the case of *thirunangai* (transwomen) communities in India, for instance, recognition and preservation of a certain kind of sexual/ritual/religious/aesthetic identity are central to the community. There exist accounts and stories of identity recognition within community memory, which have been lost or delegitimised over time and have recently been legally reclaimed through a change in constitutional legislation. Thus, a movement for identity recognition is not always distinct from a movement for change. It seems that in Appiah's model, the syntax of expression is set in reason. As a consequence, the battle for identity preservation has been identified as unproductive and possibly dangerous, and there is little room for the existence of those who are not yet able, and possibly have never been able, to articulate anything approaching belonging, and of those who fall outside the comfortable realms of inside/outside – the abject, the absolutely marginalised and the grotesque bodies of society. Thus, an LGBTQI+ movement, or a women's movement, or a *Dalit* movement will, in this framework, only be recognised as such if articulated within a specific syntax, constitutional vocabulary and given epistemology of social change. The need for identity recognition and preservation is a deeply emotional and corporeal one. For communities and peoples who have been displaced and ravaged by colonialisms, wars and genocides, the language of reasoned dialogue and social change is not only grossly inadequate but it can also be very triggering. Unfortunately, the language of reason and rationality have been used in too many violent ways and cannot be used to address the affective and embodied dimensions of non-white, queer and subaltern people's stories. We do not have the luxury of participating in the deliberative, conversational, global-democratic community that is on offer here. Hannah Arendt (2006) makes the important observation that Western civilization has always functioned with an interloping triad of authority, tradition and religion – an oft-repeated idea – nevertheless still significant. She notes that, traditionally, Western and Platonic philosophy look for the bodiless afterlife; however, the notion of hell and purgatory always threaten unspeakable bodily pain. It is this threat that is ultimately used to coerce many into understanding the "truth" which few have experienced. Over time, democracy and secularisation have rid the state of the fear of hell, but the threat of violence of bodily pain has always remained (Arendt 2006, 91–141). Conflict, violence and any embodied, material reality is thus absent from Appiah or Nussbaum's discussion where a marginalised group – for instance, a group of women or transgender sex workers – can be dialogued with from the point of view of what is reasonable and what is their *right* as humans or citizens but never from the point of view of their material realities, their physical, affective and sexual bodies and their desires. Following in the Kantian vein, the overarching thesis of these ideas is a kind of noble, "good" utopia based on reason, which will work well for many but not all, depending on whether they are deemed reasonable or not. If the minorities for whom it does not work are not "reasonable", then they require no explanations, and if they are "reasonable", then they will be engaged in dialogue and discussion. Nussbaum's argument too in this sense flattens the bases of conflict and agency in a kind of all-encompassing moral understanding of humanity which ignores materiality and power politics. This kind of compassion runs a real risk of becoming oppressive at worst and patronising at best.

The cosmopolitan narratives offered by Appiah and Nussbaum require us to think deeply about the relationships between belonging and cosmopolitanism, and what it means, as I asked at the start of the chapter, to inhabit the world with a particular set of identities? Judith Butler (2002), in her critique of Nussbaum, articulates these concerns regarding inhabiting the universal rather effectively. She argues that 'the excluded . . . constitute the contingent limit of universalism' and that 'if existing and accepted conventions of universality constrain the domain of the speakable, this constraint produces the speakable, making a border of demarcation between the speakable and the unspeakable' (Butler 2002, 48). It is precisely the problem of categorisation – deciding what qualifies to be named this and not that, why some violences are acknowledged and others summarily dismissed, and by whom – that is at the heart of this debate. Butler's contention is that, operating on an existing, a priori idea or construct of the universal means that we are strengthening and legitimising the exclusions and omissions which are an integral part of that universality. She makes a case for a nontemplate, becoming universality that is entirely conflictual. That is, an *idea of universality*, which defies existing understandings of the term. Butler calls for a fluid, open idea of universality, which is both dynamic and uncertain and always open to change. The 'performative contradiction' (Butler 2002, 50) of such a becoming, conflictual universalism is not only the challenge or articulation of the unintentionally excluded, whose status can simply be changed from unauthorised to authorised by a function of constitutionality or semantics. It is really the challenge of the intentionally excluded, silenced and invisibilised because the 'norm is [itself] predicated on the exclusion' (Butler 2002, 50) of those making this articulation. In other words, Butler is calling for the exposing of conventional universalisms. This calls for reimagining universalism as being in constant flux – as allowing for multiple articulations and imaginations of what universalism might mean, and also allowing for each of these articulations to disintegrate, making room for new ones. Engaging in the creation of a layered, open universalism will require constant movement, dialogue and understanding.

Might it then be possible to have a nuanced, polysemic notion of universality that can address some of the pertinent issues raised by particularism? Veronique Pin-Fat (2013), in her work, tackles precisely this question. Using the Wittgensteinian framework of language games, she argues, similarly to Butler, against a foundationalist, essentialist understanding of universality. For Pin-Fat, the potential of universality as an ethical possibility lies in its (im)possibility. She makes a strong argument for fluidity rather than rigidity in the distinction between the possible and the impossible, thus suggesting a 'soft' ontology for universality rather than a 'hard' one (2013, 241–257). In other words, the space for articulating dissent or voicing the feeling of exclusion is what makes universality so fragile and all the more crucial to creating dialogic possibilities. Such a view may add a valuable component to the existing arguments for a nuanced, polysemic universality. A cosmopolitan universality that acknowledges its own (im)possibility must then be perpetually open to dialogue and disagreement and be composed of the marginal as well as the mainstream. However, in reimagining universalism, we must bear in mind that the draw of a stable certainty, of the variety that Appiah and Nussbaum provide, is not easily dismissed. And it is important to recognise that situations of constant flux and change can make positions of marginality even more precarious. These last two subsections have considered some of the ways in which liberal cosmopolitan narratives respond to particular, "small", affective ways of belonging. I have focused on the moral-affective dimensions of belonging in the discussion of patriotism and related themes of identity politics, the role of the state, as well as how they complement and/or contradict the *large* visions of cosmopolitan universalism. These dimensions of identity are both materially and emotionally central to people's subjectivities, and liberal cosmopolitanisms' inability to really engage with their emotional and embodied paths stresses the importance for radically new imaginaries. In the following discussion, I examine another popular liberal cosmopolitan argument: the demise of nation state owing to the accelerated rate of globalisation and changes in social organisation. To recall my point from the introduction to this chapter, these arguments against nation bonds are also made with respect to a certain globalised, political and economic similitude, rather than an actual embodied desire for a larger connection or solidarity.

Mapping Cosmopolitan Belongings: Excising Nation from Cosmos

The nation state is one of the West's most formidable forms of political belongings, and in most cases, also the legacy left behind for ex-colonies. The liberation from colonial control was, thus, hardly total, leaving ex-colonies in a Fanonesque[4] prison, in the mould of Western political and social organisation, often in ghastly combinations of their own forms of cultural violences and hierarchies. The dismantling of the nation state is thus a monumentally significant action and a potentially radical act. However, as we will presently see, liberal and decolonial approaches to such a dismantling are markedly different, and I hope to establish that this difference once again reiterates the need for articulating new forms of decolonial and corporeal cosmopolitanisms. Following some of the ideas of the previous discussion centred on whether the affective dimensions of patriotism as a form of belonging could be compatible with liberal notions of cosmopolitanism, in this section, I address the complex politics of the nation state: the arguments of postnation and the disappearance of the nation along with "traditional" social divisions, most notably, class.

One of the main arguments in favour of the receding significance of "traditional" social divisions in formulations of liberal cosmopolitanism is the absence of certainty and the idea of risk as formulated by sociologists such as Anthony Giddens (1991, 94 98), Ulrich Beck (2006, 2007, 2009) and Gerard Delanty (2009) Brock and Brighouse (2005), to name a few. Beck (1992, 2006) argues that risk has replaced class as a new power game. Global risk, according to Beck, is a state of latent revolution where normalcy and emergency overlap, thereby dismantling "traditional" categories of conflict, or opposition. His thesis is that the "other" becomes more and more included in the face of global risk because people are forcibly thrown together and must confront challenges and problems collectively. This kind of cosmopolitanism, he argues, is nonelite, precisely because people have no choice but to engage with it. He is highly critical of nationalism, particularly within the social sciences, and like Appiah believes that people inevitably get used to change, he too believes that cosmopolitanism is always happening everywhere – a quiet, inevitable revolution that all of us participate in. Beck understands this as the cosmopolitanism of everyday life. There is, to be sure, something to be said for the drama of precarity and the forms of community that it can sometimes produce. Some of these formations of solidarity are powerful and moving and often produce radical change. However, it is both naïve and dangerous to suppose that people are not capable of working together while continuously finessing the ways in which they produce exclusions, discriminations and microaggressions. The 2017 Women's Marches across the United States of America are a good illustration of this. The precarity of the 2016 elections and the presidency of Donald Trump brought together unprecedented numbers of people, in exactly the sorts of ways that galvanise public and political resistance. These resistances stand as an extraordinary example of embodied and affective cosmopolitan solidarity and deserve to be celebrated and replicated. However, we would be doing these acts of protest a disservice if we insisted on celebrating them as monolithic solidarities where the common ground supersedes the differences. It is precisely the desire to erase marginalisations and silences in the face of the "greater" cause that perpetuates discrimination. In the forging of *large* solidarities such as this one, it is crucial to acknowledge and be accountable for the reality that women (and people) of colour were variously excluded and to recognise that being "woman" *still* refused to address the realities and discriminations faced by women of colour, transwomen and black women, particularly in North America. The absolute threat to these women's lives and bodies was not sufficiently acknowledged in this *large* show of solidarity, *precisely* because "traditional" social divisions of race, gender, sexuality and class are still very much in operation.

Nevertheless, 'enforced cosmopolitanism', according to Beck (2006, 2007), is a sociological process – it is unconscious, latent and constant. It seems to operate as some kind of transition phase before people actively choose it. Appiah's suggestions of state involvements and Nussbaum's educational reform programme are also suggestive of something similar. The idea appears to be that we need a *push* of some kind to set us on the path of choice-based cosmopolitanism. This is a kind of philosophical cosmopolitanism that helps to reform unconscious cosmopolitanism into a conscious choice; Beck terms this *cosmopolitan realism* (2006, 13–14). This act of choice is crucial to creating a strong sense of cosmopolitan belonging. The focus on choice and individual autonomy is very much a part of the liberal-rational discourse on cosmopolitan solidarity. 'Methodological cosmopolitanism' (Beck 2007, 287) is about inclusive oppositions, that is, it rejects the notion of exclusive oppositions or polarities. This is the primary way in which methodological cosmopolitanism is opposed to nationalism which, Beck argues excludes the "other" in a constitutive way – by placing them outside an actual boundary. The corollary to this, which remains unspoken, is that the formation of nation states as the swan songs of colonial occupation, allowed the colonised, albeit in often violent ways, to reconstruct their destroyed identities. One explanation for this omission might be the idea of 'entangled modernities' (Beck 2006, 4), which proposes the increased forgetting of a global past. According to this concept, the heightened performances of global risk and the "mixing" of our histories, economies and societies make the past more and more difficult to fix, and consequently, recall. At the historical level, Beck's cosmopolitanism is referencing the uncertainty and ephemeral quality of meaning, memory and identity, as well as the understanding of European modernity as an interplay of various versions of modernity. At the social level, he is suggesting that cosmopolitanism can be seen in the interaction between societies all over the world and the constant reconfiguration of core-periphery relations. And still further, at the micro level, this methodological cosmopolitanism lies in the relativising of cultural values, the experience of risk on a global scale and the self-problematisation within hitherto homogenous categories of identity. It is both difficult and painful at multiple levels to respond to the notion of forgetting. On the one hand, contemporary technologies are altering and strengthening the very definitions and capacities of memory as a mental category and process, and on the other, from sheer overload and the privileging of certain forms of documentation, many things are indeed, forgotten. Beck's theorisation of cosmopolitanism is fundamentally situated in Europe. Even in its consideration of 'entangled' modernities, it only sees *European* modernity as entangled with others, creating a clear geopolitical hierarchy within the alleged call to multiplicities. The powershifts that Beck refers to are in fact constantly taking place, but these shifts are in no way absolute, and the shift in the economic statuses of the "global south" has been accompanied by an equal, if not greater, backlash of anti-immigration policies, xenophohia, anti-black racism, islamophobia, queer-phobia and misogyny. The shifts in economic capital are in no way mirrored by shifts in cultural and symbolic capital. And finally, if, in the 'relativisation of cultural values', we also include moves to ban burqas, burkinis and the speaking of "foreign" languages on airplanes, it seems premature to make a case for the breakdown of "traditional" identity categories. In other words, global risk does not appear to be helping us connect with each other in healthy, compassionate and sustainable ways that might then move us, as a world, to *choose* cosmopolitan solidarity.

Another contemporary liberal variant of cosmopolitanism is Gerard Delanty's critical cosmopolitanism, which arises 'when and wherever new relations between Self, Other and World develop in moments of openness' (2009, 27). Delanty suggests that if we understand modernity as plural and as the absence of security in identity, meaning and memory, then such an understanding could be a basis for critical cosmopolitanism. Critical cosmopolitanism thus focuses on the relationality between cultures, rather than the differences between them. The idea behind such a focus is that all cultures share similarities in methods of problem-solving, and this is a kind of partial universality upon which a dialogic consensus can be imagined. This consensus, however, is also implicitly based on an erasure or forgetting. It is not focused on addressing or healing the psychological, emotional and spiritual wounds of violence and trauma, particularly in the cases of those who, within hetero-patriarchal political structures, are considered largely illegitimate. This idea of cosmopolitan solidarity is predicated on the idea of common global issues that all people face and advocates a focus on relationality and problem-solving. It advocates a sentiment of soldiering on together based on the premise that we live in an uncertain world of great risk and it is very important that we band together and look out for each other. There is an ahistoricism enabled by this sense of urgency and danger, which masks the very foundations of some of the risks and dangers, including, but not restricted to, colonialism, wars, genocides and systematic violence against particular groups of people.

Globalisation narratives like Beck's refer to migrant labourers, the ubiquity of world cuisines and the increasing irrelevance of class, ethnicity and the nation state as a whole. The argument that all consumption, production, desire and identity are now located globally/glocally and not just nationally/locally, while not untrue, fundamentally excludes the realities of marginalised people in the "global north", both non-white, and white. If such a cosmopolitan narrative is only selectively applicable in the "global north", then it wholly excludes the "global south" and the material and embodied conditions of life, labour and governance in the rest of the world. Beck's claim is that identities everywhere are no longer tied to locations and that workers have no national connections to their work anymore. In fact, he argues that the very concept of traditionally understood state power has been destabilised. There is both a colonial and economic elitism in Beck's observations because current political examples of several countries in South Asia, Africa and South America, as well as countries in the "global north", demonstrate that state and labour are deeply intertwined, and very often, the state becomes the sole recourse of the marginalised classes – often, but not always, to their detriment. The idea that identities are no longer tied to locations is also an intrinsically narrow view that excludes vast populations that do not live within the privileged spaces of global or international belonging, as well as diasporic, immigrant and refugee populations who live in terribly debilitating conditions. The redundancy of the nation state, as argued by Beck and others, is also strongly countered by Butler and Spivak (2007) who note that the state is still extremely significant because it has the power to banish people into a condition of statelessness. Statelessness, however, does not mean a return to bare life, because, as the authors point out, dispossession and destitution are themselves state-created limbos. The postnation argument is weakened precisely because it seems not to take cognizance of this reality at all. Butler and Spivak characterise stateless people as "dark" people, illegible humans who fail the citizenship test and therefore enter a produced status of statelessness. Dispossession in this sense is not just locational. It does not only refer to the refugee or the camp prisoner. Butler and Spivak explain dispossession as a 'departure from within . . . that demands immobility' (2007, 18). In Beck's global risk society, where enforced cosmopolitanism can gradually transform through philosophical cosmopolitanism, there is no real room for the dispossessed or preventive measures in the event of this 'enforced cosmopolitanism' turning into an autocratic, oppressive cosmopolitanism.

Beck's explanation of cosmopolitanism is inevitable and equalising; basing it on a European model of modernity, as well as characterising this new cosmopolitanism as one of *forgetting*, is deeply worrying, especially in postcolonial and subaltern terms. His allusion to a decreasing memory of a global past is an experience of either privilege, predicated upon the model of linear progress for a few elite *world citizens*, or an experience of trauma, which is not at all a forgetting, but a suppression. Violently erased and suppressed historical memory is a painful part of diasporic communities, exiled and/or refugee communities, former and current colonies and dispossessed people of all denominations, for whom the act of remembering and feeling is also one of resistance and reclamation. The dispossessed often carry the memories and stories of their homes and their cultures in their bodies. On the whole, it appears that it is 'methodological cosmopolitanism', which does much of the forgetting and leaves legions of marginalised peoples behind. The critical theoretical work of making room for corporeal cosmopolitanism requires strongly worded arguments and exposing extremely well-hidden lacunae and exclusions. I do not intend for all dialogic attempts to take this form; but, decolonial scholarship is pushing back against centuries of episte-mological privilege and violence. The charge against liberal cosmopolitanism is not that it is intentionally heartless, but rather that, because it has chosen mind over body, it cannot, and perhaps does not know how, to speak from the body. Consider, for example, the idea of the 'post-traditional society' advocated by Anthony Giddens (1991, 1994). Giddens's basic argument is that everyday living and daily experiments impact the self and identity significantly. According to Giddens, globalisation and the increase in global communication, along with the growth of human knowledge, have given rise to new notions of consent and this has led to challenging traditions, creating a 'post-traditional society'. 'Social reflexivity' (Giddens 1991, 214) is an important part of this new vision of society, and Giddens suggests that 'life politics' (1994, 93–94) should replace the view of politics in an emancipa-tory role. This accompanies the understanding of new forms of capitalism as something positive and potentially radical, capable of creating a 'generative politics' (Giddens 1994, 93–94). This new politics is described as bottom-up and autonomous, placing emphasis on individual choice and decentralising political power. Giddens advocates a democratisation of all social institu-tions, a phenomenon already visible in the sphere of families and sexual relationships – what he calls an 'emotional democracy' (Giddens 1994, 117), although these emotions are basically to do with the autonomy of the private sphere. He speaks of a dialogic democracy, where disagreement will exist but in nonadversarial forms. Giddens's articulation of embodiment and affect in terms of this nonadversarial emotionality is yet another instance of how liberal definitions of affect and vulnerability can close off narratives of liberal cosmopolitanism to other more messy, chaotic and even violent understandings of affect. Giddens is very clearly interested in the transforma-tive power of reflexivity, as well as the new forms of intimacies and recon-figuration of the autonomy of "traditional" family roles. He sees a genuine potential in these new ways of living and choosing with independence and autonomy; but, similar to Beck's vision, this appears to be applicable only to a small, privileged minority. These changes of late modernity that Gid-dens understands as enormous but ultimately positive are reminiscent of the teleological, Kantian belief in the ultimate goal of humanity: *progress*. Again, there is a clear disavowal of colonial annexation, systems of domination based on innate privilege, and so on, but this occurs without actually address-ing the life-worlds of marginalised minorities, non-white and non-Western peoples, or their narratives of modernities and histories. Giddens's focus on emotions and transformation of intimate relationships is also based on an elite, Euromerican world view of the liberal tolerance of difference, which cannot, and will not, engage with the framework of the personal as political (the feminist resistance to the binary division between private and public), or with affect and embodiment as significant markers of political identity and community building. To speak of an emotional *democracy* suggests an inherent discomfort with excesses, mess and chaos. The dependence on "choice" and reflexivity as a democratic action also means that in this conception, whatever feelings may arise, they must be contained in manageable forms. But containment is not a feature of desire or of pain, and while dialogue does require a framework of some description, if we cannot make room for intensity, then honest speech will not be possible. One of the key operating principles of corporeal cosmopolitanism is that it must be a space where honesty and integrity of speech, body and spirit are both cultivated and protected. In the next and final section, we will explore some "other" notions of cosmopolitan belongings and the possibilities of expanding cosmopolitan relationalities. These three discussions have tried to critically grapple with some popular ideas and narratives of liberal cosmopolitan belongings, and in so doing, make the case for different imaginaries of belongings. However, dialogue is *still* the focus of these discussions. It is not my intention to alienate liberal narratives or decry them altogether but, rather, to see if we can build new possibilities with existing and future stories. These are fearful times, and we must hold spaces for ourselves and each other in as many ways as possible.

Mapping "Other" Cosmopolitan Belongings

One of the main features of Kantian cosmopolitanism, hospitality, has perhaps not received as much analytical attention as its counterparts, such as global dialogue or shared normative frameworks. It is worth recalling that the Kantian notion of hospitality is also underpinned by his ideas on race, geography and "maturity", making the caveat of hospitality a wobbly one indeed – in the sense that the definitions of mature, able humans, capable of reason, and therefore citizenship, were fairly restricted. However, the notions of *making welcome*, of receiving and of friendship, are powerful expressions of love and relationality and therefore quite relevant to formulating corporeal cosmopolitanism. Hospitality sits at the interstices of ethical, moral and emotional action, and is, as such, quite difficult to qualify in practicable terms. Seyla Benhabib's (2006) use of the Kantian right to hospitality, for instance, is central to her conception of cosmopolitanism as intersecting the state, law and morality. She advocates an ethical universalism, where ethnos and nationalism are undesirable, and encourages mediation between the moral, ethical and political realms. Benhabib sees Kantian cosmopolitanism as a move towards liberalism within states, changing the locus of control from internal to external and destabilising the absolute and arbitrary nature of sovereignty, especially post–World War II. Benhabib contends that the existence of cosmopolitan norms makes it harder to justify forms of exclusion and helps balance the relationship between universalistic norms and self-understanding of local communities. In light of the growing concern with human rights and the idea that crimes against humanity are now an indictable legal offence, she advocates a transition from the 'soft power of global society to the *constitutionalization of international law*' (Benhabib 2006, 72). For Benhabib, the principles of hospitality, as articulated in human rights frameworks, are an important way in which we might establish cosmopolitan openness and relationality (the human rights framework is, of course, a contentious framework, and I examine it in greater detail in chapter five). The larger point here is to do with the legal aspect of the cosmopolitan vision, which was critical to Kant's own formulation, and I certainly consider the constitutional/legislative aspects of cosmopolitan belonging as crucial to the work that lies ahead of us. It is an extremely delicate set of balances between practicable solutions, visceral emotions, intellectual motivations and bodily inhabitations. While I am well aware that those balances cannot always be maintained, it is very important to carve out spaces for all these aspects of articulation and identity.

The conundrum of cosmopolitan belongings and solidarity are so often hinging on the binarism of sameness and difference. And in many ways, the notion of hospitality was also based on such tension. The 'right to hospitality' (Kant 2006) refers to the right of any person to visit foreign territories without fear of death or hostility. The visitor may be denied entry according to the discretion of the state but may not be harmed, unless they pose a significant threat to the state. As we have already seen, Kant's denouncement of colonial and imperialist actions by Europe as inhospitable was negated by his belief in the fundamental inferiority of non-Europeans, women and "others". Combined with his his endorsement of hierarchical power relations (Kant 2006, 48–50) makes his anticolonial sentiments partial at best and meaningless at worst. Additionally, the use of particular discourses of reason and rationality makes them very early colluders in the history of colonial othering, and if we want to rescue the notion of hospitality, we will have to embody it and restore active, deeply felt love to it. In his dual-essay publication, *Rogues* (2005), Derrida navigates the twin conundrums that form the crux of the democratic question. The first is what he calls the circularity of sovereignty's return to itself. It is a return to the 'One' (Derrida 2005, 16), or homogeneity. The second conundrum is (Derrida 2005, 28), the element of heterogeneity, the multiplicitous and the dissymmetrical. The living (zēn) of life (zōe), according to Derrida, extends beyond the human living. It is the desirous, cyclical living or the energy of living; like the thinking of thought, there is a pleasure involved in this larger living. He writes, 'We must never dissociate the question of desire and of pleasure when we treat the political, and especially the democratic, the question of conscious or unconscious pleasure from the calculation and the incalculable to which desire and pleasure give rise' (Derrida 2005, 15). These pleasures and desires are an integral part of corporeal cosmopolitanism. In so many ways, the solidarities that produce and are produced by corporeal cosmopolitanism are rooted in pleasure and desire and in the embodied, affective dynamics of coming together. Democracy, according to Derrida, carries with it the idea of self-mastery – to have the power to do as 'One' pleases, or what he refers to as *autos* or *ipse*. Freedom is impossible without a certain sovereignty of self and the very notion of freedom comes from the 'Other'. Democracy excludes people by virtue of birth, citizenship, gender and sexuality, and the very idea of fraternity itself, as Derrida points out, is both Christian and always male. This consequently means that the traditional liberal cosmopolitan extension of hospitality as a political ideal has always been restricted to men. In his *Politics of Friendship* (1993), which is an important contribution to cosmopolitan understandings of relationality between people, Derrida describes friendship as having been understood in highly phallogocentric and fraternal, or male, terms, creating the double exclusion of the feminine, excluding the male-female friendship as well as the female-female friendship. He asks, 'Why this heterogeneity of *eros* and *philia*?' (1993, 382). In chapters three and four, I examine these very questions, as we explore the cosmopolitan solidarities in communities of queer, transwomen and dispossessed, diasporic women. What happens when we re-embody these relationalities of friendship? The solidarities of corporeal cosmopolitanism are embodied and rooted in the emotional and embodied constructions of friendship, and it is important to recognise these constructions as simultaneously capable of robust intellectual dialogues, legislative and constitutional actions that are rooted in traditions of deliberative reasoning and problem-solving. Contemporary liberal cosmopolitanisms often see these constructions as constitutively exclusive, and thus, conceptions of hospitality too become distant and utilitarian. By making the issues of "otherness" through gender, sexuality and race, as well as desire, central to the question of the political in general and democracy in particular, we can challenge these liberal cosmopolitan foundations of hospitality. The liberal cosmopolitan foundations of hospitality are also reflected in the use and deployment of "tolerance" as a civic value; and as practice, is simply not equipped to build deep bonds, and solidarities.

Derrida writes of friendship as a possibility that is yet to come. It never arrives in any absolute sense – 'friendship is never a given in the present; it belongs to the experience of waiting, of promise or of engagement' (1993, 384). He likens it to the discourse of prayer in the sense that it is neither true nor false. In my own work and journeys, making a commitment to this kind of futurity has been very important. The sensations, thoughts and feelings that I explore in this book that is moving towards corporeal cosmopolitanism demands this kind of commitment to a possible future; neither true nor false but a deep, abiding desire. The unconditional right to hospitality, Derrida argues, requires an unlimited openness to the other and links this to the gift of forgiveness beyond calculation – a kind of 'transformative repentance' (2005, 149). These are the concepts that are, according to Derrida, the bases of justice, as distinct from law. The incalculable and the calculable that he argues must always be thought of together although always in tension. He suggests a 'hyperethics' or 'hyperpolitics' that contains the unconditionality of freedom beyond the subject and creating a 'hypercritical' faith that is nondogmatic and nonreligious (2005, 152). I discuss Derrida's iterations of hospitality, friendship, desire and love here at length, because they quite eloquently point to the inarticulable, but deeply felt elements of cosmopolitan belongings that we must hold on to. Although liberal cosmopolitanism operates within the constraints of particular interpretations and discourses of reason, and is, as such, conditional upon several constraints of constitutionality, law and policy, these only form a part of the cosmopolitan vision. Cosmopolitan imagination is also formed of the unbounded, unconditional capacity for conversation, friendship and forgiveness in the almost spiritual capacity that Derrida describes them. Even Kant's own description of cosmopolitanism and hospitality is not devoid of this largeness of vision. In the essay *On the Relation of Theory to Practice in International Right*, Kant (2006) searches for conditions of lovability that might make human beings worthy of love. He posits that if there are 'predispositions in human nature', which can point to the constant movement and approach of the human species towards goodness, then humankind is worthy of being loved; 'otherwise we would have to hate or despise it, whatever posturings of universal love of humanity we might be presented with as proof of the opposite' (Kant 2006, 60). Thus, the teleological view of progress and the ultimate triumph of reason become essential prerequisites to loving humanity; relating love and reason in a complex bond, where the "soft" affective dimensions of love must be sacrificed, and the firm, "objective" hand of reason and the teleological framework of progress be adopted instead, in order to fulfil the original condition of love. The point I want to make here is about the multiplicity of cosmopolitan understanding. Even though the more deeply affective, spiritual and embodied dimensions of cosmopolitan imaginations and belongings may be difficult to implement, the strength of cosmopolitan visions lies in including these dimensions in its conceptual and practical frameworks. That is to say, the practicability of cosmopolitanism should never divorce itself from the core beliefs in unbounded, unconditional love, friendship and dialogue.

Before I move on to considering some narratives of "other" cosmopolitan belongings, I want to draw specific theoretical attention to the connections between colonial difference and liberal cosmopolitanisms. Throughout this chapter, the festering wound of colonialism and racial violence has loomed large in the presence of liberal cosmopolitan solidarities, beginning with Kant himself. Coloniality and the production of otherness form part of the core of corporeal cosmopolitanism. Many of the constitutive and traumatic violences

that I referenced throughout this chapter (and will in others to come) are
directly connected to colonial difference and the creation of the racial binary.
While it is important to remember that internal hierarchies, which include
colourism, casteism, xenophobia, bigotry etc. are not uncommon in non-white
cultural histories, the particular machinations of white and non-white are of a
different description and set of consequences altogether. Coloniality is an integral part of bodily marking, difference and othering. The mind-body duality,
which dominates so much of liberal cosmopolitan thought, is predicated upon
the othering of the non-white "savage" as "body" without "mind". Walter
Mignolo (2000b) thus posits cosmopolitanism within Christianity, modernity
and colonialism, arguing that 'coloniality is the hidden face of modernity and
its very condition of possibility' (2000b, 722). Mignolo's point of departure
is the sixteenth century and the growth of capitalism through the Atlantic
trade circuit. He locates critical cosmopolitanism in exteriority on what he
calls 'border cosmopolitanism' (722) – the outside that creates the territory
of the inside. He identifies four nonlinear interlocuting moments in history:
the Christian mission of Spain and Portugal in the sixteenth and seventeenth
centuries, the civilising mission of England and France in the eighteenth and
nineteenth centuries, the modernising mission of America in the twentieth
century, and the current civilisational project of neo-liberalism. Mignolo traces
the production of the infidel, the barbarian, the foreigner and the communist
through these historical moments and points out that Kant's cosmopolitanism has everything to do with Europe and very little to do with outside of it.
Thus, in order to be truly radical, Mignolo argues that critical cosmopolitanism must locate itself firmly within colonial difference and not within cultural
relativism, which is the liberal cosmopolitan bulwark. Colonial power stems
from its ability to define what constitutes the "human". Africans, Asians and
other non-Western/colonised peoples were simply not recognised as human,
and the rhetoric of human rights was not required to address them at all. This
is precisely the point that Judith Butler makes in her work, *Precarious Life*
(2004), when she questions the premise of lives worth grieving for. Mignolo
distinguishes this by using the terms 'Ontological and Epistemological equality (2011, 279). *Being* human, and equality in an ontological sense, is a status
that *can* be accorded to all people, but epistemological equality pertaining to
legitimacy, recognition and sovereignty is an entirely different matter.

In the discussions of liberal cosmopolitan narratives in previous sections,
it is easy enough to glean that colonial difference was not the crux of liberal
cosmopolitanisms. For instance, Beck's arguments suggested that cosmopolitanism is essentially of the future, with little room for the past, and Delanty's
critical cosmopolitanism looks to transcend differences in light of a shared
normativity and political community. Butler, in her collaborative work with
Ernesto Laclau and Slavoj Žižek (2000) critiques, through Hegel, the image

of an annihilating universality which, in order to survive, has to keep erasing the wills of those it excludes, therefore becoming incapable of sustaining its original intent of denoting itself as 'self-identical to all human beings' (2000, 23). Questioning the very bases on which someone is categorised human, she argues that 'those who are dispossessed or remain radically unrepresented by the general will of the universal do not rise to the level of the recognisably human within its terms' (Butler et al. 2000, 23). Butler refers to this kind of universality as a 'spectral universality (2000, 23). While she is in agreement with Appiah's position, that all identities are formed on the basis of a constitutive exclusion and antagonism, unlike the liberal school of cosmopolitan thought, she focuses on the importance of cultural translation which many scholars ignore. Universalism without cultural translation is nothing short of imperialism, and it is here that Butler warns of the dangers of cultural translation itself becoming imperial through the imposition of *one* language – that of emancipation and "progress" on "other" worlds. In Mignolo's critical cosmopolitanism, colonial difference and history are central features. The formation of the colonial matrix of power through religion, economic control and the control of knowledge, precluded non-white people from the *nomos* of humanity itself. Thus, the postnation ideal, which liberal scholars propose, fundamentally does not make room for colonised peoples. In order to make this room, there must first be an acknowledgement and recognition that, for the most part, nation states were colonial impositions both by Europe and America upon the territories they annexed. In Mignolo's terms, the equality that liberal cosmopolitanisms advocate, is ontological, not epistemological. That is to say, being *human* is common to all, but being *sovereign* is not, and unless this epistemological inequality – the direct result of colonialism – can be addressed, there is no moving forward into cosmopolitan futures. By way of concluding chapter one and to illustrate what might constitute "other" narratives of cosmopolitanism or 'border cosmopolitanisms' (Mignolo 2000b), I discuss a few cosmopolitan narratives from the "global south". I hope to demonstrate the radical potential of these challenges to liberal cosmopolitan narratives, as well as show that the explicit corporealisation of these cosmopolitan stories is a necessary and productive movement.

The first example of such a radical cosmopolitan narrative can be found in Kalpana Ram's (2008) work, which explains cosmopolitanism as an orientation rather than a set of tenets. This orientation, according to her, has to do with transcending locality, identity and often disembodied ways of living. Ram's research is on *Dalit* women in India fighting for various rights from female healthcare to safe drinking water, and she argues that these kinds of solidarities are not a gentle and 'unselfconscious movement between the local and the global' (Ram 2008, 141) in the way that some liberal cosmopolitans suggest. It is a far more dramatic process requiring the women to 'shun and abjure all that comes under the label of tradition' (Ram 2008, 141). These women make massive and active transformations with very serious consequences in order to transcend their conditions. Ram suggests that, unlike cultural cosmopolitanism and diasporic acknowledgements of multiple homes or belongings, this cosmopolitanism is far more political. The cosmopolitanism of the *Dalit* women's movement is rooted in socialism and feminism, and both ideologies have been critiqued for suppressing rather than appreciating difference that makes it distinct from a liberal cosmopolitanism rooted in a universal shared framework of humanness. This type of cosmopolitanism, writes Ram, is 'resolutely partisan, aligned with a particular oppressed group' (2008, 141). At the same time, there is a kind of universalism that informs this alignment with the oppressed. This cosmopolitanism, rooted in constitutive difference, caste and identity politics, has fallen out of step with today's narratives of cosmopolitanism. Ram argues for the layered understanding of modernity, using the example of Christian missionaries as having galvanised the *Dalit* communities in India, who gained much confidence from them, which is quite different from a typical postcolonial understanding of the influence of Christian missionaries in postcolonial spaces. She distinguishes 'activist cosmopolitanism' from other Western and liberal cosmopolitanisms by suggesting that the latter approach the obliteration of the distinction between self and other through deliberation and reflexivity – as dialogues within the self. Activist cosmopolitanism, by contrast, 'moves by *contagion*' (Ram 2008, 151) and blurs the distinction between self and other in a large openness, by connecting the self to the other in historically specific situations such as the example of the Christian missionaries discussed previously. Ultimately, Ram is suggesting that cosmopolitanism need not be restricted to dismantling the distinction between self and other, but could also be a 'rush of identificatory emotion from self to other' (2008, 151), in the context of solidarity and collective action, which also challenges the binary division in a different capacity. Solidarity is once again tied to affect and *eros* and the question of what role it plays, especially in the context of marginalised solidarities, is a significant one[5]. However, it is important to note that the argument for solidarity based on this 'rush of identificatory emotion' (Ram 2008, 151) could also transform into an essentialised and exclusive community, where the 'truth' can be *authentically* known only by being part of the "inside". The kind of cosmopolitan solidarity that Ram describes is distinctly different from those that I have discussed thus far. The relationalities between the *Dalit* women and Christian missionaries have a long and complex history that cannot be fully elaborated upon here. However, it is important to recognise the radical, cosmopolitan nature of *Dalit* resistance to traditional Hindu caste hegemony and violence, through an alliance with English both as a language and as an alternative to upper-caste oppression. There is an intersection of global/local, with a complete unraveling of self/

other binaries on multiple levels, including ethnicity, language, nationality and culture, which, once again, points to a combination of practicable, grass-roots cosmopolitanism, with the conception of a much larger understanding of what solidarity might mean. The embodied experiences of discrimination, segregation and caste-gender violence that *Dalit* women experience as an existential reality make the articulation of solidarity both complex and rooted in material conditions of living and identity. The activist cosmopolitanism that Ram describes here is thus a layered and nuanced combination of alliances and resistances that can only be understood in terms of embodied and affective experiences of this community of *Dalit* women. This is a powerful example of how *large* and *small* understandings of solidarity are exploded and combined in ever newer ways. They are constructed and carried in the bodies and voices of this marginalised community of resisting women, giving us a glimpse of what activist, and corporeal cosmopolitan solidarities could achieve, if we recognised and strengthened them.

The next example of 'border' cosmopolitanism that I want to discuss is slightly different in that it is a biographical cosmopolitan trajectory, by way of Kris Manjapra's (2010) work on M. N. Roy (1887–1954). M. N. Roy was an anticolonial revolutionary, philosopher, freedom fighter and Marxist cosmopolitan in India and the world. Biographical narratives are an important part of the affective cosmopolitan experience, especially when trying to envision new constructs and paradigms. Roy's journeys, beliefs and experiences are also symbolic of the complex dimensions and implications of a colonised experience. Roy's story also offers an important problematisation of the debates around patriotism and nationalistic sentiment as being opposed to a cosmopolitan ethos. Anticolonial cosmopolitanisms form an important part of border cosmopolitanisms, and Manjapra's M. N. Roy is a radical cosmopolitan, a traveller of everywhere and nowhere, a figure who occupies the margin of margins. An ardent Marxist and anticolonialist, M. N. Roy was deeply engaged in the politics of the world, but he was also someone deeply rooted in the materiality of inhabiting the world as a desiring, political agent.

Manjapra characterises M. N. Roy as combining the *swadeshi* Indian independence ideals of *exegis* (interpretation and critique of religious texts) and *ascesis* (physical and spiritual rigour and abstinence). As Manjapra explains, *exegis* and *ascesis*, though very distinct from each other, were not closed off as conceptual frameworks. Though Hindu-centric, these frameworks projected themselves into the world and made connections with it. These twin concepts dominated the intellectual theatre of colonial India and elite, *swadeshi* avant-gardism, most prevalent in Bengal. This way of thinking was committed to travel, reimagining colonially imposed concepts of time-space as well as engaging in a constant re- and de-territorialisation. Some examples that Manjapra offers are those of Aurobindo Ghosh, who proposed a new kind of anticolonial universalism, Bipin Chandra Pal, who pioneered the "cult of the mother" and Benoy Kumar Sarkar, who advocated *Vishwa Shakti* (cosmic/world energy/force), urging Indians to travel as widely as possible. M. N. Roy, Manjapra observes, was vehement and passionate about the idea of India's deterritoriality. As he drew away from the *swadeshi* stance towards communism, Roy's major associations were with German fringe communists rather than the Bolsheviks. The former's mandate was focused on worker education and solidarity building, as well as the call for radical democracy, and Rosa Luxemburg, not Lenin, was their intellectual pivot. Roy himself was very critical of Lenin for propagating the dictatorship of a selective proletariat rather than advocating a focus on fostering a proletariat consciousness that was inclusive. However, his deep engagement with Europe and America did not by any means lessen his involvement with India: 'Roy's internationalism did not mean that he was rootless, exiled or distanced from the Indian anticolonial struggle' (Manjapra 2010, 80). Roy's tryst with anticolonialism and communism was a torrid one, full of fiery idealism and terrible losses, both material and ideological. These embodied, emotional qualities of Roy's anticolonial and international cosmopolitanism reiterate a real necessity to produce decolonial, corporeal and affective histories of cosmopolitan identification and belonging. As Manjapra observes, 'Roy's position as an intermediary between intellectual positions meant that Roy often broke the frame of his own way of thinking' (2010, 82). This remains one of the most critical necessities of cosmopolitan thought and makes Roy's life-work an invaluable part of border cosmopolitan narratives.

Roy's radical ideas of communism, his open criticism of Lenin and his fundamental belief that communism *had* to be freed from authoritarianism completely isolated him both from the Comintern (Communist International – an international Communist organization founded by Lenin in Moscow in 1919 and dissolved in 1943) and within Indian communist circles. He was also critical of Gandhi's notion of a frozen Indian cultural identity and his insistence on a certain notion of purity. Gandhi's insistence on a 'territorialised selfhood' (Manjapra 2010, 114), his propogation of austerity, fasting and sexual abstinence as a 'necessity for ethical political action' (114) was entirely opposed to Roy's way of thinking. These radical ways of thinking and disagreeing came at terrible prices, and often, the liberal narrative of embracing a cosmopolitan way of life completely omits the visceral hardships involved in choosing such a path. After spending twelve destructive years in prison, he resumed his critical philosophy and intellectual activism, now turning more and more towards the enervating capacities of desire and pleasure. Manjapra writes that Roy used sexuality and desire as ways to connect India to the world, by advocating an Epicurean path to freedom. Roy was 'interstitial and taboo. His life course and his political philosophy epitomised a temporality of global circulation that seemed to contaminate and infect the regimens of anti-colonial morality and discipline' (Manjapra 2010, 113). Manjapra's observations place Roy in the realm of a radical, affective and embodied cosmopolitanism that was and still is a formidable challenge to liberal imaginations of cosmopolitan solidarity. Roy's unequivocal privileging of international solidarity over nationalism made him extremely unpopular among Indian anticolonialists. He was also vociferously anti-fascist and feared that fascism was a global phenomenon, a new mode of politics, as capable of being Indian as it was German. He viewed Gandhi's call for cultural exclusivity and his *khadi* movement as cultural militarism that enforced homogeneity. Indian anticolonialists of the time were not entirely opposed to fascism; in fact, some of them actively supported it. Shunned and slandered by nearly all his colleagues and compatriots, Roy became an abject of the Bengali *adda* (an informal radical community/gathering of intellectuals popular in Bengal).

Manjapra characterises Roy as a Caliban of sorts, and as I progress through the following chapters, we will see that the figure of Shakespeare's Caliban is a recurrent one in African, Latin American and other subaltern imaginaries. The problem here was that the "major" figures of Indian anticoloniality, such as Gandhi and Rabindranath Tagore, had their own (not necessarily coeval) versions of internationalism and cosmopolitanism that suppressed other, more minor articulations like Roy's. There was a strong strand of Indian anti-colonial cosmopolitanism, as Manjapra observes, which was characterised by 'civilizational continuity' (155) and an 'exchange between high traditions' (2010, 154). It is, however, important to note that Indian anticolonialism was by no means monolithic and that there were several oppositional and subaltern anticolonialists like B. R. Ambedkar, E. V. Periyar and others. That said, it must still be understood that the strong sense of a past glory and the elitism that accompanied these strands of anticolonialism are also what made India so problematic within the racial imaginary of both Africa and the Caribbean (see chapter four). In his movement from *swadeshi ascesis* and *exegis* to communism and the eventual rejection of all of these, Roy finally advocated a radical humanism that was rooted in science, spiritualism, eroticism and class politics. He saw desire as the primary motivator of the self and as a universal energy and proposed a monism that would encompass mind and body, combining scientific rationalism with romantic faith. I recount Roy's journey here in some detail not only as an individually important narrative but also as relating to Ram's discussion of *Dalit* resistance and activist cosmopolitanism in a broader sense. These narratives also pose important challenges to the seemingly oppositional bonds of nation and world: polis and cosmos. It is clear from scholarship like Ram's and Manjapra's that cosmopolitan imaginaries and identifications have been and are incredibly nuanced, plural and open, in these "other" places. These radical, resistant forms of cosmopolitanism are indicative of a deeply felt openness and capacity to hold seemingly incompatible differences together in affective, embodied and political ways, which may then open up paths to reimagine and recombine our visions and narratives of cosmopolitanism, which make room for affective and embodied notions of political belonging and community.

As we come to a close in this chapter, I have tried to bring together some of the crucial ideas and concepts that animate liberal, Euromerican understandings of cosmopolitan identification, belonging and community, from Kant to more contemporary scholarship. These discussions have been selective and mostly in relation to questions of embodiment and emotion, and how we might reanimate the idea of cosmopolitan belonging as a corporeal, affective process. As far as possible, I have endeavoured to keep these discussions productively critical and always open to dialogue. I hope that you are interested enough and moved enough to make your way to chapter two, where I will explore some important dimensions of embodied and emotional identities. In other words, we now know that new cosmopolitan imaginaries are necessary, but why should they and what does it mean for them to be corporeal?

NOTES

1 I would be remiss if I do not mention the work of Jürgen Habermas in connection to liberal cosmopolitanism. Habermas deals with Kant's ideas in a rigorous and critical capacity, and his work is invaluable to liberal cosmopolitan scholarship. However, Habermas deals with the question of democracy, justice and Enlightenment-based liberal politics largely in relation to Europe and the European understandings of cosmopolitanism. The logics of the Enlightenment, reason and rationality form the core foundations of his work, and, as such, there is no real opening in which to situate the conversation around embodiment and emotions in relation to Habermas's cosmopolitanism.

2 "But if you believe you're a citizen of the world, you're a citizen of nowhere. You don't understand what the very word 'citizenship' means." (Theresa May, 2016) For the complete speech see: http://www.telegraph.co.uk/news/2016/10/05/theresa-mays-conference-speech-in-full/.

3 For a detailed and nuanced examination of Rabindranath Tagore's relationship with cosmopolitanism, see Rahul Rao's *Between Home and the World* (2010) and "Postcolonial Cosmopolitanism: Making Place for Nationalism" (2013).

4 Frantz Fanon's work documents, and theorises the horrific extent of psychic and physical wounding as well as severe self- abnegation that racist colonial violence perpetrates upon, and produces in colonised peoples. See: Black Skin, White Masks (1952), The Wretched of the Earth (1961).

5 For a nuanced exploration of the politics and processes of marginal solidarities, and how they emerge and dissolve in strategic ways, see: Sandoval, Chela. 1991. "U.S. Third World Feminism: The Theory and Method of Oppositional Consciousness in the Postmodern World," *Genders* (10) 1–24.

Chapter 2

The Anatomy of Abjection

Contextualising Exclusion, Corporeality and Emotions

So much for telling stories about cosmopolitanism; I must now turn to that which forms the basis of my call for corporeal cosmopolitanism: bodies and feelings. This chapter aims to provide theoretical and conceptual contexts to embodiment and affect as constitutive elements of political identities and solidarities. It examines the connections between the intellectual tenets that underpin liberal understandings of cosmopolitan solidarity and the ways in which these tenets have excluded corporeality and emotional identity-scapes. As chapter one has demonstrated, the core discourses which fuel liberal cosmopolitan conceptions are predicated upon the hierarchies of mind-body dualism and the supremacy of certain discourses of reason which inherently delegitimise the body. This chapter examines some of the logics of delegitimisation and exclusion. I characterise the elision of the body through some oft-used theoretical lenses of otherness and exclusion in contemporary scholarship, in order to unpack the structures of such elision. That is, how can we understand this kind of extreme marginalisation? What might it look and feel like? This chapter also considers cultures of embodiment that are or were not influenced by certain Euromerican discourses of scientism and the Enlightenment, to gain a sense of the particular ways in which liberal cosmopolitan narratives exclude embodiment from their framing of *large* solidarities. I use feminist scholarship around the material and conceptual acts of embodying and explore ways in which we might *corporealise* cosmopolitan belongings. Once again, turning to decolonial and "other" narratives of cosmopolitan solidarities gives us an idea of how these stories, which are not rooted in spaces of liberal, hetero-patriarchal and elite white privilege, are already articulating the body and emotions in their formation of communities, though not always in overt and conscious terms. These are the stories which pave the way for the following chapters, where I consider specific sites and communities which

provide us with blueprints, directions and hope for corporeal cosmopolitanism. My imagination of corporeal cosmopolitanism, as briefly examined in
the introduction, does not maintain strict definitional boundaries between
embodiment and corporeality and affect/emotion. They can, and do, mean
different things, but I am interested in the relationships between them and
the spaces they can create and hold within cosmopolitan narratives. As Sara
Ahmed (2014) so aptly describes, emotions *shape* the surfaces of our bodies and the interactions between them in physical, social, sexual, emotional,
economic and cultural contexts. Emotions circulate among and between
bodies – both in solitary and social ways. Emotions and bodies belong in the
messy matrix of identity, community formation and political belonging, in as
equal a capacity as the 'mind-reason-intellect' complex. Indeed, as feminist,
poststructural and postcolonial scholarships argue, creating hierarchies and
exclusions among emotions, thoughts and bodies only serve to limit and skew
our understandings of the processes of identity and community formation and
political belonging. Such hierarchies and exclusions also form the bases of
violence and marginalisation, on multiple levels, in material, emotional and
epistemological experiences. Making corporeality and affect a core part of a
new understanding of cosmopolitanism requires some understanding of *why*
it is so important and the histories of how bodies and emotions have been sys-
tematically excluded and delegitimised as sources of identity, experience and
thought. The discourse of marginalisation that surrounds the body – pathologising
and delegitimising it, relegating it as a category to medicine and biological
science or to desire, sin and irrationality – has silenced ways of knowing and
belonging that do not fall into public/political/rational/male realms. It is these
articulations that are relevant to the understandings of cosmopolitanism and
what it can mean to think about ideas of global ethics, *human* communities
and the weakening of territorial boundaries. Elision lies at the heart of this
discussion of the construction of knowledge in general and cosmopolitanism
in particular. To understand the relationships between the exclusion of the
body and cosmopolitan narratives, I first explore the understanding of exclusion in relation to the body, in selected Western and postcolonial scholarship,
and then proceed to discuss it in specific relation to liberal Western thought,
and consequently, liberal narratives of cosmopolitanism.

The logic of exclusion is predicated on difference, and the most visceral
form of difference is often located in the body. If exclusion as a practice is
understood as being based on differences mapped and marked on the body,
then the theorisation and treatment of the body itself become highly significant in understanding its elision. I therefore briefly explore some pre- and
post-Cartesian theorisation of the body, specifically within European imaginaries, and contrast these with non-European imaginaries of the body. I do
this to highlight the problems of the body within Euromerican epistemological

positions and also to draw attention to the seriousness of colonial violence and its contribution to these epistemological positions with respect to the body and its political valence. In the third section, I explore some relevant ideas in the work of two feminist scholars, Elizabeth Grosz and Moira Gatens, both of whom explore the body and corporeality as legitimate, generative sites of knowledge and experience. This is where we will consider what the process of corporealising might entail and why it is so vital to reimagining cosmopolitan notions of community and belonging. There is an enormous amount of scholarship around the processes of embodiment and corporealisation within queer and feminist studies. However, I restrict myself to ideas which address the delegitimisation of the body within the political. I also examine the specific problems of Euro-American epistemology in eliding the body and link it to larger questions around political agency and ethics of the body. Grosz and Gatens's ideas about embodying the political are rooted in a critique of Enlightenment-influenced liberal political epistemologies, which is why their work enriches the framing of corporeal cosmopolitanism. Since much of the work of building corporeal cosmopolitanism must happen through conversations with and divergences from liberal cosmopolitan narratives, it becomes important to conduct critical dialogues which speak to the specificities of liberal cosmopolitan framings.

The concluding section of the chapter, as previously mentioned, explores these connections between corporeality, affect and cosmopolitanism through some postcolonial and decolonial narratives of cosmopolitan belonging, travel and exile. These narratives intersect with corporeal politics and affect, acknowledging their importance, without making embodiment an explicit part of their cosmopolitan vision. However, they do bring aspects of corporeality, grief and desire into their formulations of cosmopolitan communities, emphasising the necessity and potentials for corporeal cosmopolitanism. To corporealise is a crucial process. Rather than creating an isolated or bounded space exclusive to the body and affective assemblages, to corporealise an idea, discipline or theory means something far more. It requires us to make corporeality and emotions integral to how we comprehend or come to "know" something. The *presence* of the body and emotions must be revitalised in that they must be allowed to extend beyond their physical, biological and gendered limits, either as dead matter or as mere carriers or effects of the causal mind.

THE MECHANICS OF EXCLUSION

What does it mean to *exclude*? What shapes and forms do the damages, violences and silences of exclusion take? To place outside is to necessarily create a boundary and a dichotomy of the permitted and the denied. Here, I critically explore some Euromerican understandings of exclusion with particular reference to corporeality and affect and the ways in which they both open up and close down cosmopolitan thought to an embodied, affective understanding. I do this partly to provide a little intellectual context to some contemporary conceptions of otherness and exclusion in Euromerican scholarship. But I also want to remind us that though these conceptions are highly critical of liberal dualisms and hierarchies, it does not immediately follow that these critiques can be absorbed into critical corporeal cosmopolitanism in an unproblematised fashion. The objective is to find conversant spaces where questions of embodiment and corporeality directly challenge or destabilise the liberal foundations of cosmopolitanism but in ways that will allow for genuinely radical formulations of political community and belonging.

Exclusion and elision, in many ways, constitute the boundaries of belonging, and I try to unpack the contexts and effects of these processes. There is a particular quality of isolation that marks the ways in which certain exclusions take place. Some exclusions carry a powerful moral charge of loathing and visceral hatred, making them a more complex terrain than other kinds of more subtle exclusions. Julia Kristeva's (1982) theorisation of the abject speaks powerfully about the exclusion of bodies and emotions – particularly women's bodies. It is a frequently used classic text, though still relatively new to liberal cosmopolitanism (see Nyers 2003). To cast body and affect as the abjects of cosmopolitanism is to suggest that they are always present at the edges of cosmopolitan narratives but never permitted to enter or be part of them. They are, in a sense, made conspicuous by their absence. Thus, they both form a solid critique of and provide the opportunity to reimagine cosmopolitan solidarities. Kristeva places both affect and a visceral physicality at the centre of exclusion. The abject, for Kristeva, is what destabilises the distinction between subject and object, inside and outside. It is always associated with desire, an amputation of the self, discarding that which is mourned, feared and loathed. The abject is seen not only as the banished but also as something that taunts and challenges from the borders of its expulsion. The abject:

> is not the white expanse or slack boredom of repression, not the translations and transformations of desire that wrench bodies, rights and discourse. . . . Not me. Not that. But not nothing either. . . . A weight of meaninglessness about which there is nothing insignificant. . . . On the edge of non-existence and hallucination, of a reality that if I acknowledge it, annihilates me. (Kristeva 1982, 2)

Spat out in terrified revulsion and rejection, speakability or acknowledgement of the abject will be an acknowledgement of an abnegated, loathed self. The abject, in Kristeva's work is deeply tied to the self, but in a relationship of fear and loathing. Fear shrinks the body (Ahmed 2014), and it is this shrinking, this withdrawing in revulsion from that which is part of us, and yet expelled, that makes the abject so compelling and so complex. The abject is marked by its exclusion; its absence makes it a presence, perhaps even a haunting. The absent presence of the body and emotions in much classical, liberal political and social thought invokes a similar kind of image. This inability to articulate material, lived experiences and feelings, as part of political identity or thought, is at the heart of liberal cosmopolitan narratives, and that focus on unspeakability is why I use Kristeva's idea of abjection as a way to understand this elision. It is important to remember, though, that, to be abject is also to be locked in a perpetual *outsideness* as a way to desta-bilise the "inside". That is to say, the dismantling of the inside, still requires the positionality of the outside, which is (potentially) an indefinite extension of binary subjectivity. While I certainly see abjection as a way to effectively describe the ways in which corporeality and assemblages of feeling have been othered, I do not see it as a way forward, in terms of building corporeal cosmopolitanism.

In an attempt to place abjection in an explicitly political context, Kristeva (1991) framed the foreigner as abject, making the connection between excluded bodies and notions of citizenship and belonging. The political framing of abjection connects to the discussions around citizenship vis-à-vis cosmopolitan belonging from chapter one. Liberal narratives of cosmopolitan belonging are not really equipped to deal with abjection as a political condi-tion, and, if we follow Kristeva's argument, this applies to "foreigners" as an ontological category. The foreigner is always the other, defined negatively as being not one of "us". Traditionally defined by law of blood, it is defined in modern times by nationality and statehood. The foreigner is either deemed harmful or beneficial, rejected or conditionally assimilated; 'The foreigner is thought of in terms of political power and legal rights' (Kristeva 1991, 96). In other words, the very existence of foreigners is predicated on law. Ancient Greek and Latin cosmopolitanism, as well as proto-Christian move-ments, sought an inclusion beyond law, to make the foreigner equal to the citizen, but only within the bounds of a specific territory – city or religion. This in turn gave rise to a new set of outsiders and heretics, outside this new boundary of selective inclusiveness. This way of defining inclusion is always predicated on some form of exclusion, and that exclusion will always make itself conspicuous by its absence. Thus, foreigners are perpetually causing the state to confront the "other" and the non-state. Kristeva distinguishes the citizen from the human, identifying the rights of a citizen as superior to the rights of a human, an observation made by Mignolo in his discussion of onto-logical and epistemological equality (see chapter one). In fact, it is well worth considering if there truly exists a functioning set of rights that will apply to humans who are not citizens. For, without that kind of belonging, how "human" are we, really? To not be a citizen, then, invariably means to not be fully human. This question of whether the noncitizen is *fully* human becomes ever more prescient as the political rhetoric around immigration and refugees pushes these "others" further and further away towards the inhuman condition of stateless abandonment. In a related capacity, Partha Chatterjee (2004) makes an interesting distinction between citizens and populations. He argues that citizens are morally constructed, while populations are a gross mass of people empirically determined – a number of bodies. This distinction is also at the heart of the distinction between so-called developed and developing countries in the sense that the association between citizenship and the "first world" seems to be a given, while the "third world" is often identified with an excessive population, a teeming, uncontrolled mass of people. Thus, the citizen is a complete human with complete rights, while the "third world" is precarious, full of too many imperfect people in failing democracies, or worse, non-democracies, making them alien, and often, less than human. The criteria for entrance and hospitality have settled into an organised xenophobia, profiling bodies as illegitimate on the bases of skin colour and/or religious faith.

Major political decisions such as Britain's decision to *exit* Europe in 2016 and Donald Trump's ascension to presidency in 2017, in the larger context of a substantial move towards the political right, have further weaponised the body of the *foreigner-as-threat*. The renewed pledge to maintain the integrity of the "inside" has strengthened the divides between citizen and human far more acutely than we might have anticipated. The *noncitizen* is ultimately illegitimate. They cannot participate or speak in legal processes that decide the outcomes of whether they will be permitted or denied. Thus, the protection, the entry and the potential eradication of the foreigner are all decided in absentia. Seeing as the request for political membership is so far divorced from any notion of equal choice; it is difficult to see how liberal cosmopolitanism is able to justify these means as a foundation for equal cosmopolitan status. Kant's understanding of hospitality works only in an ideal situation of equality, where the request to enter a territory or state is just that – a request to visit or trade. Contemporary political realities could not be further from this ideal. The foreigner inevitably belongs nowhere, and lives as an "other" among others. Kristeva (1991) alludes to Freud's concept of *heimlich/unheimlich* or 'uncanny strangeness' (170) in describing the foreigner as symptomatic and symbolic of the idea of strangeness within the familiar; that is, the uncanny strangeness of the foreigner is experienced by the "us" as something that was once familiar, then expelled, but now threatens to become familiar again. For Kristeva, "othering" is a deeply gendered process, and women are always more vulnerable to this negative rhetoric of otherness, because they are always already foreign and abjected. I unpack the gendered nature of othering in chapters three and four, where I focus on sexuality, femininity, transgender and women's experiences to highlight the impact of eliding the corporeal in cosmopolitan thought. For psychoanalytical approaches, the real threat lies within ourselves. The fear of the foreigner is ultimately the rejection of otherness within ourselves; the other is our own unconscious. Abjection in Kristeva's work is more concerned with *where* it is located – the space of exclusion, rather than its identity per se or *who* the abject is. What this means in relation to the excluded body in cosmopolitanism is that we may be able to account for bodies *as such* – the refugee body, the mutilated body, the prisoner-of-war body, the terrorist body, the raped body and so on. However, there is no spatial recognition of the body as an experiential and epistemological site within cosmopolitan identity production and creation, and that is one of the things that corporeal cosmopolitanism would address. As I argued earlier in this chapter, abjection, while useful, is not the kind of politics that I want to base corporeal cosmopolitanism on. Abjection places the revolutionary potential of the abject at the heart of its own rejection – that is, being reviled makes us powerful in some ways. The problem with this framing is that it is conducted from one side of the spectrum and does not pay enough attention to the complexities of what abjection does to the abject, aside from excommunicating it. Kristeva's psychoanalytical approach suggests that the expulsion of the abject is a manifestation of the expulsion of the self, and there is a sense of loss and amputation as the abjection occurs. Since the abject loses both legitimacy and speakability, we are unable to fully explore the ways in which the subject, which performs the expulsion actually, interpellates and produces the abject. That is to say, the "other", though recognised and legitimised in some senses as the *abject*, still remains mysterious, unspeakable and primal, though not in an intentionally derogatory way. If corporeal cosmopolitanism was to adopt this kind of a position, it could not be decolonial. It would still need to essentialise corporeality in an exotic or mysterious way, making open dialogue a real challenge.

Another articulation of such extreme otherness is exemplified in Giorgio Agamben's work about the Holocaust and Jewish prisoners in concentration camps, he writes of the *Homo Sacer* (1998), which also attempts to express this sense of absolute exclusion. *Homo Sacer*, simultaneously hallowed and cursed, can be killed with impunity, but never sacrificed or murdered simply because they are the absolute abject. Agamben (1998) describes the *Homo Sacer* as one who is absolutely and irrevocably excluded or set apart. Although there are some important and complex overlaps in Agamben's work between *Homo Sacer* as both sovereign and abject, here, I examine the latter. The *Musselman*[1] (Agamben's term for the abject camp prisoner) is expelled to the space of the concentration camp where she or he ceases to be human. This understanding is critically important as it follows the earlier discussion around the relevance of being human without being a citizen. It also follows,

in a perverse logic, that citizenship can alone authorise the state to dehuman-
ise its citizens or those humans that it considers a threat to its statehood. That
is, only the state has the power to banish subjects into statelessness (see Butler and Spivak 2007; and chapter one). Jyotirmaya Tripathy (2014) describes
this as the power of the state to 'un-modern' (8) its abjects, which Tripathy
illustrates through state torture of the "terrorist" body:

> if the body is constituted meaningful within modernity and its demands in terms
> of ideal citizenship, it must also be subjected to a spectacle of un-moderning
> once it becomes useless for the state. (Tripathy 2014, 8)

There is an important link here between citizenship and "first worldness",
which is particularly relevant to liberal cosmopolitan notions of belonging.
The citizen is understood through their relation to reason, progress, development and modernity. They are a modern subject par excellence, invested
with all the rights – both moral and corporeal – of a citizen. The citizen, as
Kant also observed, is protected by constitutional right and cannot be easily
injured, at least by law. The abject/terrorist/foreigner/refugee, on the other
hand, is not a citizen. They do not bear the moral or bodily rights of one who
belongs to the state, and therefore receives no protection. Their body is bare –
merely human and therefore open to any form of use, misuse and abuse. One
of the major problems with the postnation arguments of liberal cosmopolitanism that were discussed in chapter one is that while their critique of the nation
state is well made, they do not account for the absolute capacity of the state
mechanism to make and unmake the bodies of its citizens. Even in the case of
arguments that were more sensitive to the complexities of nation, borders and
identity, the understanding of cosmopolitanism is fundamentally premised
on a liberal democratic order. This means that the inclusion of people into a
democracy is based on membership, while noncitizens are outside the realms
of includability. They are bare bodies, carrying stories of travel, globality,
exile and internationalism in visceral, corporeal forms that need to be articulated and witnessed.

When Agamben (1999) recounts the stories of survivors – those who used
to be *Musselmann* or the abject – what is difficult to fathom is how exactly
this process of being *der Musselmanner* ends. For if the survivor tells only the
shadow of a story, and indeed, often feels compelled to do so, she or he is still
separate from the *Musselmann*. The survivor conceives of the *Musselmann*
as separate and other – not as part of themselves, because the *Musselmann* is
unspeakable. They have no purpose or aim but to survive, and the testimonies
tell the readers that the *Musselmann* cared nothing for life in the sense of being
human or retaining humanity. The accounts tell of desperate snatches for extra
helpings of food, a complete destruction of selfhood and dignity; the blank

vacancy and the revulsion they caused to those around them. This is indicative of the extent of state power and its capacity to render subject as object, and object as abject. Agamben (1999) writes, 'the Muselmann, [is] the "complete witness", making it forever impossible to distinguish between man and non-man' (47). Ultimately, in some sense, the *Musselmann* is "imagined", because we are incapable of comprehending *Homo Sacer* in her or his reality: a reality that the state creates but expels outside its own bounds, simultaneously destroying the delineations of inside and outside within the self. The brutality involved in the destruction of the self-other delineation is even more profound than it appears in Kristeva's work. While we must be careful not to disavow *any* part of the horror endured by victims of genocidal violence, it is also important to note that this conception of absolute otherness is made possible only through the annihilation of "other" bodies. The sense of irreparable internal fragmentation, which Agamben captures when making the distinction between survivor and *Musselmann*, is a theme that repeats in many strands of postcolonial and decolonial writing. Frantz Fanon's (1963, 2008) analyses of this absolute splintering, through his pioneering work, are an important part of the beginnings of anticolonial scholarship. He wrote both evocatively and powerfully against the brutality of dehumanising black peoples, and the ways in which slavery and racist violences completely decimated any sense of self-identification in black people. Even the ways in which the black self is put together, Fanon argues, are fundamentally violent. Black peoples have been allowed no other possibilities, or frameworks, to imagine or experience their material, spiritual and emotional bodies. The extent of physical, mental and spiritual wounding is, according to Agamben, beyond description, or speech, and yet, we *must* speak it. As Fanon argues, this articulation is likely to be bloody, violent and painful, but it *must* happen. Corporeal cosmopolitanism is envisioned as a dialogic space and not a violent one, but it must be prepared for the possibility of confrontations, explosions and volatilities. Corporeal cosmopolitanism cannot embrace the politics of abjection because the abject-as-revolutionary still makes the violation and destruction of the "other" a necessary condition of its existence.

The politics of exclusion in both Kristeva's and Agamben's work are a powerful reminder that the imagination of community, at any scale, is a monumentally difficult endeavour. In envisioning otherness this way, the mere notion of speech, let alone dialogue, seems an impossibility. As we have seen, where cosmopolitan belongings are concerned, one of the difficulties with the Kristevan abject and the Agembenian *Musselman* is that they are in a state of permanent inarticulability, forever beyond the limits of language and of comprehension. There is a kind of revolutionary potential in their incomprehensibility, but the idea that one must remain in a state of abjection to *be* a resisting subject simply supplants one violence for another. In my own conception of corporeal cosmopolitanism, I do not consider these discourses of othering as generative ones, though they are important. Corporeal cosmopolitanism must decolonise its conception of otherness. Only then will otherness be embodied and articulate, able to speak the unspeakable and build a politics of resistance. The dualistic conception of difference and otherness will coerce our narratives into a single story,[2] and corporeal cosmopolitanism stands resolutely against the tyranny of *the* single story.

The next few chapters are a detailed exploration of this narrative multiplicity, and we will look at the myriad ways in which communities tell their stories of dispossession in assemblages of relationality rather than structures of commonality. Before we move forward to decolonial multiplicity, however, I want to acknowledge, in some small way, the ideas of Mikhail Bakhtin, a Russian literary theorist, whose work on dialogicity was an early and radical approach to otherness. For Bakhtin, dialogue and exchange are central to the creative process and living itself, and I draw on some of his ideas for how to conceive of dialogue in corporeal cosmopolitanism. In his work on the grotesque body, Bakhtin (1981, 1984) combined the notion of the abject and the corporeal, allowing the body to mourn its abjection as well as celebrate its connections and inclusions, through his theorisation of the grotesque. He viewed the abject, the bizarre and the totally rejected in a somewhat celebratory manner. There is an obvious danger in uncritically celebrating "otherness", and I do not adopt Bakhtin's framework into my own work in its entirety. However, his conception of the grotesque body issues a powerful counter to the visualisation of the "othered" body as broken, fragmented and exiled. Bakhtin's grotesque body was a *becoming* body. This body was all about opening, and penetrable surfaces – the mouth, anus, bowels and genitals – places of fluidity and exchange, where boundaries are effaced. The grotesque body is utterly unconcerned with smooth surfaces, it does not speak to smooth categories of commonality like the humanness of liberal cosmopolitanism. The grotesque body speaks to a different scale of universality in the sense that for Bakhtin, it is cosmic and timeless, unlike the new or modern body, which is closed, clean, smooth and complete. In the following section, where I discuss different cultural and spiritual conceptions of body, we will get a better sense of this kind of cosmic, mythic largeness, which is very different from liberal notions of universalism and commonality. The Enlightenment body has no protrusions, bulges or growths, delineating it very clearly from what is *not* part of it. The grotesque body, on the contrary, is always connected to other things; it can escape into and is part of the carnival, a celebration – a time outside time. The grotesque body speaks in many tongues, existing in what Bakhtin terms a *heteroglossia* (1981, 270). Gary Morson and Caryl Emerson explain the grotesque thus:

> A grotesque-word matrix drags the messy body into territory previously occupied by disembodied, hierarchical word systems. It spreads obscenities

throughout learned talk, and degrades language in order to transform abstract thought into something more material, concrete, and widely shareable. (Morson and Emerson 1990, 438)

The grotesque body demands that we radically alter our approach to corporeality and fleshliness, and that we make eroticism and desire an integral part of how we understand the world. The imagery of the grotesque is such that by its very existence and its appalling candour it breaks the fragile walls that maintain structures and norms. For Bakhtin, the presence of and dialogue with what is other, strange and abject are crucial to understanding the self. The "other" holds knowledge of the self, a 'surplus of vision' that is inaccessible to the self; 'mere negation . . . can never produce a meaningful word' (Morson and Emerson 1990, 42), which is to say, an oppositional stance does not necessarily or ultimately lead to the creation of anything new. There is little meaning in prolonged confrontation or violence as short-term reactions rather than longer term responses. There is no point in empathetic understanding of the "other" because it is not dialogic, and dialogue, for Bakhtin, is paramount. According to Bakhtin, cultures always contain multitudes of potential meanings and the capacity for exchange that they may not be conscious of. The perceived existence of an outside, for Bakhtin, creates the potential for dialogue. It is an important reminder that, while the constitutive outside – the abject and the marginal – is critical to the formation of identity, it is not necessarily always a negative thing. It also reminds us that celebrating differences or the liberal penchant for tolerance and dialogue with the other can sometimes turn into something of a tyrannically polite straitjacket. The grotesque, for Bakhtin, is dramatic, revolutionary and joyous. The grotesque is so transgressive and alien that it escapes the very confines of categorisation. This dramatic escape is made possible in what Bakhtin calls carnival, and in carnival, there is a moment – a potential – for dialogue and a possible, if momentary, dissolution of self-other boundaries. Bakhtin's characterisation of the grotesque is a profound understanding of dialogic conflict, far ahead of its time. His insistence on dialogue at every stage makes him a useful interlocutor to open cosmopolitan thought up to embodiment and affect. Bakhtin's commitment to honest, open dialogue; emotional excess and embodied, desirous engagement are important elements in the conception of corporeal cosmopolitanism, and allow for the transformation of the abject into something far more powerful and agentive.

In a different capacity, the discussions of activist and anticolonial cosmopolitanisms (see chapter one) also recast abjection in an alternative light. A good amount of contemporary subaltern/postcolonial scholarship is committed to the voice of the most marginalised – in a sense, refusing to allow the abject to remain so. These resistances, interestingly, are all centred around corporeality, and the body is crucial both to the performance and articulation of exclusion. They seem to say: "Our languages may be alien, and incomprehensible to you, but we will keep on speaking, until we are seen, and felt, and heard". The *Zapatista* movement in Mexico; the *Dalit* movement in India; the queer and transgender movements in Pakistan, Bangladesh and India; and the Black Lives Matter movement are only a few powerful examples of these abject articulations. While abjection is certainly an important reminder of the constitutive violence of exclusion and describes the extent of its cruelty and dehumanisation, it ultimately closes off the possibility of articulation. The abject remains a haunting, ghostly presence, albeit a powerful one. The abject is also restricted in terms of how its relationship is to embodiment and emotions – viewed through Kristeva's or Agamben's theoretical lens, there seems little room for a joyous, loving articulation of resistance. This suggests that the abject can only challenge through the affects of pain, fear and violence, which seems not only restrictive but also unsustainable. One of the reasons I am drawn to the prospect of corporeal cosmopolitanism as a framework, is its commitment to speech, and love. It may be that we discard the word in favour of a new one, but until such time, I will retain cosmopolitanism, both as a reminder of the spaces that it *could* open up and also of the ones it has closed off. If we want more conversations, we must learn new languages and open ourselves to different ways of doing, being and knowing.

How we go about actually achieving these conversations and *visibilising* these suppressed realms of knowledge and experience is part of the journey of envisioning corporeal cosmopolitanism. Foucault's (1972) concept of 'subjugated knowledges' becomes particularly relevant here to understand the body as a site of excluded, silenced knowledge. In his work on sexuality, Foucault makes the connections between body and knowledge, and body and experience, quite clear. Our bodies are material, discursive and affective entities, which interact with and affect material, intellectual, political and economic realities. For Foucault, subjugated knowledges are buried in historical events and contexts that are seen as "low" or "naïve" knowledges within formalised knowledge systems. They are seen as a 'historical knowledge of struggles' (Foucault 1980, 83), minor knowledeges (see also Deleuze and Guattari, 1986) that oppose the science- and/or rationality-driven canonical knowledge of institutions. These subjugated knowledges are often stored and remembered in affective and embodied ways. If we graft this understanding of subjugated knowledges on to the body, we can comprehend it as a crucial site of resistance and an active producer, as well as a recipient of knowledge and experience. But what happens when we place subjugation as an oppositional category to the mainstream – that is, minor as an oppositional category to major?

R. Radhakrishnan (2007) asks whether subjugated knowledges are a kind of deconstructive, internal abjection or do they come from "outside": a 'disinterested space that functions at a "panoptic" remove from the object of criticism?' (Radhakrishnan 2007, 33). Subjugated subject positions are often forced into a binaristic position of the grand other – 'the realities of "others" are essentialised into a grand alterity . . . which itself is nothing "other" than the ruling ideology in an antithetical or "reverse narcissistic contemplation" of itself' (Radhakrishnan 2007, 33). The mode of articulation, then, is still unchanged, making the minor knowledge part of the same grand narrative it tries to escape, similar to the discourse of abjection. This questioning of the category of subjugated knowledges is an important one. I do not want to place "the body" as an oppositional category, or corporeal cosmopolitanism as a kind of absolute, binaristic challenge to liberal cosmopolitanism. That would place it within the same strictures of a certain kind of alterity, which I discussed previously as described by Radhakrishnan. In another piece, Radhakrishnan (1996) writes with regard to the production of minor knowledges that, 'the more the "subject" produces knowledge about itself, the less it is able to assume political agency on behalf of that very knowledge' (1996, 2). This produced minor knowledge, therefore, has a complex and conflictual relationship with its producers, sometimes unable to assert itself as a carrier of minor agency, because of the structure or language in which it is forced to produce that knowledge. Translated into my concern about embodiment and emotions, I do not want to envision the body and affect as ossified realms of knowledge production, which will challenge the Cartesian binarism in an oppositional capacity. Not only will that potentially mean a collapse into the existing binary all over again but it also places embodiment and feeling into a matrix of production, an already problematic space as far as the body is concerned. As Radhakrishnan explains, the production of knowledge within an ideological framework, no matter how subversive or minor, often falls into the trap it sets out to avoid. That is, the process of subject production through the creation of these knowledges demands a certain mode or form of articulating identity, of 'imaginary identification' (Radhakrishnan 2007, 11), which ultimately conforms and 'reproduces the very modes of production that brought them into existence' causing them to 'finally neutralise themselves' (11). It is for this reason that I am invested in the corporealisation of cosmopolitanism as an organic process in flux. *Corporeal cosmopolitanism* is a term that marks the constant becoming of that process; I do not intend it to become a fixed point of body or affect as knowledge.

The whole point of the Foucauldian celebration of minor knowledges is the articulation of knowledge with no need for a single spokesperson, which, in many instances, is lost. It is worth noting then, that the problem lies in the very structure of the binary major-minor dynamic, with the major rhetoric production being essential for the minor to produce an authentic, grand account of alterity. This is ultimately what Foucault is arguing against, when he frames power as generative – a flow of energy that cannot be frozen into binarism. Radhakrishnan makes a case for the poststructural subject who constantly rebels against the authority of naming and reminds us of the instability of the known. Although I want to move away from the label of a poststructural subject, I am certainly reaching for an understanding of the body and affect as central producers of and participants in knowledge and experience, particularly in the realm of the political, as entities which form the core of cosmopolitan dialogue, of building communities and expanding the notion of belonging. The problem with this kind of poststructural fluidity is closely tied to the politics of recognition: to visibility, acknowledgement and acceptance. In order to be deemed legitimate, the body cannot speak in minor tongues, and so it is this impasse that once again forces the body either into invisibility or into submission. For Foucault, as it is for Friedrich Nietzsche (1968), the very idea of "truth" is produced through power, and power is exercised through truth. It is important to note that Foucault and Nietzsche deal with truth as a particular, discursive regime of power, and that other disciplines such as material and analytical philosophy have very different, equally complex approaches to the understanding of truth. However, within the discursive formulation of truth, in order for the body to be visible and legitimate, it must conform to a given, acceptable mode of articulation, which may well strip the body of corporeal materiality, desire and affect. Balibar describes minorities as a 'normalised exception' (2002, 152). With the classification of individuals becoming more and more complex and slippery, we are increasingly turning to a fictive or constructed universality where normalisation is the key to being equal. Balibar writes that, 'normality is the standard price to be paid for the universalistic liberation of the individual from immediate subjection to primary groups' (2002, 162). This means that the body as a marker of heterogeneity has to be absorbed into the rhetoric of standardisation. Power too, in its new global manifestation, has become far more sophisticated, but Balibar (2005) is quick to remind us that no matter how poly-centred, power is an apparatus that is meant to disintegrate complexity and heterogeneity. The new regimes of power depend on bodies rather than resources. They use bodies as mass, undifferentiated reservoirs where data can be harvested and then used for extremely subtle mechanisms of surveillance. In an almost extreme turn towards hyper-Cartesianism, the body becomes ever more conspicuous by being increasingly *invisibilised* and delegitimised as a mode of existing and knowing. In a twisted ontological justification, the body achieves a kind of legitimacy through delegitimacy. Like the minor subject straitjacketed into grand alterity, a narrative that is fundamentally opposed to it, the body too finds itself in this kind of a meta-trap, where the only way it can be articulated is through a disarticulation. It is from within these complex networks of biopower, technology and institutional control that embodiment must find other ways of expressing and articulating itself. The shifting boundaries of what embodied identities entail require corporeal cosmopolitanism to be both mutable and vigilant.

What follows in this next section is a brief exploration of some trajectories within European knowledge and thought, since they form part of the bases of how the body and affect are (un)treated in liberal cosmopolitanisms, as well as some alternatives to those conceptions of the body which support the idea of a corporeal cosmopolitanism. This move to corporealise is both difficult and often maladroit. The refusal to set the body up as a "minor" figure in opposition to a "major" discourse risks total nonrecognition or incoherence, neither of which is particularly desirable in the generation of a new imaginary. The process of corporealising cosmopolitanism needs more than an inclusion of the body and affect; it requires a questioning and transformation of what cosmopolitan belonging entails.

BODY STORIES ACROSS TIMES AND PLACES

This section is a brief, selective discussion of the different ways in which the body has been narrativised in mainstream European and non-European imaginaries. The history of the body is a colossal field of enquiry, and I do not intend to investigate or encapsulate it in any major detail. I am merely providing a few snapshots of this history, as an example of the ways in which the body has been expelled and reclaimed at various points in social, political and academic narratives, and presenting some context of this history in cosmopolitan thinking. In order to corporealise cosmopolitanism, we need to have some comprehension of the ways in which the body has been represented and understood. It will also be useful to identify those conceptions that have influenced liberal cosmopolitan understandings the most. Some of the discourse around the body in the sixteenth century – *baroque embodiment* as Dalia Judovitz (2001, 4) terms it – had not yet fully embraced the dualism that was to change the imaginary of the body, after Descartes. The understanding of corporeality was far more fluid and open, and the body was considered as an important part of creative work. Michel de Montaigne, for example, decried what he termed 'inhuman wisdom' (Judovitz 2001, 2), which inhibited the agency and experience of the body and created a hierarchy of mind and body. For Montaigne, the text itself was corporeal and was mediated by the fluidity of language, where imagination or *fantasie* constituted both perception and experience. Judovitz writes of Montaigne's narrative: 'Fantasie, the imagination, makes desire tangible as embodied form, thereby bringing representation within the purview of the body' (2001, 24). Montaigne's basic tenet of fluidity extended to sexuality where the so-called distinction between the sexes is irrelevant to sexual identity. It is rather the ultimate fluidity of sexuality making it exchangeable and reversible that characterises it. In reconstituting language and the body in his essays, Montaigne reconstituted the very basis of conventional knowledge.

The seventeenth-century Cartesian body however, provided the more enduring and influential account of the body and its place in human life and progress (See Holliday and Hassard 2001). It is also the one that we see most frequently reflected in cosmopolitan narratives of solidarity, belonging and community. The Cartesian body was conceptualised as mechanical, rather than experiential, and the instrumental body was, in effect, severed from subjective existence. Knowledge, intellect and reason came to be the valued traits of human existence, and corporeality and embodied ways of knowing lost their significance. The processes of perception, imagination and memory were absorbed wholly into the realm of the "mind", thereby effacing the body as a legitimate site of knowledge. The Cartesian body was thus an enclosed, discrete machine, an object of mechanical logic, piloted by the mind, rather than a site of knowing, feeling and experience connected to the larger cosmos. Even speech became a special faculty of "reason", alienating the body even further as a legitimate mode of articulation. In his *Meditations*, Descartes (1911), comparing the body to an intricately made clock, writes, 'I consider the body of a man as being a sort of machine so built up and composed of nerves, muscles, veins, blood and skin' (Descartes 1911, 30). Although Descartes' work is contingent upon the philosophical, scientific and religious discourses of its time, like Kant's work, Descartes' work is also voluminous and complex. It is the legacy of the Cartesian body – that is so powerful in mainstream contemporary social and political thought – to which I am drawing attention. Descartes argued powerfully for a constitutive split between mind/soul and body, designating the mind/soul as the eternal, immutable divine substance, while the body was a superb machine – wondrous, but ultimately divisible and perishable. It was mental examination that aided us in understanding the truth about the world around us, and the body was not an integral part of such an understanding. Although Descartes was keenly aware of the interrelationship between mind and body, ultimately he argued for their irreducible distinction: 'it is certain that this I [that is to say, my soul by which I am what I am], is entirely and absolutely distinct from my body, and can exist without it' (Descartes 1911, 28). The subsequent interpretations and internalisations, of what became Cartesian duality, produced a binarised view of social and political processes, elevating them to the realms of reason, rationality and the mind, and alienating them from the realms of emotions and corporeality.

Although we do see a return to the body, via philosophers such as Nietzsche, who brought forth a sharp critique of mind–body dualism in the eighteenth and nineteenth centuries, this return was reflected more in the humanities and arts than in social and political thought. Maurice Merleau-Ponty (2002), for instance, insisted that all consciousness is perceived and therefore embodied. Merleau-Ponty's work on experience and perception uses the body extensively. The body is what we see and experience the world with; it is also how we experience the "other". He writes, 'My body and the world are no longer objects co-ordinated together by the kind of functional relationships that physics establishes' (Merleau-Ponty 2002, 408). The body and the world thus move towards and anchor each other, and there is no experience or perception without the body. Nietzsche's focus on the desirous, passionate and experiential body is present throughout his work. Part of his extensive critique of Abrahamic and Christian religions, too, was based on what he perceived as the Western, Christian inability to enjoy and celebrate the body and desire. However, as observed earlier, this return to materiality and the body was not really reflected in sociological and political under-standings of humanity, society and sociopolitical life, and it is only with the advent of feminism, poststructuralism, postcolonialism and queer studies, that we witness a reclamation of the body and emotions as legitimate bearers of sociopolitical experience and identity.

In order to illustrate the previous point a little more in detail, we will now consider some non-Cartesian, non-Euromerican representations of embodi-ment. Coloniality and non-Western experiences, knowledges and imaginaries play a crucial role in my understanding of corporeal cosmopolitanism. These knowledges are, of course, too extensive and plural to map in any one way, and I only try to provide a small window into the invisibilisation and subjuga-tion of these voices and bodies, and how the recovery of these knowledges might help to create corporeal cosmopolitan spaces. With this in mind, I want to consider some non-Western bodyscapes that provide completely differ-ent alternatives to the Cartesian binary and help us foreground a corporeal, embodied sociopolitical imaginary.

If we consider the descriptions of the body in indigenous American and Mesoamerican narratives, Sylvia Marcos characterises the 'conception of corporeality' as 'embodied thought' (2004, 313). Marcos speaks specifically about *Nahua* epistemologies where she explains the fundamental duality of *Nahua* creation myths. *Ometeol* was the original duality who subsequently engendered more dual divinities of life/death, sun/moon and so forth. Marcos argues that Mesoamerican duality is vastly different from feminist theorisa-tions of duality, primarily because it is fluidly bipolar, where male and female aspects are always in transition but mediated by a dynamic equilibrium. In a framework radically different to the Greco-Roman one of either/or thought, Mesoamerican cultures are also primarily oral, lending them even more fluidity. Equilibrium in Mesoamerican thought, Marcos clarifies, is not the excluded middle of logic. It is a deep engagement with both extremes, a con-versation with the emotional range. The body in *Nahua* cosmology is open to the cosmos; it 'combines and recombines in endless play' (Marcos 2004,

320). The existence of the Western "I" is negated in *Nahua* cosmology, as well as any privileging of spirit over flesh. The poets of Hindu *Bhakti* from the sixth to the fifteenth centuries, CE too, as Menon (2012) notes, rebelled against the rigid categorisations of body and sexuality. Indeed, the mode of devotion for many of these poets was through passion and a fervent *love* for their gods and goddesses, through their erotic bodies and souls. This calls the body and soul – gross materiality and ethereal divinity – to reside in the same space – that of the body – allowing for the interplay and dialogue between self and universe. There is an ease which operates here between *eros* and cosmos, which indicates that the body does not need to be separated from matters of spirit, or expansive, even infinite universality. This provides a powerful counter to the Cartesian requirement of separation, or submission, of body to mind/soul. *Mahadevi Akka* wrote of Lord Shiva[3] in this poetic verse, or *vachana*:

> Thy love has pierced me through and through.
> Its thrill with bone and nerve entwine.
> I rest a flute laid on Thy lips.
> A flute, I on Thy breast recline;

The movement between God and devotee, man and woman, human and nonhuman are all called to the same space here, paying little attention to the categories of organisation. Nivedita Menon (2012) succinctly refers to the post-Cartesian categorisation of corporeality, gender and sexuality as part of 'the constellation of features that we term "modernity"' (Menon 2012, 1). She references a number of precolonial African societies which were marked by hierarchies or categories of occupation, seniority or wealth, rather than gender. For example, one Western anthropologist's search for "women" in the *Ga* tribe of Accra, Ghana, led her simply to traders, which is not tied to corporeality, rather than women, which is. Similarly, Menon also notes that *Yoruba* language is gender free, while among *Igbo* people, roles of husband, master, head of the household and so on are also not gendered. It is important to understand the particular role of sexism and misogyny in the discourses of the Western, Christian body as distinct from other spiritual and religious cultures. Even later critical scholars like Nietzsche or Foucault, while noted for their radical emphases on desire, corporeality and pleasure, are made conspicuous by their silence around women's experiences of the body, desire, sexuality and pleasure. Corporeality, embodiment and affect do not exist in a nongendered vacuum. They are deeply gendered and sexualised spaces, and must be understood within the complex matrix of reason, rationality, and heteronormative masculinity, where they are rendered inferior, as well as effeminate. That is to say, the privileging of reason over emotion and mind over body is also a privileging of a certain kind of masculinity over femininity. Gender thus forms an important part in the imagination of corporeal cosmopolitanism. (I examine this further in chapter four). The fact that women's bodies face a double exclusion – both by way of the broader elision of the body and in the particular ways in which female embodiment and sexuality is suppressed, demonised and sometimes obliterated – is part of the legacy of the absent body in the political.

The relationship of gender to body also forms an important part of corporealising cosmopolitanism. When we consider the process or action of corporealising, it is important to ask what this corporeal form entails. Resolutely committed to queer feminist notions of corporeality as I am, I do not envision a *smooth*, unblemished, closed body for corporeal cosmopolitanism. The liberal cosmopolitan imagination of the body is not always intentionally complicit with a hetero-patriarchal view of embodiment, because that is what the post-Enlightenment, Cartesian body subscribes to. The connections between hetero-patriarchy and embodiment are significant to the process of corporealising and it is important to be critically aware of how patriarchy colludes with other forms of oppression to render the body illegitimate. Paula Gunn Allen, in *The Sacred Hoop* (1986), identifies traditional tribal communities as *gynocracies*, and the destruction of indigenous American society as an act of *gynocide* rather than genocide. Several Amerindian beliefs placed women as the source of thought and she was symbolic of far more than fertility and childbearing. She was the creatrix of ideas and thought, which were also the cause of creation, thus undoing the stereotypical connotations of sexuality as animalistic and instinctive. Humans were created in this cosmology not by copulation but by singing or breathing life into inanimate beings. *Mother* was used as the highest term of respect and imbued with enormous ritual power, rather than biological or sentimental power. The decimation of Amerindian society thus took place through the destruction of its women when patriarchy infiltrated it and replaced the female goddesshead with a male godhead. Allen notes that 'the root of oppression is the loss of memory' (1986, 213) and the systematic obliteration of women, physically, culturally and ideologically, ensured the whites' victory against Amerindian people. Amerindian cosmology advocated universal harmony, a kind of spiritual cosmopolitanism where harmonious movement was more important than nomadism. The metaphor of connectedness runs through Amerindian thought. Multiplicity in gender, sexuality and desire was not only accepted but also revered. In fact, gender designation did not happen through physiological designation but through dreams and the kinds of play objects a child chose. The effects of hierarchical, binarised distinctions cannot be ignored, and the possibility of a more open, fluid space that is capable of accommodating these different multiplicities is significant to envisioning corporeal cosmopolitanism.

In *Embodying Gender* (2005), Alexandra Howson argues that all Western thought is grounded by the Platonic distinction between soul and body, along with the Christian notion of body as sin, predating Descartes's influential work. The subsequent privileging of vision and the eye further delegitimised other ways of experience, excluding nonvisual sensory experiences and emotional experiences from the realms of thought and rationality. The revival of biological determinism also contributed to sanitising the body, erasing its differences and allowing it selective entry into the realm of civilised reason. Howson writes, 'Consequently, the body's materiality has to be managed and contained in sexual encounters in ways that conceal its noises, discharge . . . and presented as a civilized body' (2005, 78). For Howson and many trands of feminism, the exclusion of women in the sociopolitical realm is always tied to the female body as a site of sexual excess and unreason. She argues that the entire notion of ethics is entwined with embodiment and that 'the rights of access which women now have to civil, economic and political participation are based on a model of contract that denies the specificities of female embodiment' (82). The female body has been the site of several political struggles, and the body has been used as the basis of exclusion in a variety of situations. Writing about body politics and reproductive rights, Wendy Harcourt (2004) argues that 'women's bodies are the first place that define political struggle . . . the body is the site for struggles over modern/ traditional – or hybrid-identities' (292). The female body in globalisation must be examined as an epistemological site in its cultural and ideological context. Harcourt sees the body as being inextricably linked to public, political and community spaces where the questions of choice and rights play out. The bodily experience of particular bodies perceived and lived as female construct a concept of self and place that has a political meaning and is based on fleshly experience. 'As feminists, it is important to validate this specific bodily experience constructing a concept of self and place that forms the basis for political actions' (Harcourt 2004, 292). Women have been admitted into liberal institutions based on the tenet that they are not actually very different from men and on 'their ability to emulate the capacities associated with male privilege' (Howson 2005, 92). In other words, the standard for inclusion has always been proximity to maleness. The significance of gendered exclusions within the political has been clearly articulated earlier. This brings us, as Howson and Harcourt argue, to the question of ethics. Global ethics in liberal cosmopolitanism are considered to be polyphonic and heterogeneous, but based on some kind of a shared normativity, usually stemming from some common moral conception of the human. While the idea of a shared normative framework and the belief in collective humanness that is still capable of accommodating difference are promising in many ways, their inability to interact with the question of corporeal ethics or an ethics of the body presents a challenge. If we follow the narratives of Gun Allen, Howson and others, it seems that the very notion of ethics involves embodiment and affect and is intricately tied to action and the being that *does*.

For cosmopolitanism to take cognizance of corporeality, we will require a closer examination of the notion of ethics in relation to the body and affect, and consequently, what constitutes "humanity". Agamben (1998) makes a distinction between *Zoē* and *Bios* – the bare life and the political or "good" life. *Bios*, has long been the standard of what humanity may constitute through many centuries of social and political thought. As discussed previously, it has been considered suitable to include only those facets of humanity that are capable of citizenship and of being rational and moral through 'impartial reasoning' (Held 2005). In other words, "man" is primarily a political animal, and this precludes *Zoē*. *Zoē*, for Agamben, precedes reason, much like the Nietzschean Dionysian (Nietzsche 1995). As we follow Howson's argument, it becomes immediately obvious that, first, the body has been completely distanced from the conception of ethics. And, second, the discourse of ethics around the body is so blatantly discriminatory and constitutively violent in its subjugation of corporeal expression, desires and affect in general and even more so with respect to women's bodies, not to speak of other kinds of bodies. To corporealise a way of being, doing and thinking requires reimagination in many senses. Thus, a corporeal reimagining of cosmopolitanism also requires the creation of corporeal ethics. Every argument and formulation of liberal cosmopolitanism, especially in contemporary scholarship, grapples with the reconciliation of tensions. These tensions are often located between the nation state and democracy, boundedness and territoriality, and difference as such, on the one hand, and the construction of a universal moral normative order that appeals to the very constitution of *humanness* rather than humanity, on the other. The focus on universally shared norms, a dialogic possibility and conversation is central to liberal cosmopolitanism, and, therefore, bringing corporeality into dialogue with the question of humanness is crucial.

This section has considered the damage that mind-body dualisms can cause, and how effectively they can silence and exclude the body, rendering it extremely difficult to reclaim and re-establish it as a legitimate site of experience, thought and identity. The play of creation, sexuality, rationality, thought and dreaming, in these non-Euromerican cosmologies and cultural imaginaries is invaluable to the creation of corporeal cosmopolitanism and the kind of ethics it must embody. It is vital that corporeality, emotion, embodiment and resistance are constitutive to corporeal cosmopolitanism, in the same way that existing discourses around constitutionality, reason, rationality and democracy are constitutive to liberal cosmopolitanism, and that all of these discourses are able to engage in an *equal* dialogic capacity.

BODY AS VERB: *DOING* CORPOREALITY

This section tries to discover and conceive of how to corporealise – that is, what does the process of corporealisation entail, so that we may gain some insights into how to corporealise cosmopolitanism. There is a plethora of relevant and interesting work around the subject, though I have chosen to explore some ideas that seemed most productive to the conversations around cosmopolitan identities and belonging. To this end, I focus my discussion around some helpful concepts in the works of Elizabeth Grosz and Moira Gatens. In my reading of Grosz and Gatens's work, I found their analyses particularly useful in identifying the specifics of a process – some guidelines on how to corporealise. Both scholars are concerned specifically with issues of sexual difference, women's bodies, the problems of dualism and the sex-gender distinction. They see corporeality and the ethics of corporeality as being central to the feminist position and to political participation. Grosz in particular writes specifically of 'corporealising feminism' (Grosz 1994). The previous section has already introduced the importance of gender and patriarchal collusions within modern liberal conceptions of the body and embodiment as such. Much feminist thought and literature engages with these questions from a variety of perspectives, but I want to focus specifically on some feminist responses to Cartesian dualism and how it affects our perceptions of the body, gender and sexuality.

The French Feminist scholarship of Hélène Cixous, Luce Irigaray (1985) and Kristeva, whose work I have already explored at some length, was emphatic about the importance of the body in creating a new feminist politics. There are important criticisms that must be made of their work about both essentialism and whiteness, which form an important core of corporeal cosmopolitan understandings. However, I want to use Cixous's ideas in *The Laugh of the Medusa* (1976) because of their relevance to the process of corporealising. Arguing for a new form of writing – of, by and from women – Cixous advocates the process of *l'ecriture feminine*, where she insists that women must return to writing from their bodies, which they have been abjected from (1976, 875). Cixous advocates an 'erotogeniety' (876) of identity, accepting the erotic and the sexual as crucial markers of writing and producing identity. This is a point that is poignantly and emphatically made, several times, over the course of chapters three and four where both queer and cis-women of colour assert the connections between body, emotions and spirit in articulating solidarities and resistances. Cixous writes, 'By writing her self, woman will return to the body which has been more than confiscated from her, which has been turned into the uncanny stranger' (1976, 880). One of the ways in which we might bring the body back, as Cixous suggests, is by writing in, with and through it – a process that several feminists, particularly non-white feminists have embarked upon with powerful results. For Cixous, the sexual is central to women's identities. The multiplicity of female sexual pleasure (vaginal, clitoral and more) means that there is not a "centre" that organises things around itself. Cixous suggests that the male body is centralised and organised around the penis and is the structure of phallogocentrism. Without setting too much store by biological essentialism, what Cixous is suggesting is that, the 'erotogenetic' heterogeneity of the female body and female desire is what gives them the revolutionary potential for a new politics. I want to suggest that the corporeality and affect as sites of experience and being are both capable of this heterogeneous porosity. Making the sexual, erotic and affective central to our experiences, identities and politics means that we necessarily make room for multiplicity and openness. Because the body is porous, fluid and constantly traversed by desire, it is particularly important to understanding boundaries, *eros* and violence as political affect. Without this body syntax, much of what liberal cosmopolitanism proposes and argues for remains in the masculine, phallogocentric realm of "logic/rationality" that cannot, and will not, admit other kinds of speech. In other words, the body possesses an autonomy that precedes language and discourse as it is shaped by *malepolitik*. It is this autonomy of the flesh that corporeal cosmopolitanism must recognise and imbue. 'Memory of the flesh . . . which has no discourse to wrap itself in? That which has a place, which has taken place, but has no language? The felt which expresses itself for the first time. Declares itself to the other in silence' (Irigaray 2001, 43). The phrase *memory of the flesh* is both evocative, and I believe, central to the process of corporealisation. As Paula Gunn Allen (1986) argues, to forget is to be oppressed, and, it is in this sense that the memory of the body, flesh and feeling, must be invoked and reclaimed as part of our personal and political inhabitation. Elizabeth Grosz (1994) evocatively posited the body as both thing and non-thing, and elucidates the ways in which it disrupts certain discourses of philosophy which style themselves as disciplines of the "mind". It is ironic indeed, that memory, which has such an important bond to the body and empirical materiality, should be so utterly sundered from bodily experience. Descartes, argues Grosz, did not achieve the separation of mind from body so much as the superiority of mind over body. The separation had already been achieved in Platonic and Aristotlean thought. What Descartes did most effectively, notes Grosz, was link this separation to the foundations of knowledge and, by removing the "soul" from nature, he achieved the mind-body hierarchy. Sex and sexuality were identified as instruments and laws through which the body was controlled and consequently influenced knowledge creation. 'Knowledges, like all other forms of social production, are at least partially effects of the sexualized positioning on their producers and users' (Grosz 1994, 20). The link between the marginalisation of embodiment, desire and sexuality, on the one hand, and the development of a "mind"-centric knowledge, on the other, is a strong theme in Grosz's work. In fact, it is the powerful indictment of mind-body dualism in her work that I find particularly productive in making a similar case for corporealising cosmopolitanism in resolutely nondualistic ways.

For Grosz, the body is a threshold between binaries, blurring the lines between interiority and exteriority. In her own arguments, Grosz draws on Spinozan monism as a counter to Cartesian dualism, to emphasise this point. Spinoza collapsed the mind-body distinction by arguing for both as extensions of a singular, indivisible substance. He understood the body as a process, rather than an implement, thus displacing the primacy of the psyche over the physical body. This nonhierarchical understanding of the body-mind complex allows us to envision selfhood and identity as the complex, layered processes they really are. Much of this fluidity is captured in different narratives and cultural tropes of non-Western and indigenous people's knowledges, and, it is a combination of these different nondual narratives that will form the body politics of corporeal cosmopolitanism. Grosz uses the phenomenon of phantom limbs to illustrate this blurring of corporeal, material and imaginary realities. The phantom limb is an anomaly – experienced as real but *visibly* absent, and explicable both physiologically and emotionally. It is in this sense that it is both spectral and material, and thus defies the premises of binarised, or oppositional, language. Grosz collapses the subject-object/mind-body distinction in this way, arguing that the subject and object are 'inherently open to each other' (1994, 103). The image of the phantom limb is particularly appealing to me because along with a strong sense of blurring boundaries, there is also a strong presence of desire which propels the reality of the "phantom" limb. A certain sense of ghostliness, a visceral memory of something which used to be, is recreated as a haunting, a presence that is not governed by optics but by feeling. The metaphor of the phantom limb speaks poignantly to the ways in which corporeal cosmopolitanism might open itself to embodied and affective assemblages. The Möbius strip is another image that might be useful to envision the body as part of lived experience and knowledge, as a canvas and site of inscription – an assemblage and a constant becoming. Grosz uses the image and concept of the Möbius strip – the paradoxical surface with only one edge and one boundary to explore the unboundedness of the body-mind complex. The Möbius strip can be made out of a strip of paper which has two sides and two edges. A single twist is made in the strip, and the edges are then glued together, producing a new surface and shape with only one side and one edge, even though we seemingly began with two distinct sides. Grosz uses this to illustrate the complexity of the relationship between mind and body, as surfaces both open to and continuous with one another. They feed into one another, and produce and create one another, in a relation of constant becoming and movement. The Möbius strip is an intriguing and apt metaphor to explain the paradoxical, yet inextricable, link between the material and nonmaterial, the real and imaginary, the physical and mental, and is also helpful in demonstrating the complexity of corporealisation.

Following this poststructuralist engagement with corporeality is a useful way of exploring the different levels of fluidity and unboundedness within Euromerican scholarship, which very effectively counter the dualistic impulse. Deleuze and Guattari (2004) conceive of the body as flows of energy – they describe the body as rhizomatic, without beginning, middle or end; rootless and unfixed, yet alive and generative. For Deleuze and Guattari, the body is always defying hierarchies and entirely constructed of flows; it is always desirous, pulsating and extraordinarily *alive*. Every single body has a history, geography and biography that could be traced, making it impossible to create any single set of norms or indeed a category within which to *fit* the body. The body is an erotic, desirous and sexual entity, and Deleuze and Guattari describe the notion of selfhood as contiguous with the universe. We are all part of an enormous connected plane of intensities and desires. It is desire that generates the flows and the becomings of self and cosmos, and as such they cannot be separated into neat containments. I am not advocating a complete departure into the poststructuralist lava pool of endless viscosity (extraordinary though it can be). A move like that might take us too far away from the more pressing particularities and politics of community building and sustainable solidarities. I do, however, want these discourses of constant breaking-and-reforming to feed into the ways in which we understand embodiment, as a constantly moving, thoroughly *alive* phenomenon. Grosz reminds us that desire is neither opposed to the real nor is it a "lack", as psychoanalysis often describes it. It is something that creates and sculpts reality, bringing assemblages together, making them and unmaking them, fashioning them into ever-new assemblages. By envisioning the layers of subhuman and suprahuman, of which the body could easily be a part, Grosz (2002) decentres the subject as our sole focus. If we can break the causal relation between subject and othering, causing what Grosz terms a Nietzschean, 'dramatic and untimely leap into futurity' (2004, 466), we can better understand the kind of deep body autonomy she argues for, in trying to envision a process of *corporealising*.

To reiterate my earlier concerns, this is a highly poststructuralist description of a radical notion of singularity which contains multitudes – and as such, it frames political, social and economic life too, in the same matrix of pulsating, desiring energy. This view has been extensively critiqued as elitist and fanciful, not cognizant of real power inequalities, structural violences and marginalised peoples and communities. The reason I have discussed the body in this mode is to demonstrate the importance of the interconnectedness of our existences; the intertwining of material, intellectual and spiritual realities and variables. I want to carry this complexity of interconnectedness into the process of corporealising cosmopolitanism.

Desire forms an important, pleasurable and joyous experience of embodiment as political inhabitation, and corporeal cosmopolitanism is ultimately desirous – a space of *eros*. We must also bear in mind some other, less pleasurable, though equally constitutive, elements of embodiment: pain, violence and trauma. These affective experiences are integral to memory and identity, and are viscerally inscribed upon the canvas of the body. The tortured, or violated, body, particularly if it has been abused by the state, or other forms of hetero-patriarchal domination, is a crucial manifestation of political identity and participation. The connections between the body and law are thus indispensable to the constitutional focus of cosmopolitanism. Gatens (1996) argues that law itself has been inscribed on the body canvas for centuries of "civilization". Punishment, torture and cruelty have been part of law-making from very early times, and Gatens argues that the law today is 'no less corporeal, no more cerebral, just, or fair than it has ever been' (1996, 134). Rather, there has been a 'kind of social sublimation, a desensualization, and a series of refinements to these processes of social engraving of the law on bodies' (Gatens 1996, 134). This is in keeping with radical contemporary views on how power has refined itself through modern and technological modes of surveillance, and that its hold on our bodies has intensified, rather than diminished. In other words, the gross, bodily violence of law has been sublimated, making it less ostensibly violent, in terms of the methods employed to control bodies, but actually far more invasive and insidious. The use of "security" technologies – microchips, retinal and body scans, the gathering of data by Internet companies and a whole variety of surveillance techniques – facilitates the monitoring, regulation and control of the corporeal. This in turn is subjected to the complete authority of the state. To contextualise this in terms of the tensions between liberal cosmopolitanism and the state, we are left with a crucial gap within liberal cosmopolitan narratives that cannot address these issues because it is not open to the corporeal and the affective dimensions of political life. The perfunctory banishment of the nation state is more a question of form. That is, there is no indication that these modalities of state control will in any way be diminished or resisted. And as the discussions in chapter one indicate, some liberal cosmopolitan arguments seem to suggest that these technologies might be useful in creating cosmopolitan ways of living. It is worth reminding ourselves that liberal cosmopolitanism is no supporter of autocratic state control, and its focus on individual freedoms and use of Kantian hospitality are intended to protect bodily autonomy in a rights-based framework. However, the whole framework is premised upon binaristic distinctions of mind-body, public-private and group-individual, which limit its capacity to engage with these corporeal and affective dimensions of political identity. Thus, we cannot escape the new technologies of corporeal surveillance to which so many of us are subject, especially in light of racial/ethnic and class profiling as well as gender and sexual policing. The liberal call for bodily autonomy will simply not suffice. Our resistance techniques must possess a queer-black-feminist and affective understanding of what bodily autonomy means in historical, political and cultural contexts.

In this context of violence against bodies, the processes of grief, pain and mourning are also critical to understanding what it means to be human, and in building solidarity – both dimensions that liberal conceptions of cosmopolitanism cannot fully process. Judith Butler, in *Precarious Life* (2004), writes of the grievability of a life as a crucial part of humanness. There is a tenuous sense of "we-ness" in loss; and where loss is felt, so too are desire and love. Liberal cosmopolitan narratives are unable to address this angle of conceiving belonging and solidarity precisely because they are unable to speak with corporeality and affect. Mourning, according to Butler, does not occur with the hope of replacement or substitution of loss, but rather as an acceptance of possibly irreversible transformation, something I discuss in subsequent chapters in greater detail. This situates the sense of community and solidarity very squarely in emotional and material experiences, which are also normative, ethical and moral in nature. This normativity, ethicality and morality, however, are radically different from the creation of a shared normative culture based on reason. However, this kind of solidarity also embodies the spirit of critical cosmopolitanism, which is one of ongoing openness, change and uncertainty.

Having explored some aspects of the connections between embodiment, affect, identity and political participation, I now explore the particular relations between the gendered body and its exclusion from the political. Corporeal cosmopolitanism, as I have already argued, must have a strong understanding of, and vigilance towards, the machinations of hetero-patriarchal violences, and queer-up to these oppressions of gender binaries and violences. Gatens (1996), in her work, argues that the body politic (à la Hobbes's Leviathan) is quite emphatically based on the male body, for there is no female Leviathan to speak of. The universal body, in this context, is an unequivocally male body, and it is worth noting that this male body is not a particularly nuanced body, meaning that it does not allow any scope for multiplicity or difference from the prescribed performance of a certain kind of masculinity. Another story of the body politic (Gatens 1996) is traced back to the legend of the Greek goddess *Athena*, who sprang fully grown from her father's head, which had to be split open with an axe. The city of Athens owes its name to that story. Despite a female protagonist, here too, Gatens notes that the body politic is fundamentally masculine – it is unbirthed and motherless, and circumvents the messiness of an embodied, affective femininity. The birth of Athena is also a clear equating of the masculine with the noncorporeal, unequivocally identified as the mind. The female body, as a body of fluids, flows and leakages, is not conducive to the creation of the political, and Grosz (1994) argues that the fluids originating in a male body are seen more as raw materials for reproduction than fluids in their own right. That is to say, women are considered to be made of the messy fluidity of the corporeal, while men simply dispense of it, to enable reproduction, but are not messy or fluid themselves. That corporeality and embodiment are more closely tied to women rather than men is fairly clear. The assertion of this discourse of hetero-patriarchal masculinity precludes the body by privileging the mind, and causes schisms, amputations and wounds within people's identities and the ways in which they fashion their political lives. As Gatens correctly points out, 'our political vocabulary is so limited that it is not possible, within its parameters, to raise the kinds of questions that would allow the articulation of bodily difference; it will not tolerate an embodied speech' (Gatens 1996, 26). This poignantly conveys the impasse that we face in raising 'these kinds of questions', since the space from where the questions emerge is already always delegitimised. Making the intervention, that is, breaking through the densely protected mire of the political, itself then becomes a battle about legitimate/comprehensible discourse. If the questions are not presented in the permitted language, then they are summarily dismissed. However, cosmopolitanism's continuing commitment to dialogue and openness provides a hopeful (if small) space to break this impasse of incomprehensibility. I do not envision corporealisation as a process parallel or unconnected to the processes of legality and constitutionality, simply because it then runs the risk of being pronounced impracticable. Corporeal cosmopolitanism, in my understanding, must be a process of resistance and challenge, and a queering of existing structures of legitimacy. However, I do not imagine this resistance as a closing off or a shutting down. Rather, it must be a process that is able to speak to and understand the impasses, oppressions and silences in liberal cosmopolitan narratives and carry its core strengths along, rather than alienate it altogether. In order to arrive at such a possibility of openness though, we must first listen to these stories of bodies in our disciplinary and intellectual archives, and find ways to re-engage them as legitimate sites of experience and speech.

This section has tried to examine some possibilities and theoretical processes that might help us with the move towards corporealising cosmopolitan notions of belonging and identity. However, the presence of embodiment, desire and affect is not entirely new to all narratives of cosmopolitan experience, even though it may not be explicitly stated. As we pick through the threads of postcolonial and decolonial cosmopolitanisms, we will see how they invoke elements of affect and embodiment, and thus help us to move towards more concrete articulations of corporeal cosmopolitan experiences of living and being.

CORPOREALISING COSMOPOLITANISM:
POSSIBILITIES AND INSPIRATIONS

The attempt to articulate a method, or process, of how to corporealise cosmopolitanism has required crossing, recrossing and erasing several disciplinary boundaries. The process of corporealisation is by no means restricted to cosmopolitanism alone, and so I have looked to various places to gather different approaches towards how to *corporealise*. For instance, material culture and the ways that the disciplines of anthropology and archaeology engage with narratives of travel and journeys, both of objects and bodies, often precede and challenge the liberal-modernist discourse of cosmopolitanism and shared cultural norms. Materiality and embodiment are becoming increasingly popular as research methodologies in a wide variety of disciplines. This is both encouraging and really helpful, as it offers a much wider canvas from which to draw on, as far as corporealising cosmopolitanism goes. I first came across Engseng Ho's (2006) work through a colleague's recommendation in response to some questions around coloniality, memory, and materiality. I found Ho's approach to incorporating materiality into the historio-cultural and political identities and affiliations of people both evocative and productive. The connections that are drawn between objects, travel routes, trade histories and nomadic identities in Ho's work really speak to the imaginary of corporeal cosmopolitanism. The realm of materiality is, as such, largely excluded from many contemporary narratives of cosmopolitanism, and in this I refer to both the corporeal and the inorganic, which often carry important implications for the former. Indeed, I am reasonably certain that a corporeal narrative would be very incomplete without inorganic materials, which are constitutive of the body. Materiality constitutes fleshly corporeality and the experience of the body as valuable. The ways in which objects, geographies, clothes, food and so on permeate and produce the body and its histories are very important to the formation of cosmopolitan hybridity and solidarities. The imposition of a linear temporality and the positioning of cosmopolitan narratives within the chronology of ancient Greece, the Enlightenment and Euromerican modernities have implicitly barred other formations of cosmopolitan communities to speak their stories. Consider, for instance, the understanding of mobile communities within the framework of globalisation and modern technology. The relinquishing of memory, in this presentist view, poses severe restrictions on how we may conceptualise alternative paradigms of bodily travel, movement and sharing which have been in play for centuries.

An excellent example of how exclusionary such a presentist narrative is can be demonstrated in Ho's (2006) work. Ho documents the transnational, cosmopolitan events that take place within an ancient diasporic community, the *Hadrami*, in Yemen. He recounts the immense solidarity that arose across the Middle East in response to the desecration of the grave of a Sufi saint, the *Adeni* (sacred to the *Hadrami*), by orthodox Islamic groups who saw the saint as a foreigner and blasphemer. This diasporic community, whom Ho terms the 'society of the absent' (2006, 3), has an ancient history of travel and movement. The place of their settlement, which is not the same as their home, is also the resting place of, and pilgrimage centre to, thousands of worshippers of the *Adeni*. The desecration of the grave marked the rise of this large solidarity, highlighting the significance of graves as symbolic of life and memory in the lives of these mobile communities. The significance of bodily remains, material memory and the process of mourning uniquely explain a particular sense of identity and identification (Butler 2004). The naming of the dead during the time of pilgrimage embodies and enshrines them in memory, and the place of pilgrimage itself becomes one of eternal return, marked with the significance of embodiment and ancestry rather than territoriality or nationhood. Each pilgrim brings a new set of experiences every year and forges a fresh bond with the departed. Ho's observations are particularly relevant to my conception of corporeal cosmopolitanism because they bring to the fore the intensely complex relationships that communities have with the notion of belonging and how the physicality of space, both in absence and presence, affects it. The material, corporeal manifestation of land, whether the return is possible or not and whether it is mythical or not, is very important to community identity. The actual, metaphorical and ritual journeys to *home* must be part of a cosmopolitan imaginary, no matter how global they are. These kinds of journeys and movements do not fit the typologies of mobile or fluid communities as we understand them in a postmodern, globalised, advanced technological society, à la Beck or Giddens, and yet their fluidity and mobility are undeniable. There is a powerful and enduring connection to material embodiment, memory and emotion within the *Hadrami* community, both in their older and contemporary cosmopolitan forms. The practices of the *Hadrami* provide us with an example of cosmopolitan solidarity that is equally invested in change, mobility and internationalism, as well as the embodied, affective and even rooted dimensions of their identity. It also flags up the importance of materiality in a larger sense in creating solidarities and communities, especially among diasporic groups and communities, which I explore in chapter four in greater detail.

There is a growing number of non-Western cosmopolitan narratives that have picked up on these themes and present a variety of histories of cosmopolitan values and living from all over the world. The first part of this chapter has explored the exclusion and invisibilisation of the body as a site of legitimate experience and knowledge. I have also considered a selection of European Enlightenment and non-European conceptions and relationships to embodiment and corporeality. Both of these form the basis of why it is important to remember cosmopolitanism and corporealise it. The section which followed was an attempt to investigate the processes and methods of *how* to corporealise: what it means and how we might achieve it. This final section, therefore, explores some cosmopolitan narratives which have recognised the importance of materiality and embodiment in some way, as indicative of both a possible move towards, and highlighting the need for, corporeal cosmopolitanism.

The first example of such a narrative deals with the particularities of urban life in Mumbai, India, and the hyperembodiment that homelessness produces (Appadurai 2002). The absence of belongings, a physical home or objects forces homeless people into a situation where their bodies are their only materiality. There is a particular material relationship to different states of dispossession: from the grimmest of social housing to pavement dwelling. Appadurai (2002) presents a compelling story of the city and its innumerable contradictions: its mythical Bollywood character; its dark, underworld connections and ultimately, the multiplicity – though not always celebratory – of its people. There is a single line in Appadurai's essay which captures very poignantly and viscerally the place of body in our engagement with cosmopolitanism. He writes of street life and the different kinds of homes in Mumbai, from the government's housing colony flats, to the tenements and slum neighbourhoods, to pavement dwellers and finally, public sleepers: 'Public sleeping is a technique of necessity for those who can be at home only in their bodies' (Appadurai 2002, 66). The point he makes here is to do with the ways in which the homeless and poor in Bombay, carry their "homes" within their bodies. This understanding of body-as-home is important, particularly when we think about the travelling bodies of the homeless and poor, as well as refugees fleeing violence or poverty. Here, corporeality and affect form the basis of the cosmopolitan experience, and it is the body that becomes the holder and marker of global movement and multiple belongings. Particularly significant here is the repeating refrain of the Kantian right to hospitality where a stranger has the right to feel at home, however far she may be from the physical location of her home. Much of cosmopolitan literature in fact draws from travel and exilic literature – stories of people who have challenged the very notion of a stable home. What kind of a cosmopolitan, then, is the public sleeper whose body *is* their only home? This opens up a space for the interpellation between home, body and affect, where the notion of home is inseparable from that of the body. This is even more acutely highlighted here because the pavement sleeper quite literally has no physical home. Their body, as a bearer of memory, pain, violence and desire is where they dwell at all times. Extrapolated to the larger question of belonging and community, how could we possibly imagine a cosmopolitan sense of belonging without considering one of the most crucial markers of belonging – the body?

Embodiment challenges and deepens the dimensions of cosmopolitan belonging in many different ways. The previous illustration considered the meanings of urban cosmopolitanism as an experience of pain and vulnerability, and how a cosmopolitan viewpoint would respond to the notion of a community in pain. I now proceed to discuss some examples of embodied cosmopolitanisms that place erotic desire at the centre of their notions of cosmopolitan communities. As we have seen earlier in this chapter, the erotic and desirous energies of embodiment and emotion form a very important part of understanding corporeal experience. Decolonial feminist understandings of identity, solidarity and community are founded on the erotic and affective potential of people, to forge deep connections and bonds as well as to perform resistances and revolutions. The body is thus seen as an extraordinary medium of openness, connection and sharing, as well as the marker and bearer of all manner of differences. Mamadou Diouf's (2002) work on the Senegalese *Murid* diaspora explores the importance of eroticism and desire as a crucial part of the discourse of community identity and belonging. Diouf explains the cosmopolitanism of the *Murid*, a Black African Islamic community known for its diasporic networks of trade. The *Murid* transform the cities they live in, he explains, creating a home enclosure of exclusive social and cultural identity, performing rituals and traditions that contribute to the strength of their identity. As a trading community, they are both ubiquitous and fluid – their nomadic status contributing to their image as a global presence. However, the *Murid* are tied to their spiritual heartland or *Touba*, to which they make an annual pilgrimage. The identity formed by this community, then, belongs to a unique temporality and modality. They do not follow an assimilation or absorption model, and instead add on their identity to the global diasporic network in an informed, deliberate way.

The most interesting element in Diouf's work, for me, however, was his discussion of the conception of eroticism as a particularly unique marker of identity amongst the *Murid*. The *Murid* conception of eroticism, argues Diouf, does not lie in nudity, but more in accessorisation and transformation. The idea of nudity and sensuality in the *Murid* imaginary, which Diouf extends to an African conception of the erotic, is very different from the West and heavily influences the different kinds of Islam practised in Africa. According to Diouf, eroticism in the African cultural milieu is more tactile, based on touch and smell and influenced by piercings, perfumes and sometimes even ritual tattoos or mutilations rather than visual stimuli. The erotic archetypes of *drianke* (symbolised by a plump, curvaceous woman) and *diskette* (depicted as a slim, angular woman, conforming more to white, Western beauty standards) are equally prevalent in the African erotic imagery. That Diouf chose to focus on the significance of the erotic, as an identity marker of the community, is a significant move away from traditional conceptions of identity-based solidarity and bonding. The consideration of the sexual and the erotic is an oft-ignored aspect of social and political life within contemporary liberal cosmopolitanism and provides another instance of the significance of corporeality and affect in the political. What can we learn by focusing on a community's perceptions of the erotic? The discourses of sexuality, desire and sensuality affect relations of gender, sex and standards of beauty and self-perception in significant ways. The conception of desirability which Diouf describes will make a significant difference, for instance, to the ways in which both female bodies and the male gaze are conditioned, as distinct from other cultural/social milieus, which are saturated with visions of the slender but strategically curvaceous female body. The difference in the erotic perception of visual versus tactile is also significant in the sense that it affects the way in which stereotypes of beauty, sexuality, appearance and gender regulate and divide people in communities. What has this got to do with cosmopolitan belonging? You may wonder.

As one reads Diouf's account of *Murid* cosmopolitanism, the main attempt appears to be to illustrate the specificities and uniqueness of the community's identities and practices. The choice to prioritise desire or not, say reason, or rationality, or modernisation, as a core facet of cultural identity, offers a completely different insight into the shapes of and structures of gendered relations and intimacies. In other words, do these conceptions of eroticism and desire offer more possibilities for building solidarities? I argue, in a word, *yes*. In this particular illustration, this is most clearly demonstrated in Diouf's description of the phenomenon of *goor djigen* or close female bonds among the Senegalese where there is an extremely close relationship between women who consider each other to be twin souls. There is something deeper than friendship in these bonds, often involving a close emotional as well as physical relationship, which may be sensuous but not explicitly sexual in heteronormative terms. More importantly, they cannot be directly equated with a commonly understood Western feminist understanding of sisterhood or lesbian love or desire, which means that they resist the kind of cosmopolitan generalisation under the Western banner of queer movements or communities, which advocate the rights of women and alternative sexuality. The larger point that I am interested in here – and one which is crucial to corporeal cosmopolitan identities – is that eroticism itself functions as a domain of resistance. In this case, *goor djigen* subverts both popularly propagated, patriarchal, Islamic belief systems and the liberal restrictions of an LGBTQI+ framework.

The discourse of a Westernised globalization propagates very specific norms of "progressiveness" and desirability. It promotes particular narratives of beauty, attractiveness, desirability, health and sexual practices that are being disseminated across the world through a multitude of media forms. These discourses limit and constrict the possibilities of different kinds of bonds, even within "progressive" communities of feminists, queer people and sometimes even people of colour. Take for example, the extremely problematic but popular perception of the *hijab* as a symbol of "conservatism" or "restriction of freedom" in many Western liberal, feminist discourses. In Diouf's description, the *hijab* emerges as an incredibly subtle performance of embodied female agency. The *hijab*, explains Diouf, can be worn in ways to both convey disinterest towards, or protection from, an unsolicited sexual or desirous gaze, as well as to indicate interest or enhance sexual and erotic appeal. This is certainly an absent narrative, in the popular discourses of hijab-wearing that white, Western countries promote. The banning of wearing the *hijab* in certain European countries has, on the contrary, been justified on the basis of a secular notion of "equality" between genders and religions. Clearly, the *hijab* is a far more nuanced cultural artefact, which also resists and responds to oppressions on the basis of both religion and gender. One is also resolutely unconvinced by the liberal progressive impulse to be "tolerant" and permit the wearing of the *hijab* as a matter of personal choice. If anything, "toleration" is even more dangerous, if it is only a fragile veneer of civility waiting to implode. If liberal discourses hope to produce lasting solidarities by misnaming ethnic prejudices and white Western cultural imperialism as cosmopolitanism, then they are bound to fail. The discourse of "toleration" is really the relegation of complex cultural artefacts like the *hijab* to the realm of "personal choice", thus stripping them of political affective meanings and agency. It is the silencing of an important mode of identity and solidarity-building, and one which women use to negotiate their autonomy on their terms. By the same token, this is not at all a move to promote an uncritical and essentialist caricature of gender and "femininity" in non-Western and Islamic communities as unproblematic. This particular critique is of Western liberal interpretations of gender and sexual relations in non-Western, non-White communities, but that does not negate the work that all communities must do, in relation to gender, female and queer oppressions. That is the mandate of an intersectional, corporeal cosmopolitanism: it must make space for these critical conversations as well. For corporeal cosmopolitanism to build functional solidarities, it must actively engage with these particular cultural modes of embodied, desiring bonds and intimacies. It is not tolerance but deep engagement and emotional, bodily involvement which will strengthen communities. Diouf's work shows us ways in which to imagine the identities and solidarities that are possible within communities by asking questions that would certainly not form a part of liberal cosmopolitan understandings of either community or solidarity. This is an approach that corporeal cosmopolitanism might benefit from, in its attempts to create dialogues across different communities and cultural spaces.

This chapter has tried to weave together a framework of why and how we might envision the corporealisation of cosmopolitanism. As I have demonstrated, contemporary liberal narratives of cosmopolitanism do not take cognizance of the body and affect as autonomous, legitimate sites of experience. The long-standing liberal tradition of cosmopolitanism in the last few centuries has ensured that the body and affect remain severed from the political, rendering corporealisation neither easy nor coherent. Like the disjunctures and fractures with which the body is rife, its entry into, and dialogue with, cosmopolitanism too is highly fraught. However, as we have seen, there is also enough recognition, across communities, scholarship and disciplines, to articulate embodiment and affect as legitimate sites of knowledge and experience. Chapters three and four are the *sites* in which I locate the theoretical combinations and critical reflections from this chapter and chapter one. I explore two different communities through these theoretical lenses and attempt to draw out the strong and vibrant practices of embodied and emotional belonging, and large solidarities that exist within them. The hope is that such practices, along with, those of many other communities can be drawn together in relationships of love, difference and resistance, and articulated as a new movement: towards corporeal cosmopolitanism.

NOTES

1 This use of the German word for 'Muslim' to describe concentration camp prisoners is a deliberate move to allude to very particular processes of political violence, incarceration and dehumanisation. I do not wholly agree with this usage, but find it quite telling in this specific context.

2 For an eloquent, (though not exclusive) articulation of why "single stories" are so damaging, see Chimamanda Adichie, https://www.ted.com/talks/chimamanda_adichie_the_danger_of_a_single_story.

3 For the complete verse, see: http://www.virashaiva.com/akka-mahadevis-vachanas/.

Chapter 3

Occluded Rainbows

Queerness and Cosmopolitan Solidarities in India

A commitment to dialogue is extraordinarily complicated. It requires as much speech, as it does silence. It can be frustrating, exhausting and not always possible, or productive, in the end. My own political relationship to cosmopolitanism is messy and fraught, and its commitment to dialogue, and my desire to discover this relationship fully, is what holds me in this space. Chapters one and two have been an attempt to think through the possibilities of transforming cosmopolitanism, and decolonising the understanding of dialogue itself. Chapters one and two have also tried to show why and how the experiences of the body and the work of emotions are so central to political identity and belonging. The attempt to corporealise cosmopolitanism is shaped by a feminist and subaltern ethos, not least because there is a constant and inherent imperative throughout this book, to dismantle distinctions between political and personal notions of identity and community. When we consider the identities and lives of disenfranchised and marginalised peoples, the barriers between public and private, and between personal and political, are practically nonexistent. Just as the ontological security of the citizen far exceeds that of a bare human, we see that vulnerable communities are accorded few privileges of privacy; if we think of queer people's sexual lives, refugees in new countries, traumatised/marginalised women, black communities, indigenous communities, or the economically disenfranchised, the implications are not dissimilar. When the "worth" of certain kinds of lives is deemed less than elite, white, male and heterosexual lives (in varying combinations), then they are required to prove themselves constantly worthy and authentic in legal, political, social and moral realms. For them, there are no political rights that protect their safety, privacy or personal choices – that privilege is only accorded to those who are deemed worthy of state protection and full citizenship.

Chapters three and four, therefore, are an exploration of how these divides between the personal and the political are not only fictitious but also actively dangerous, for people whose bodies, sexual choices and skin colours are not, and have never been, matters of so-called privacy. Indeed, it is this binary of public and private that has permitted so many marginalisations, abuses and violences towards the "personal". To this end, these chapters are about the stories of marginalised communities, from marginalised spaces in the "second" and "third" worlds; indeed, they may even be described as border communities in their so-called home cultures, or as peoples of multiple abjection. I have chosen these particular stories not because they are among few such narratives but because they spoke to me so powerfully, in my own search for ways in which to corporealise cosmopolitanism. For the excluded and marginalised, bodies and feelings *are* politics, and building political communities and solidarities can only be possible if all our political identities are acknowledged and understood as embodied, affective and material constructs. In other words, the construction of corporeal cosmopolitanism is only possible if we consider all these aspects of personhood and community to be contiguous and open to one another.

In an attempt to demonstrate this contiguity, this chapter examines some of the lived, personal-political realities of queerness in India, with a particular focus on transwomen's (also referred to as *thirunangai, aravani, hijra* and so on in various parts of the country)[1] communities in southern India. Having grown up in southern India myself, I am a little familiar with queer communities here and have formed many bonds and friendships over the years. Many of the insights I have are owed to queer friends and colleagues, from numerous conversations, over shared commitments, fears and joys.[2] The focus on *thirunangai* communities is motivated by the very particular ways in which the political and personal collapse into each other in the lives of *thirunangai* women. Another reason for the focus on this particular community is the recent legal/constitutional developments with relation to transgender persons' rights. The history of transgender communities in India is vast and complex, with multiple cultural, regional and linguistic variations all across the country. I only examine a very limited set of narratives in my own work, as they relate to how we might reconfigure cosmopolitan solidarities. I use the legal-constitutional space to critically explore the implications of a democratic constitutional framework that is committed to the inclusion and recognition of equal rights, and what role it plays in fostering cosmopolitan solidarity. Overall, it appears that legality, in its very formulation as a framework, is unable to acknowledge the corporeal, sexual, affective and cultural dimensions of the *thirunangai* community and the multiplicity of transgender and genderqueer identities. This, ultimately, renders it inadequate, and potentially harmful, in the struggle to create a space of equality, love and dignity for queer and transgender communities in India. This is not in any way to disparage the significance of legal/constitutional change, but rather to point out that liberal cosmopolitanism's dependence on the state, and constitutional understanding of equality, is inadequate in terms of creating the depth of dialogue and solidarity that we require.

Once again, the literature of this area is both vast and multiplicitous, and my objective here, broadly speaking, is to demonstrate the connectedness between political, corporeal and affective dimensions of identity and community building. We have already seen that the liberal discourse of individual rights and choice has played an important role in constructing contemporary understandings of cosmopolitan solidarity. It is little surprise, then, that queer movements in various parts of the world and many LGBTQI+ solidarities have either been co-opted by, or subscribed to, the label of a certain kind of popular, Western liberal, elite cosmopolitanism in the sense that they are not restricted by geography, ethnicity or culture, and are potentially capable of fostering a transnational "Queer Unite!" kind of solidarity. The liberal espousal of the freedom of "personal" choice in the "private" realms of religion, ethnicity, race, sexuality and gender, creates an illusion of openness and equality. It suggests that so long as liberal democracies are founded on constitutionality, tolerance and an equal rights framework, they protect these "individual" rights. Because organised movements for queer rights and freedom are relatively recent, they are also those in which community and identity politics have been articulated in the kind of liquid and fragmented modernity that so many liberal cosmopolitan theories promote. Queer solidarity also challenges "traditional" hierarchies that are built along the axes of class, race, ethnicity, gender and nationality, making them particularly compatible with a cosmopolitan articulation of "modern" community building. However, both queer literature and the discussion so far have demonstrated that gender and sexuality are deeply rooted in corporeal, emotional and spiritual experiences of selfhood and community, and to that extent, the inability of liberal cosmopolitan discourse to deal with these experiences makes its engagement with queerness somewhat restricted.

To be clear, queer solidarity is enormously significant and radical. It has opened up a whole new set of understandings of community building, belonging, kinship, and politics that challenges sexist, hetero-patriarchal and rigidly categorised ways of living. Queerness resists fixed understandings of identity based on narrow interpretations of solidarity and creates spaces of interlocution and dialogue where a multiplicity of people occupying a very diverse set of socio-economic, gender, sexual, political and cultural positions can potentially create new kinds of belonging. That is to say, queer solidarity, because of its unique location within the margins, is capable of transcending many conventional markers of solidarity, including sexuality and gender, which queerness challenges and subverts. However, as with any kind of large-scale movement, queer solidarity can also be co-opted into a deracinated and celebratory understanding of "managing" difference if articulated as a purely "personal" choice as sometimes happens with liberal cosmopolitan narratives, rather than as an embodied, political, and psycho-affective experience. It is also important to account for the very particular trajectories – especially in terms of race, gender and class – of articulations of queer solidarities, and how those articulations have been erasures, and supplanted other narratives and understandings of gender and sexual fluidity. This has been rather dramatically and controversially conveyed in Joseph Massad's (2002) work, where he accuses the 'Gay International' (Massad 2002) of absolute, Western cultural imperialism. Massad's critique is broadly located in an Arabic Muslim context, and he argues that Muslim, male same-sex desire has been orientalised in queer Western scholarship and turned into an exotic desire. He also argues that Western queer literature conflates ancient, modern and contemporary Islamic approaches to, and practices of, queerness, making it a flat, ahistorical and monolithic realm. While this is not an uncommon or inaccurate postcolonial critique, Massad's critique seems to border on an essentialist understanding of who can and cannot speak with "authenticity" about Muslim same-sex desire. He also has little to say about the work of other queer, Muslim scholars and their critical understandings of queer identity and community in the Arab world.

Massad's broad argument appears to be against the politics of naming – that is, the 'Gay International' has produced these same-sex identities of homosexual, gay, lesbian and so on, forcing people to conform to these categories under duress, while also condemning any cultural framework that does not accept these identities as conservative or closed. The broader claim is that these Muslim sexual choices resist Western naming, which are an attempt to stabilize desire, and that this resistance and 'polyamorphousness confounds gay (and straight) sexual epistemology' (Massad 2002, 364). Further, Massad argues that this "Western" imposition has been co-opted by elite and middle-class Arabs, leaving working-class men who practise same-sex relationships in a vulnerable position. The nuances of queer, or any kind of liberation politics, especially as they emanate from the West are very complex, and Massad's point about how they affect doubly marginalised, working-class Arab men who are particularly vulnerable, is a crucial one. However, one must wonder what Massad's critique of middle- and upper-class Arabs adopting this 'Western' queer identification means in the larger context of freedom of sexual and gender practices. On the one hand, his point about upper-class Arabs being able to identify as gay, or queer, is important in terms of examining the inequalities of class and the problem of class privilege within queer movements. On the other hand, not only does this convey the problematic idea that queer identification as a whole (in a political sense) is white and elitist, and therefore condemnable, but it also, more importantly, strips non-white, working-class or otherwise marginalised people, of their own agency and choice with regards to queer identification.[3] My interest in Massad's argument is threefold: firstly, I want to highlight some of the important criticisms he makes of white privilege and the politics of queer taxonomy as it is constructed in liberal, white Western discourses; secondly, I want to ask what implications these criticisms have for the possibility of dialogue and solidarity within the queer movement in the sense of it a large, cosmopolitan solidarity; and thirdly, I want to ask how both these positions sit with the understanding of queer and LGBTQI+ movements as examples of global cosmopolitan solidarity. The politics of corporeal cosmopolitanism are resolutely decolonial, queer and feminist. While it is clear that all of these terms have complex histories and multiple interpretations, I hope that my use of the terms is clarified and elaborated through the course of my writing. Thus, while I take Massad's critique of Whiteness, Western taxonomy imposition and the dangers of fetishising non-white same-sex desire very seriously, I want to be very careful not to essentialise the "West" versus the "non-West", which simply falls into the same trap that Massad is ostensibly critiquing. I also want us to think about what these kinds of borders of cultural geography mean, and whether it is possible to critically recognise and acknowledge them, without reifying them. The worlds we inhabit are frighteningly complex, violent and chaotic, becoming ever more connected, aware and full of new possibilities and dangers. Now more than ever, collective action, resistance and solidarity are critical personal and political acts that we must perform, and for that reason, shutting down dialogue on the basis of essentialised differences might not always be the best course to follow. I am not, by any means, suggesting that dialogue is the *only* course to follow – there are points at which dialogue is neither possible nor advisable. Those times *must* be recognised and defended. The time for corporeal cosmopolitanism is when dialogue is a productive possibility. Resistance to hierarchies of power and inequalities of gender, race, sexuality, caste, class and body is vital, but resistance is also strengthened by sharing and through acting together. It is in this spirit that I believe corporeal cosmopolitanism to be one such critical, open and dialogic space that can hold difference, resistance and conversation simultaneously.

Constitutional and/or state recognition and protection is an extremely important part of identity and community formation, as well as fostering a sense of belonging among marginalised communities. This is particularly important for queer and variously identified LGBTQI+ people, because of the ways in which the state has suppressed, punished and criminalised same-sex and queer desires in various ways. However, it is equally important to remember that state support and protection belong to a particular political discourse and framework, and constitutional support is certainly not always essential to queer desire. It is also worth noting that many people reject traditional labels of heteronormativity, as well as labels of queerness, or same-sex desire, and I use queerness as an indicator of non-heteronormativity, and not as an imposition on people's identities. With such a multiplicity of dimensions, this chapter focuses on racialised, subaltern experiences of queerness, in order to explore solidarity that is deeply imbricated in fleshly, affective and cultural experiences.

The trans-identities of *hijra* and *thirunangai* communities are complex and varied. *Hijras*, according to Claire Pamment (2010), perform a kind of burlesque femininity by challenging the norms of traditional femininity over and above the more complex rejection of and yearning for traditional masculinity in themselves and their lovers. The British colonial administration notified *hijras* as a criminal tribe (S. Narrain 2003), a view carried forward by postcolonial administrations as well. The political interventions of the *hijra* community therefore become very significant, threatening the political status quo at multiple levels. In Pakistan, *hijras* are denied permission to participate in the election process; they go to voting venues anyway, dancing and singing (Pamment 2010) – criticising the state that denied them citizenship, creating a satirical, humorous denunciation through performance, an act of carnivalesque defiance. The *hijra's* body, here, becomes a very important bearer of political resistance. In fact, the resistance is coded in the very liminality and non-categorisability of the corporeal. In a liberal cosmopolitan framework – which believes sexual preference and gender identity to be a matter of individual, personal choice – the crucial critique that occurs through the inhabitation of a non-cis identity and body highlights the inadequacy of understanding sexuality purely as a "personal" choice. The *aravani* body complicates this notion of choice and reaffirms the need to corporealise political identities and solidarities. I have chosen to explore the community in Tamil Nadu because of the state's ostensibly progressive position and its early legislation around transgender peoples vis-à-vis the moral strictures, oppression and policing of bodies and desires that are simultaneously forced upon same-sex and queer-identified peoples.

The first section begins with a brief and selective description of the history of the queer movement in India through the work of South Asian scholars and queer activists. This provides some culturally specific context to the kinds of queer solidarities that have emerged in India. The queer movement in India has a diverse and complex history replete with contradictions of cultural authenticity, class and caste, all of which are borne by the body, and all of which are rather obfuscated within the celebratory narrative of liberal queer solidarity. This is particularly significant within the context of trans/*hijra*/*aravani*/*thirunangai* communities. *Hijra* is a term more popular in the north of India, while *aravani* and *thirunangai* are specific to Tamil

Nadu, which is where my analysis is focused. However, I use all four terms interchangeably throughout my work (although it is worth remembering that they do not always hold equal meanings in all places and times).

The second section is a discussion of the legal and constitutional activism around queerness in India in order to highlight the corporeal implications and unaddressed problems within the legal/constitutional framework. I examine the implications and consequences of Article 377, which pertains to the criminalisation of same-sex relations, the Supreme Court judgement, followed by a Bill of Rights to acknowledge, support and protect the transgender community, and subsequent criticisms of this Bill. This section examines the queer-phobic constitutional syntax that is neither willing nor able to transform its language in order to actually engage with queerness, the right to self-determination and indeed, the right to life and personhood. This discussion is also indicative of a larger conundrum. That is, can (and if so, how?) corporeal cosmopolitanism engage with the language of legality in productively critical ways?

This is followed by the third section, which explores examples of identity constructions amongst transgender communities within different cultures. I look at some "Western" and Victorian constructions of genderqueerness as well as examples from different times and cultural spaces (see also Towle and Morgan 2002). I also examine some mythologies and cosmologies of transgender communities in South Asia. The purpose of this section is to provide some background to processes of identity formation, and also draw attention to the specificities of these processes in different cultures. These stories hold enormous emotional and spiritual value to communities and are an important part of solidarity building. Liberal narratives of cosmopolitanism, by addressing LGBTQI+ movements as flat, "global" solidarities, miss these vital nuances and are therefore unable to build more lasting and relational solidarities based on these specificities, rather than a bland kind of generality. It is also clear that these affective solidarities are perfectly compatible with legal and constitutional transformation.

Finally, in the fourth section, I discuss the narratives of *thirunangai* women from Tamil Nadu. I focus specifically on these transwomen's narratives, in light of their activism, particularly in Tamil Nadu, to gain rights as markers of their political citizenship, which then set a precedent for a National Bill of rights – for voting rights, ration (subsidised food) cards, employment, property rights and so on. To highlight the complexities of solidarity within the *thirunangai* community, I explore narratives from different socio-economic and cultural spaces, and the kinds of discourses that are employed by women who have chosen to appear in public, and share their stories in one way or another. Elite class positions, particularly in postcolonial societies, tend to dictate the appropriation of a certain narrative of western liberal, individualistic ideology, thereby doubly abjecting socio-economically disadvantaged trans communities and placing them outside the space of legitimate articulation.

I use both media representations, and autobiographical narratives to explore the creation and understanding of solidarity, which draws the realms of affect, politics, body, desire and constitutionality together in a space of experience, dialogue and articulation. This final section, drawing from these multiple queer stories of belonging, abjection, loss and triumph, tries to envision corporeal cosmopolitanism as a space of radical compassion and resistance.

QUEER/LGBTQI+: NAMING AND ORGANISING IN INDIA

The officially recorded queer movement in India is quite recent: the first reported queer demonstration took place only in 1992 (Narrain and Bhan 2005, 6) and this makes it a crucial as well as a critical factor in the discourse around both democratisation and cosmopolitanism, particularly because, as I have argued previously, the queer movement can easily be envisioned and understood as a cosmopolitan movement both in productive and not so productive ways. The process of unpacking the nexus between these marginalised spaces and the discourse of democratisation is aided greatly by the work of feminist and queer theory. The space of ambiguity, in this case, is inextricably linked with desire and emotion, and the presence or lack of it, within the framework of political thought, including its more inclusive strains. As Butler (2004) notes, the public sphere is constituted very selectively, including and excluding acts and articulations by legitimating certain kinds of actors, suggesting that, even a space of legitimate, constitutional debate is informed by deep-rooted normative, ethical and moral functions. The following lines, although slightly lengthy, express very accurately the excluded zone inhabited by non-beings:

> If violence is done against those who are unreal, then, from the perspective of violence, it fails to injure or negate those lives since those lives are already negated. But they have a strange way of remaining animated and so must be negated again (and again) . . . they are always already lost or never 'were', and they must be killed since they seem to live on stubbornly in this state of deadness. Violence renews itself in the face of the apparent inexhaustibility of its object. (Butler 2004, 33)

That is to say, if the object of violence is not recognised as legitimate, then violence ceases to be violence: it ceases to be perceived as such. The legitimising function is almost always linked to normative or moral codes, which in turn are inextricably linked to a question of power: who exercises it and how they choose to do so?

The objective here is not to analyse the queer movement in India as an historical or sociological phenomenon. Rather, the intent is twofold: the first objective is to present broad strokes that highlight some of the issues that have been central to queer politics in India, which may then be extrapolated to a broader application of those issues, and to consider the question of desire as such and how to conceive of the narratives of desire and the corporeal within political thought. The tendency has always been to treat issues of sexual choice as a matter of individual rights and the notion of toleration. There is, however, a deeper question about the definition of what constitutes the "right" *kind* of desire. The inherent hetero-patriarchal violence in defining desire is simply sublimated when it is cast within the framework of sexual or individual rights, and it is to this unrecognised violence that attention must be drawn. While there is clearly an acknowledgement of the affective and emotional element within political community and action, there is no clear idea of how to locate or engage with desire, particularly so-called transgressive desire, within the context of a political framework like cosmopolitanism, dialogic and interactive though it claims to be. The second objective is to examine the queer movement within the context of cosmopolitanism. Indeed, the queer movement is doubly relevant in this particular case *because* of its connections with cosmopolitanism. It has, in some parts of the world, been a movement that has achieved a certain sense of global community and solidarity, and opened up a progressive and alternative space, which has been based on open cultural communication, dialogue and interaction. Although this is not without its problems, expansive and dialogic solidarity is not something to be dismissed. Legislative and constitutional changes have also been fought for and achieved in various countries including, more recently, India. The shared problem-solving methods that Delanty (2009) speaks of have very much been a part of the queer movement world over. However, as the Indian case demonstrates, even a movement that is so close to the cosmopolitan ideal looks very different when the cultural specificities of queer politics in India are considered, where some of these specificities by virtue of not fitting the paradigm, or being irreconcilable, simply become invisible or excluded – a transgression within a transgression, as it were.

The queer movement in India began as a response to a long history of violence both against queer desire and its association with HIV and AIDS. In more recent years, however, the movement has moved away from this restrictive discourse into the affirmation and celebration of identity and queer desire. It is not in fighting for sexuality as a matter of personal choice or right but in questioning the entire framework of hetero-patriarchal definitions of sexuality, desire and love, and the ways in which they are graded, normalised or pathologised. The 1990s were a period of political, religious and sociocultural upheaval in India, and this extended to controversies and violence against the queer community as well. There were many recorded incidences of right-wing extremists such as the *Shiv Sena*'s vandalising and persecuting of the queer community, the ban on Deepa Mehta's film *Fire* in

1996 and so on. *Fire* (1996) raised special moral outrage because it was not only a story of queer desire and love, but of queer *women*, which was even more insidious to dominant narratives of "Indian" culture. This insistence on the "non-Indianness" of queer sexuality led to a basic problem at the level of articulation, because the use of any Western theoretical construct – that is, LGBTQI+ or Queer frameworks – became confirmation of its foreignness. The politics of naming *can* be a problematic Western construct, but it can also make visible the sexual and moral prejudices of a queer-phobic society and state. As Narrain and Bhan (2005) correctly point out, the problem that mainstream society has with queerness has less to do with the sexual act itself and more to do with ways of living and loving.

This state-led abnegation of queerness is also discussed in Nivedita Menon's (2005) work, where she discusses the larger problem of addressing sexuality in India. She points out that even in so-called progressive circles, sexuality is always trivialised as being a manifestation of identity politics and therefore accused of taking away from a more encompassing unity of "citizenship", which is presumably more pan-Indian, whatever that might entail. The idea that the articulation of core marginalisations, which dwell in the realm of the "personal", ultimately breed disharmony when brought *out* and that we must suppress these demands for justice and desire in favour of a "greater", more worthy solidarity is rather insidious. This kind of an argument puts the issue of sexuality on the defensive at all times, constantly forcing it to be justified and legitimated: 'the normalisation of heterosexuality is at the heart of patriarchy. Patriarchy needs the institutions of heterosexuality to survive' (Menon 2005, 34). This move of normalising and policing sexuality achieves a double objective in that it delegitimizes and pathologises queer sexuality and desire on the one hand, and it removes any desire or pleasure associated with heterosexuality, on the other. By laying the emphasis on a singular, restrictive view of family and the centrality of procreation, heterosexuality becomes reified into a hetero-patriarchal institution that serves purely as a mechanism to negate and delegitimize any other conception of sexuality and is itself stripped of any sexual agency or pleasure. The emphasis here is on the erasure of desire.

The systematic erasure of the desiring, pleasurable body from the realm of politics and political discourse has serious implications for us. As Akshay Khanna (2005) points out, there is a kind of hegemony in using the term *human rights* to articulate sexuality and desires. He insists on retaining the focus on sexuality, especially in the Indian context where the moral-cultural rejection of queerness as being Indian makes it very easy to ignore the issue altogether, by simply relegating it to the broad rubric of human rights. That is to say, tokenistically including sexuality and sexual desire as a small part of what constitutes the human allows the repeated elision of the body as autonomous, desiring and political. It is the spurious notion of civilization, which provides the measure by which the human is defined at the same time that a field of would-be humans, the spectrally human and the deconstituted are maintained and detained, made to live and die within that extra-human and extra-judicial sphere of life (Butler 2004). Butler (2004) further argues, quite accurately, that to envision a category of human, there must first and foremost be an acceptance of heterogeneous values at that level before we address any other forms of pluralism or heterogeneity.

CONSTITUTIONALITY, LEGAL REFORM AND COSMOPOLITAN SOLIDARITY

We have already considered the significance that cosmopolitanism places on legal and constitutional dimensions of creating dialogic possibilities. I, therefore, now turn to the constitutional dimension of the queer struggle in India. The legal-constitutional changes that queer communities in India have been fighting for are extremely important to the recognition and acknowledgement of queer lives. The first legal matter is to do with an article that was written into the Indian Penal Code and amended as recently as 2009. Section 377[4] of the Indian Penal Code places homosexuality alongside rape, bestiality, child abuse and any 'unnatural' sexual act, and has been a major violence against, and concern for, the queer movement for many years now. It was as recently as 2010 that Section 377 was brought up in the legal forums of India as being violative of the articles protecting fundamental rights of citizens in the case of adult, consensual sex. While Section 377 was ultimately not revoked, the Supreme Court did pass a landmark judgement in favour of the legal recognition of transgender people in 2014, which was then followed by a constitutional Bill of Rights in 2016. Historically, it is true that few actual convictions have been recorded under Section 377, and this fact has been used as an excuse for refusing to amend the article. However, this law has functioned as a terrorising panopticon for queer people everywhere in India. It has pathologised queerness outside the court, making criminals out of non-heterosexual people and nonentities out of women and transgender communities who did not even feature in the legal or sexual vocabulary until very recently. The inclusive transformation in laws and the constitution highlights the importance that cosmopolitanism places on constitutionality in combating violence. The sense of a democratic, globally shared victory and dignity that it has brought is unquestionable. Narrain and Bhan (2005) evocatively point out that India is a country whose legislative/penal system is modelled on the West, England in particular, and which seeks to equal and emulate Euromerican Western economies and societies in several ways. Yet, in the realm of sexual choice, the *Western* label is decisively degenerate and culturally inferior. This schizophrenic relationship to the "west" is a familiar trope in many postcolonial nations, and one that has had and continues to have devastating consequences for its peoples.

In July 2004, the Tamil Nadu State government sanctioned the right of *aravanis* to choose their gender as male or female along with free or subsidised housing. This was among the earliest legal measures taken in regards to transgender communities in the nation. In 2006, a second Government Order was issued to improve *aravani* lives: punitive measures were issued against schools and colleges for not admitting *aravanis*. Loans, subsidies, rehabilitation and the 'upliftment' of *aravanis* became a priority. In May 2008, the *Aravani* Welfare Board was constituted along with reservation for *aravanis* under women's reservation quota (Vasudevan and Govindan 2010). In 2010, the *Aravani* Welfare Board granted *aravanis* the right to a voting card, ration card, free operations and other financial subsidies (Priya Babu 2014; personal conversation). This year also marked the beginning of media interest in *aravanis*, both in film and television (Priya Babu 2014; personal conversation). Vasudevan and Govindan (2010) note that although these civil and legal measures were a landmark achievement in the *aravani* struggle, the language of rehabilitation and upliftment suggests that the state considered them fundamentally pathological. Unable to contend with the critical issues of body and desire, the state sanctioned sex reassignment surgery, while constituting a panel to counsel *aravanis* against it. The problem then, was the lack of intersection between the moral and politico-legal realms. The lack of a political vocabulary to address embodiment and desire is a clear factor in the failure of state and civil intervention to fully grasp the complexities of sexuality, gender, body and identity that form the core of queer identity and politics.

In 2016, the Indian parliament passed the Transgender Persons (Protection of Rights) Bill,[5] which, upon first glance, appeared to guarantee equal rights, redressal of justice, protection and support to the transgender community. But, as critics argue, this has been revealed to be more platitude than law. The 2016 Bill was meant to be the consolidated result of the actions in Tamil Nadu (discussed earlier), proposed bills in 2014[6] and 2015,[7] as well as a Supreme Court ruling on Transgender Rights on 15 April 2014,[8] which was a landmark judgement. The Supreme Court judgement (2014) decreed that Transgender people have the right to self-identify, and offered them both full and free access to medical and sexual healthcare, as well as 'protection from fear, shame, depression, social stigma' (2014; see appendix A), and so forth. However, as many queer activists and scholars have argued, there is no clear indication, other than broad directives to the state and central governments, as to *how* these laws and rights would be implemented and guaranteed. The 2016 Bill, however, reneged on the Supreme Court Judgement, the previous bills, as well as critical, expert feedback from queer communities, trans-activists, and policy makers. The 2016 Bill revokes the right of transgender persons to self-identify, and instead calls for 'state-based certification',[9] suggesting that one's gender and sexual identity are subject to medical or external determination, and potential pathologisation. This is a strategy of surveillance, indicative of the state policing and controlling people's bodies, determining normalcy and abnormalcy in people's intimate and affective identities. The Bill has also been criticised for excluding intersex people, as well as transmen, and other non-cisgender persons, and focusing on "transforming", and "equipping" transgender people for society. This continues to place the onus of "deviance" in the transgender body, rather than recognising that it is the larger societal structure and norms that create the marginalisation of queer and transgender people in the first place. There are no clear penalties for the violation of this Bill, and the remit of protection against violence has been described as blurry, at best, and only covers physical violence, leaving no recourse to seek justice against emotional, sexual or verbal violence. It also does not provide room for domestic violence, and violence perpetrated by birth families[10].

Perhaps what is most disturbing about this Bill is that it entrusts the implementation of these measures and the protection of transgender people to states and state bodies – particularly the police – as well as birth families, when the vast majority of documentation of violence against transgender people has been committed *by* the police and immediate family,[11] leaving the victims neither recourse to justice nor access to their chosen trans-families and communities. *Thirunangai* women are frequent victims of rape and violent assault owing both to instances of sex work, (which is often the sole recourse to livelihood), and to incidents of hate crime. Sex work is illegal in India, making the transgender community even more vulnerable and multiply punishable. An article in *The Hindu* (2013), narrates the following: '*In Naz Foundation v. NCR Delhi*, an affidavit was filed by Kokila, a hijra, detailing the horrific rape to which she was subjected. She was anally raped by ten goondas and subsequently brutally sexually assaulted by policemen inside the police station. The police tortured her with a burning coir rope' (Mundkur and Narrain 2013). When we consider these facts in light of some liberal cosmopolitan narratives, such as Appiah's, it is quite clear that state intervention and involvement are both problematic and potentially deadly in these cases.

What is most glaring and revealing about these constitutional measures, is that Section 377 was not amended, which means that same-sex relationships, desire and love remain a punishable offense in the Indian State. While the 2015 Supreme Court judgement regarding transgender people ruled that no one can be discriminated against on the basis of nonconformity to gender-binary stereotypes, the confinement of this to transgender people suggests that there is no real understanding of the slippages, relationships or nuances of sex, gender, sexuality, gender presentation and gender and sexual identification. This is, perhaps, one of the clearest examples of how legal/constitutional change is deeply inflected by moral and normative imaginaries, which are far more powerful than the law. Queer cosmopolitan solidarities most definitely need constitutional and legislative change, but those changes can *only* be brought about with a deep engagement, and conversation with, corporeality, affect, gender and sexuality. Fighting for queer rights as a matter of private sexual choice will do nothing to dislocate dominant social norms and morality. Rather, it will only invisibilise queerness further, disabling the space for protest, now that the law has prevailed. As Bhan notes, 'The law is not an objective and autonomous space but an institution firmly located in prevailing social hierarchies' (2005, 43).

I make these observations within the larger context of law-making and protection of human rights and human dignity and safety, which are all part of the cosmopolitan vision. The laws against sexual assault, rape and violence are based on global laws and UN-based policies pertaining to the same. The protection of human lives, rights and dignity are generally considered parts of the shared normative project of cosmopolitan ideology and ethics. This shared project also believes that dialogues around constitution and legality are significant issues. Given such a framework, we see that it is not simply cultural specificities and particularities that will affect this globally shared normativity. Liberal cosmopolitan frameworks are also affected by deeper epistemological elisions and an invisibilisation of the entire presence and performance of body, sexuality and affect that underwrite the very conception of rights and dignity. It is this larger ideological elision that requires both our attention and the need to revisit the politics of naming and categorisation that will ultimately open up a space for cosmopolitanism to engage honestly with the tensions of marginality and liberatory politics.

STORYTELLING AND IDENTITY-MAKING: MYTHOLOGIES, COSMOLOGIES AND LIFE STORIES

Various regions and cultures of the world possess stories of transvestites, "eunuchs", hermaphrodites or trans-people, often viewing them as other-worldly beings, outside the constructs of human or "natural" existence, describing gender fluidity as magical and powerful.[12] These stories form an important part of particular cultural imaginaries and can provide important context, both to the histories of marginalised communities and the ways in which the presence of such marginality in religious and cultural mythology can often be a convenient cover for violent attitudes towards gender and sexual fluidity. In Western scholarship, Magnus Hirschfield was among the earliest scholars to use the term *transvestites* in his work of the same title (1991, first published in 1910). The text is described as progressive, for its time, and the author attempts to dismantle the stigma attached to transvestism. However, because it is such an early work, gender binaries are very clear and male superiority is still conformed to, for the most part. For example, the author comments that frailty in a boy child was frequently the cause for cross-dressing and bringing him up as a girl, because his nature and physique were better suited to being a girl. Hirschfeld also notes that the Bible condemns transvestism as an abomination unto God, although, he also describes a Catholic sect in Dalmatia, where women could choose to be reborn as men, and the priest would transform them. If the women (now men) were found to be pregnant after their transformation, then they were executed. There are also similar cases in Mahayana Buddhism (Paul 1981) where women could be reborn (in this life) as men to pursue their spiritual goals. These accounts of fluidity are, however, rooted in the belief that the female body is considered inferior and therefore incapable of spiritual rigour, and it is important that we make and retain this critique. In their work on female transvestism in early modern Europe, Rudolf Dekker and Lotte Van de Pol (1989) note that female transvestism was far less objectionable than male transvestism, as the woman at least, was aspiring to a so-called higher ideal. Transvestism could have also been a disguise for homosexuality, as the dominant norm of heterosexuality along with the dictates of the church prevented women from even considering the possibility of *tribady* as it was then termed: 'Therefore, it is logical that those women would think: if I love a women [*sic*], I must be a man' (Dekker and Van de Pol 1989, 57). These accounts of transvestism in the Victorian era are relevant to the processes of colonialism, and consequently to how transgenderism was perceived in colonised spaces, because these were the prevailing norms and beliefs about gender and sexuality, which made their way to the various colonies that Europe subjugated. They also underline the need of that era to conform to prevailing systems of religious belief and reproduction. These dictated that women dressed as men had to live as virgins, and male transvestites often lived with their wives and children, turning their choices into an acceptable anomaly, as long as it did not go against the so-called natural order of life and religion.

There are many more extensive accounts of gender nonconformity in other societies. For example, Kathryn Ringrose (2003), in her work on the eunuchs of Byzantium, examines the possibility of Byzantine society being founded on a different gender construction altogether, and of eunuchs being officially present as a third gender. Emasculation and effeminacy are the symbols of the most taboo process – that of losing one's "manhood" or virility. The eunuch of Byzantine, according to Ringrose, was 'a perfect servant of God or of his secular master, one from whom lifelong loyalty is expected' (Ringrose 2003, 2). They were a functionally legitimate group with clear roles to perform within their society. Eunuchs were classified as erstwhile men, and hermaphrodites were considered special and "naturally whole", as opposed to boys who were deliberately castrated. The author affirms that eunuchs were not explicitly excluded anywhere in society, but by virtue of being the "perfect servant", incapable of participating in domestic functions of reproduction and the like, they were excluded from that entire social sphere. The "otherness" of the eunuch was both feared and revered, and they were often looked upon as other-worldly and associated with angels because of their physical appearance and the fact that both hermaphrodites and angels were seen as created by divinity, and not of this world. This action of dehumanisation, which, in many cases is precisely what deification sets out to achieve, plays an important role in the politics of exclusion in relation to queer communities. Ringrose also raises the important point that negative attributes such as excess of all sorts and selfishness were considered to be the flaws of women, while all positive attributes such as loyalty, management skills and intelligence were attributed to the male part of the eunuch. This is a powerful reminder of why we must always be wary of situating Byzantine's or any culture's gender constructs as unique or separate from any other. While cultural relativism is an important tool and one often invoked both by cosmopolitanism and its critics, it is important to remember that stigma, particularly gender- and sexuality-related stigma, is not an isolated phenomenon. 'The term *eunuch* carries a powerful psychological charge in our society, just as it often did in the ancient and medieval world. It implies far more than sterility. It implies loss of masculine affect' (Ringrose 2003, 14). This is also a notion that runs through the core of the body politic and the nation politic that cannot tolerate the liminal, the "disfigured" or the uncategorisable. Liminal bodies destabilise the sand-scrawled boundaries and white picket fences of nations and kingdoms so carefully guarded by guns and phalluses. Byzantine may have created an institutionalised place within its society for eunuchs, but that does not in any way mitigate the obvious discrimination and othering directed against them. For even though they were powerful, the power was not theirs to keep or wield, and at no point did they cease to be a marginalised group, framed within the language of lack and degeneracy.

Contemporary religious discourse, including Catholicism, has several religious leaders, and *gurus*, speaking in defence of queer people and queer sexuality. The *hijra* and *thirunangai* communities in India tell of several different stories in Hindu mythology. It is worth noting that much of the scholarship on *hijra* and *aravani* communities make references only to Hindu mythology,[13] although there are several references to *hijras* as an important part of Islamic and Mughal history in South Asia. One such story involves *Arjuna*, a well-known, and stereotypically hetero-masculine warrior hero from the epic *Mahabharata*, who was cursed by a beautiful celestial woman, *Urvasi* to live as a eunuch when *Arjuna* rejected her advances. *Arjuna* thus lived as the beautiful woman *Brihannala*, in exile, teaching dance and music to a princess, as well as helping the king of the land vanquish his enemies (See Menon, 2006a). In yet another story involving *Arjuna*, *Aravan*, son of *Arjuna* and *Uloopi* (princess of a great serpent kingdom), *Aravan* came to aid his father, in the great battle of *Kurukshetra*. The machinations and deceptions of war dictated that for *Arjuna* and his brothers to win the war, a voluntary human sacrifice must be made. *Aravan* complied, on the one condition that his wife mourn him, after his death. *Aravan*, at this point, was unmarried, and so, *Krishna*, who is both a popular Hindu god and a character in the epic *Mahabharata*, transformed himself into a beautiful maiden, *Mohini* and wed *Aravan*. There is also a hidden point here about the *legitimate* fulfilment of *Aravan*'s sexual desires. Upon *Aravan*'s death, *Mohini* mourned *Aravan* with all the wrenching grief of a newly widowed woman. To this day, an annual festival in *Koovagam*, in Tamil Nadu, is largely dedicated to *aravanis*, who come by the thousands to perform and embody ritual love and loss of their beloved *Aravan*, from whom the term *aravanis*, the wives of *Aravan*, is derived (Menon 2006b).

Yet another story comes from the Hindu epic *Ramayana* (Vālmiki 2000). Here, the protagonist *Rama* (also an incarnation of *Vishnu*) was unjustly exiled through the schemes of his stepmother. As he left, the whole city made to leave with him and he implored the *men and women* to return to their homes. *Thirunangais* alone were able to accompany *Rama* as far as they were able, since they were neither men nor women. Blessed by *Rama*, they waited for his return, establishing their supreme devotion and earning *Rama*'s special affection (*Ramayana*, Vālmiki 2000). The *Bahuchar Mata* temple in Gujrat, the *Siva-Sakti*'s in Andhra Pradesh, *Jogappas* in Karnataka and Krishna worshippers and followers of the saint *Chaitanya* in West Bengal are all examples that demonstrate the engagement of dominant religious and spiritual literature with gender and sexuality. This could very easily create the false sense that Hinduism is somehow less discriminatory towards non-heteronormative sexual and gender identification, and it is important to guard against this tendency, because it is patently untrue. Contemporary Hindu rhetoric against queerness, and sexual desire in general, counts decisively against such a tendency. The religious accent on transgender mythology in India lends it a certain cultural specificity and context, but is not at all indicative or in keeping with the ways in which transgender and queer people are treated in contemporary Hindu discourse and practice. It is important to remember that Hinduism by no means controls, dictates or sanctions trans-identities, and many *aravanis* are Muslim, Christian, Jain, Sikh, Atheist and pan-religious. There is a strong critique against the saffronisation of the *thirunangai* identity by *savarna* castes (ritually "upper" caste),[14] which is extremely important within the politics of resistance, as well as the creation of embodied and affective solidarities. This critique is specific to the Indian queer and trans-gender context, and I am unable to address its full implications here. I do, however, want to clarify that I have not provided the above-mentioned Hindu cosmologies as a way of reifying or exoticising transgender communities in

India but more as a set of particularities that inform their histories and also to highlight the ways in which transwomen communities have been typecast. Mythological and cosmological origin stories can sometimes serve as important ontological narratives, as Jennifer Ung Loh (2014) notes in her work, and it is in this capacity that I have recounted some of the popular cosmologies. Gayatri Reddy (2006) notes that Islamic and Hindu practices form part of a continuum among Hyderabadi *hijras*, who identify as Muslims and follow Islamic practices but also believe in Hindu Goddesses and participate in Hindu festivals. As Jeff Roy (2014), in his work on transgender communities in India, describes it, 'the lines separating religion, class, caste, language, and most importantly gender, are quite permeable'.

Identity-related legitimacy is by no means restricted to mythological cosmology and the performance of *hijra* identities in Pakistan and in Mughal- and Nizam-ruled India. The narratives and practices of *hijras* vary within South Asia (Pamment 2010). However, ritual dances, songs and blessings at gender-liminal moments such as the birth of a child, where the child's gender is as yet unknown, or a marriage, where the sexual union of the couple and consequent procreation is undetermined, tend to be common in many places. Muslim *hijras*, particularly in Pakistan, certainly do not use *Hindu* myths to strengthen their legitimacy or origin (Pamment 2010). It is important to understand that *hijra* communities in India are multireligious, and there are large communities of Islamic clans all over the country, but the religiosity of the *hijra* community, much like their gender and sexual identities, is varied and layered. In autobiographical narratives, we see evidences of several religious and cultural practices as far as their own rituals and beliefs are concerned, even though they may primarily identify with one religion. Many Muslim *hijras* legitimise their identities by referring to their historically important place in the Mughal courts as political functionaries, advisors and harem guards, very reminiscent of Ringrose's account of the Byzantine Empire. Unlike the Hindu origin myths, this carries no magical or mythical significance, but rather a political one. In early Islam, *hijras* were said to have guarded the *Ka'bah* and other holy sites, particularly tombs, which fortified their connection with the liminality of death (Pamment 2010). Contemporary *hijras* associate their fertility blessing/cursing powers as a compensation given by *Allah* in lieu of their own inability to procreate. In Pakistan (and parts of India), *hijras'* link with death has also created a connection with *Sufism*, and many *hijras* ritually commemorate the death anniversaries of *Sufi* saints (Pamment 2010). *Hijras* in the Mughal period (sixteenth and seventeenth Centuries) also occupied powerful political and advisory positions, and some were also sexual partners to Mughal rulers (Roy 2014). Much mystical poetry and faith was based in *eros* and love for the divine, often scrambling or transcending gender. Significant as these cultural specificities are, as mentioned earlier, it is important not to glorify them as part of a mythical/ traditional glorious past, given the patriarchal, heteronormative structures of the South Asian societies. It is also useful to remember that the traditional kinship networks of *aravani* communities, *hijra jamaats* or *parivaars* – that is, traditional trans-families and hierarchical kinship systems – can sometimes be cruel and oppressive to their family members. This critique from within the *thirunangai* and *hijra* communities is vital to understanding solidarities in these transgender and queer communities, and it is important to consider the space, or lack thereof, for these narratives and imaginings within a liberal cosmopolitan framework. These cultural specificities and complex critical dialogues within and without the community are powerful illustrations of how affective solidarities may function in critical cosmopolitanism.

THIRUNANGAI REPRESENTATIONS AND NARRATIVES IN TAMIL NADU

In recent years, India, and consequently Indian media, has seen a small but marked focus on rights and legislation regarding the body and sexual rights. Much of this media attention has been sensationalist, insensitive and some-times dangerous to victims of gender and sexual violence. But some of it has been productive and important. The *thirunangai* community in South India, especially Tamil Nadu, has also been a part of this media attention. The voices of protest and resistance, and the right to be *visible*, have been reflected in media presence, though moulded within specific narratives, often of sensationalism and exoticisation. The media representation of transwomen in India, and Tamil Nadu, could be cited as a popular cosmopolitan narrative, in that it denotes a certain *kind* of visibility and acceptance. However, as we shall see, this visibility is riddled with problems and multiple kinds of dis-crimination. *Thirunangais*, as previously discussed, have held a Janus-faced ritual/religious status in Indian society, and their ritual liminality is directly connected with their bodies and sexualities. Revered, reviled and feared, all at once, the lived realities of this community pose a direct and significant chal-lenge to the ideological framework of cosmopolitanism, which seeks to estab-lish a community and set of ethics built on *humanness*. For the *thirunangai* community, the question of personhood and what constitutes being human in terms of maleness and femaleness is a deeply fissured and painful one. Although the Supreme Court has legally recognised the right of *thirunangais/* transwomen to lead equal lives, there is, as discussed earlier, no indication that there is an understanding of what *gender nonconformist personhood* actually means. This suggests that the constitutional inclusion of transwomen has been as exceptions, rather than as norms.

I want to begin with two examples from television media, which I broadly identify as being part of the popular cosmopolitan narrative of transgender representation. I want to emphasise here that I use *popular cosmopolitanism* as a reference to the popular, cultural understanding of what cosmopolitanism means in an everyday sense. In common parlance, cosmopolitanism conveys a sense of modernity, globalisation, diverse populations, an acceptance of transgressions, high fashion, access to English media, Western consumption practices and a kind of ubiquitous urban equality that advanced capitalism confers upon us all. These everyday understandings of cosmopolitanism are not unconnected to its political/philosophical articulation, and I would venture to argue that liberal cosmopolitan narratives like those of Beck, Delanty and even Appiah (see chapter one), are fairly compatible with the popular understanding of cosmopolitanism. In this context, these media narratives of transwomen serve as powerful illustrations of how cosmopolitanism – as a kitsch phenomenon in popular and Western media cultures – has clearly influenced and induced what are routinely perceived to be extremely conservative and repressive political and media cultures to open up and challenge existing norms and morals governing gender and sexual identity. The two television narratives I discuss were both talk shows on Tamil media channels. The first was titled *Ippadikku Rose* (Yours, Rose), a talk show broadcasted by Vijay TV (part of the Star Television Network) from 2008 to 2009, and was the first talk show in India to be hosted by a transwoman. The second, entitled, *Natpudan Apsara* (Affectionately/In Friendship, Apsara) aired on *Thanthi* TV (a relatively newer channel) from 2013 to 2014, and was the second such occurrence in Indian media. The pioneering nature of these media representations, at a time where *thirunangai* identity and existence were still constitutionally illegal, makes them significant. My emphasis is on the discourses of the television shows and the representation of transgender identity in them, rather than the specific identities of the presenters, although these separations can never be absolute.

Ippadikku Rose features Rose Venkatesan, a transwoman, born and raised in Tamil Nadu, who studied and worked in the United States of America for some years. Venkatesan[15] is a highly educated, well-spoken woman, fluent in English, and presents as a middle-/upper-class woman. Impeccably dressed in beautiful designer clothes, and with a poised, confident demeanour, she addresses several socially significant issues such as dowry, marital violence and education, as well as narratives of marginalised women in her show. The films she chooses to feature also tend to be socially relevant and gritty. Venkatesan is very clear about her agenda; she wants to be in 'mainstream' media, a transgender heroine-figure proving that transgender people are 'the same' as everyone else (*Ippadikku Rose* 2008b). While she does address the issues of her identity, it is not the most significant issue; the major project is to do with mainstreaming and normalising. In fact, she explicitly states in one episode of her show that people form judgements and opinions about others just by looking at them. She goes on to say 'even when you look at me, you judge me by the standards of the common *aravani* community at large. This is wrong. You must look at me through *ordinary* [my emphasis] eyes' (*Ippadikku Rose* 2008a). This discourse of normalisation is one that we hear both from Venkatesan and Reddy. There is a very specific appeal to the liberal idea of *humanness* as a denominator of equality – an appeal to sameness, rather than difference, as a way to join and connect us all. There is also an important emphasis on individuality and separation from the 'common community', which is part of the neo liberal discourse of autonomy and individual uniqueness. There is, of course, the danger of an elitist, smooth move towards the flattening of particularities and corporeal specificities, and lived experience, but one of the things that this may be a response to is the fetishised sexualisation of transgender bodies. It is important to pay attention to the politics of embodiment and the move towards corporealising political identity, and cosmopolitan solidarity must be clearly distinguished from the fetishising of bodies, feelings and sexuality. Thus, the appeal to humanness is not problematic in and of itself, and is an important part of the cosmopolitan imaginary. The objective of this book is really to find ways to re-examine the liberal idea of humanness that Venkatesan and Reddy argue for, and try instead to posit a feminist queer understanding of solidarity as an affective, embodied ideal that is also composed of the nonhuman: the abject, the grotesque, the liminal, the animal and the cosmic.

Ippadikku Rose's portrayal of "traditional" transwomen's communities and kinship groups are quite clearly conveyed through one of the episodes (*Ippadikku Rose* 2008c). In this episode, Venkatesan invites three *thirunangai* women, and we see the very interesting pattern of how the image of the "traditional" *thirunangai* community is represented. The three guests of the show were Sri Devi (a former model and member of a traditional *hijra* family or *jamaat*); '*Living Smile*' Vidya, author of the book *I am Vidya*, a published author, artiste, and transwoman; and Hema, a schoolteacher who lived a life of total acceptance thanks to her social worker mother, open-minded friends, and a lover who became her husband and finally adopted a child with her. Hema's story is portrayed as the 'fairytale' story, as Venkatesan herself quips. The *normalcy* of Hema's life as a heterosexual woman is repeatedly emphasised in the show. Vidya's story, though very sorrowful, is ultimately triumphant, as she is a published writer with a family on the cusp of acceptance, and has a partner. Sri Devi's story as a *Jamaat thirunangai* or a *thirunangai* living the "traditional" way is portrayed as the sad life, the life without freedom, choice or love. The bias against this traditionalism, though never explicitly stated, becomes quite clear as the episode progresses. This is not to suggest that the

Jamaat or kinship system of the *thirunangai/hijra* communities is in any way beyond reproach and, indeed, many *thirunangai* women have chronicled their painful experiences of oppression within these hierarchical kinship groups. These observations are meant to draw attention to the importance of habitus, and the material, social and cultural capital in the lives of these transwomen. Liberal – elite narratives of normalisation, equality and sameness, thus exclude and marginalise the complex politics of acceptance, identity building and belonging derived from these traditional kinship systems which, often without economic capital, possess some ritual and cultural capital that acts as protection to poor, abandoned, and severely marginalised transwomen. These kinship systems also acknowledge and celebrate the embodied, affective, sartorial and sexual elements of transfemininity as unique and powerful, something that many thousands of transwomen from economically marginalised, nonurban backgrounds in India may never have experienced in their younger years. These are intimacies of identity creation, production and performance that can never be captured by the liberal discourse of normalisation and multiculturalism, or the "toleration" of difference.

At the end of the episode about *thirunangai* women's lives, Venkatesan appeals for humanity, compassion and empathy from every one of her viewers to stop perpetuating this violence against a fellow human being. The idea that *thirunangais* turn to sex work for no reason other than poverty is also clearly established, thereby also linking it to depravity brought on by suffering, deserving of compassion, rather than judgement. At no point are the affective or sexual dimensions of sex work addressed. At the launch function of *Ippadikku Rose*, Venkatesan very carefully explains what it means to be a transgender person so as to avoid media misrepresentation: 'Everything that people know and learn is through the media, and their opinions of *aravanis* are formed through the media' (*Ippadikku Rose* 2008b). She then states that the only thing that transgender communities in India lack is access to opportunities. Given the right opportunity, transgender people can be just as, if not more productive than, men and women citizens. She also goes on to state that the lack of a family makes the *thirunangai* a potential model citizen, able to contribute entirely to the economy and country, with no thought to savings and family obligations. This rhetoric is not dissimilar to older, neo-liberal arguments of the gay community as economic assets to society, both as earners and spenders, as well as not having children. This strongly liberal-capitalist narrative of transwomen as efficient capitalist subjects, whose biggest hurdle is an absence of opportunities, is in keeping with a modernised, Western-capitalist discourse of equality based on productivity. However, there is a curious inflection of nationalism so characteristic of postcolonial national imaginaries, when Venkatesan adds, 'India as a country was fully supportive of the transgender people *ages* back. But the culture has deteriorated over the years because of various foreign influences' (*Ippadikku Rose* 2008b). This coexists in a precarious balance with Venkatesan's own persona that is crafted by Western media, in her excellent command of English and the stylish clothes she wears. It is superseded entirely by selective espousal of nationalist sentiment that India *used to be* an accepting and progressive country, before the advent of "foreign" influences. The most interesting nuance here is the one that complicates the understanding of liberal equality, and tolerance itself. In this, it is Appiah, rather than Beck, Delanty or Nussbaum, who has a clear understanding of the importance of patriotism, ethnic identity and national identity, particularly to former colonies. That is to say, even the elite liberal cosmopolitan narratives of the "global south" differ quite significantly from those of the "global north", with regards to national, ethnic and cultural identities. What I want to draw particular attention to here is the ahistorical, and colour-blind approach that white, Western liberal narratives can have to cosmopolitan solidarity, rendering them incompatible even with equivalent discourses of the non-West. Once again, we circle back to the issue of reckoning with the embodied and affective dimensions of colonial history, which even the most liberal elite populace of the non-West will not disavow. Indeed, for most elites in former colonies, modernity, Westernisation and fierce nationalism coexist in remarkably noncontradictory ways.

The second, more recent television show, *Natpudan Apsara*, was hosted by Apsara Reddy, a well-known and popular journalist, and an emerging political figure. Reddy is an English language journalist, who also spent considerable amounts of time in parts of Australia and the United Kingdom, which, she describes as being instrumental in shaping her trans-identity.[16] If *Ippadikku Rose* was attempting to normalise transgender identity by engaging with pressing social issues, *Natpudan Apsara* carries that message even more strongly. This show is a celebrity chat show, featuring a whole host of actors, directors, musicians and other artistes, many of whom are personal friends of Reddy's. The format of the show is plush and glitzy, and it even has a segment where a tarot card reader is brought in to predict the futures of her celebrity guests. There is a lot more spoken English on the show than in *Ippadikku Rose*, and the entire aesthetic of the set and show are to do with showbiz and celebrity buzz. There is no attempt to tackle gritty social issues or politics here, and in this sense, the show is pure entertainment, featuring both novelty and celebrities, something that Reddy herself comments on in an interview.[17]

Reddy's guests are mostly friends, owing to her long experience and elite position in popular media, and the show is very much about celebrity candour and sharing, much like any other chat show of this genre. The questions are mostly around the guests' personal lives, romances, sorrows, their professional careers and talents. The tone of the conversation is unerringly light and breezy (*Natpudan*

Apsara 2013a and 2013b), and always careful to avoid overly painful or difficult moments. With many of the female (actor) guests, conversation is around appearances, fashion, perfectly sized bodies, diets and complexion. In one interview with the actress Simran, Reddy remarks that Simran was her aesthetic inspiration when she went through her transformation into a woman. With her frequent references to "us girls" and "girl talk", Reddy exudes an easy, abiding confidence, effectively dismissing any questions around her trans-identity as anything out of the ordinary, often pointing out that she has never faced any real discrimination, and that confidence and self-belief is all one really needs.[18]

In a series of candid interviews about her own life story, Reddy also emphasises the importance of family and familial support in being a transwoman, and her own family's invaluable love and support of her choices, a luxury that is afforded to very few transgendered people. Reddy's acknowledgement of the pain and struggle of being transgender is emphatically overshadowed by her insistence that it is ultimately a glorious experience. She writes: 'So *pain* is the *last thing* you should associate with me. Yes every transsexual goes through a battle to relate her personal feelings to the society and often to his/her own family. But certainly that is what makes us that much stronger and wholesome' (Reddy 2012).

Reddy's cultural, symbolic and economic capital are absolutely crucial to her identity as a transwoman. While strongly supportive of the need for awareness and antidiscrimination campaigns, Reddy is also clearly critical of aspects of the "traditional" transgender community's practices. There is a sense that coming together and fighting the good fight is the most important thing, and that the identity politics of minoritarianism are divisive in relation to that larger cause. This is broadly in keeping with the liberal call for equality that is focussed around rights, rather than a shift in the ontology of political identity. 'But the transgender community does very little for itself. I think it is a sisterhood that promotes prostitution, begging and harassment . . . I feel ashamed to say I am a part of the transgender community' (Piu, 2016). By distancing herself from an articulation of transwoman identity that is clearly identified as vulgar, backward and unmodern, one sees a clear distinction between a certain *kind* of "traditional" transfemininity and a more "modern" articulation of transfemininity. This narrative of transfemininity asks for a seamless normalisation and a smoothness, which simply allows transwomen to be successful, confident and strong individuals, capable of achieving greatness: 'I'm asking you to step back, withdraw from the world for a moment and drop the gender roles. Ignore the fact that there are homosexuals, bisexuals, heterosexuals and polysexuals out there. Ignore the fact that we are Asian and European, American and Australian' (Reddy 2012).

These ideas reiterate the belief that "we" can be joined in a common bond of humanity that is ultimately homogenous on some level. There is a clear echo of the Western liberal cosmopolitan mandate of transcending national identities and boundaries, in order to unite as humans. This is a powerful way in which the radical politics of queerness is co-opted into elite articulations of liberal tolerance, and vague, universalistic solidarities.

These next two narratives that I want to discuss are markedly different from the previous ones. They are autobiographical works, both in print media, and tell very different stories of being transwomen. Revathi and Vidya[19] are by no means an exhaustive representation of the *thirunangai* community, but both women are radical activists and powerful voices, in the struggle for transgender and queer rights in Tamil Nadu and India. Their contexts, and narratives, challenge and unsettle many of the premises of trans-identity, and the normalisation of transwomen in Indian society. Revathi and Vidya also emphasise the urgent and increasing need for community organisation, and collective protest, along with a strong critique of heteronormativity, class privilege and patriarchy.

'*Living Smile*' Vidya narrates, in her memoir, *I am Vidya* (2007), her journey from being identified as the only "son" of a corporation sweeper and his wife, their pride and joy, to the arduous, but ultimately joyful metamorphosis into Vidya. I want to examine the particular experiences of Vidya and Revathi that converse with the liberal discourses of transfemininity discussed in the previous section, and how these diverse experiences can inform and challenge the notion of an embodied and affective cosmopolitan belonging. Inclusive politics, as we have seen, cannot simply anchor around the loose rubric of identity as a personal choice and a consequent protection of individual rights. We need a far more engaged political dialogue and discourse which addressed the corporeal and emotional dimensions of gender and sexual identity. The fleshly, affective experiences of these transwomen are so foundational to who they are and, therefore, constitutional moves to protect and include them must engage with these experiences. This would, of course, require a far deeper epistemological shift in the way that the politico-constitutional matrix deals with issues of identity, gender and sexuality. The constitutional cornerstone of "choice" must be imbued with the affective and corporeal dimensions of the people making that choice.

In her description immediately preceding what could barely be described as a medical procedure to transition, Vidya writes of the room she was asked to wait in: 'Our predecessors in the room had scribbled their names on the wall, presumably because they feared they could die on the operation table. That was their way of ensuring the survival of at least their names after the hazardous operation we call the nirvana' (Vidya 2007, 12).

At a time when the *thirunangai* community had not yet been granted any rights of belonging or citizenship, Vidya's words convey a deeper fear – one of erasure. In a world where the *aravani* woman could not exist as anything without her deadname (that is, birth, male name) the scrawled female names that all *thirunangai* women choose to name themselves became their only markers of identity, the identity of what they consider their true selves, unacknowledged though that may be by society or constitution. The incanting of names as a practice of remembrance, rooting and identification has been discussed in chapter two with relation to Ho's (2006) work on the *Adeni* and how the names of thousands of saints are chanted, keeping the spiritual memory of the community alive, but in Vidya's case, the names mark more than remembrance. They signify a legacy and a history – a proclamation of self that has been eternally negated by the world in which it has tried to exist and flourish. Vidya then goes on to describe her sense of peace and belonging once the operation was complete. Brutal and painful though it was, the operation was, for her, the confirmation of her gendered and sexual selfhood, and tied to this was the notion of bearing pain and its relationship with being female. Vidya notes that while the transgender woman is incapable of menstruation or childbirth, the pain she bears through this operation is symbolic of the pain that women go through in childbirth and labour, and this in itself is a very interesting kind of corporeal understanding of what "womanhood" entails. It is important to pause here and think about the absolute threat to life and safety in these situations. Though not all transwomen go through surgical procedures, the right to inhabit a body that matches ones gender and sexual identity is a basic human right. In India, as Gee Imaan Semmalar[20] notes, these surgical procedures, that is, the so-called medical ones, are exorbitantly priced and extremely risky, offering equal chances of successful reassignment and horrific mutilation. This highlights one of the most apparent distinctions between the narratives of economically and symbolically privileged transwomen and of severely marginalised transwomen, who are in fact, the majority. In Vidya's narrative, there is a clear emphasis on the gravitas of being the only "son" in a poor, rural family, following the birth of a stillborn boy baby. Vidya's father was an abusive man, broken both by the death of his wife and his crippling financial circumstances, which caused him to project all his desperate dreams and ambitions ruthlessly on to his only living "son". Vidya bore the brunt of being the alpha male heir, which is pressure enough on its own, combined with the struggles around her essentialised xgender and sexual identities; she writes that her very existence became unbearable as she grew older. The smallest acts of being teased at school and college and being romantically paired with girls whom she considered her close friends, were intolerable. Vidya writes, 'To you, I may seem to be a man, but I am a woman at heart. How can I tolerate any suggestion that I am in love with a woman?' (Vidya 2007, 56). This brings us to a strange kind of understanding of liminality that lies at the heart of many *thirunangai* narratives. Unlike some Western articulations of queer solidarity and pride that are based on the fluidity of desire and the acceptance of liminal performativity as a way of being, many *thirunangai* narratives can be rather heteronormative in their articulation. The notion of "homosexuality" or same-sex desire is, for the large part, not acceptable to many in *thirunangai* communities because they simply consider themselves women who are attracted to men. In Vidya's case, she does not disavow same-sex desire per se but does so for herself. There is an important tension here between the fluidity and fixity of gender, sexuality and desire, in the sense that, on the one hand, they can all be manifested in infinitely different ways, but on the other, they form an important core of a notion of self, and are therefore, also stable choices that individuals make for themselves. Being labelled "lesbian" is not an easy negotiation within the *thirunangai* community. The term *sapti majaa* or vaginal/clitoral pleasure is a derogatory term used to describe a *thirunangai* who desires cisgender women (Srijith Sundaram 2014, personal conversation). This humiliation of expressing desire for other women is deeply tied to hetero-patriarchal discourse, which spares no gender or sexual orientation. That is, if a *thirunangai* truly feels like a woman, and went through the process of transitioning, how can she be a *real* woman if she does not desire a man? The absolute diktat of heteronormativity in this scenario cannot be ignored, particularly because it subjects the desires of the body to the will of heteronormative discourse. In a bizarre reification of gender and sexuality, this is a hetero-sanctioned gender fluidity that will not permit sexual fluidity. The heavily religious, ritualistic and casteist dimensions of traditional *thirunangai* communities may also contribute to this rigidity and conservatism in sexual expression. It is also possible that this *straighting* of transwomen, as it were, has allowed the Indian legal system to create a false dichotomy allowing the constitutional recognition of transgender identity (though there is a clear exclusion of transmen), and rights but not same-sex desire. It also seems apparent, as observed earlier, that this has led to the omission and silencing of transmen, intersex and many others on the trans-spectrum. This points out a crucial slippage in the legal/constitutional dimensions of cosmopolitan reform, in the sense that, without the corporeal and affective know-how around trans and queer identity, these legal measures are likely to do more harm than good.

However, this kind of complex reification is by no means a phenomenon unique to southern India. Megan J. Sinnott's (2004) work on transgender identity and lesbian relationships in Thailand also points to similar hegemonic structures at work. In this space, *Toms* are "masculine" *women* and *dees* their "feminine" women counterparts. Sinnott writes, 'Thai *toms* simultaneously claimed an ambivalent gender identity that refused to accommodate itself to any category and claimed an unalterable masculine identity' (104). *Toms* and *dees* explicitly reject the concept of lesbianism, deeming it a Western construct and an unnatural phenomenon, echoing the *aravani* views on same-sex lesbian desire, and Massad's critique of Western nomenclature. *Toms* play stereotypically masculine roles and are usually the active partner in sexual relations. Sinnott notes that 'the ability of *toms* to penetrate their partners (symbolically, perhaps, with a dildo) was important to *toms* even though most *dees* did not need or even want penetration' (106). This brings a very particular sexual dynamic to the fore – there is a relationship between penetration and power as masculine, and the *dee*'s passivity as feminine, requiring her to accept the *tom*'s penetration, despite the fact that she did not 'need or want' it. The metaphor of penetration for territorial conquest, power and domination, the politics of consent and the complexities of pleasure and desire, make this complicated territory rather difficult to navigate. While I have no intention of foisting a heteronormative discourse on to a dynamic that is clearly both multiple and layered, I also do not wish to dismiss the influence it wields on our lives of desire, pleasure and embodiment. What this then means, is that *toms*' and *dees*' participation in the larger framework of queer solidarity or sexual/gender choice is far more complicated and *must* be culturally situated. A cosmopolitan acceptance of *aravanis* would then have to entail a cosmopolitan dialogue about the nature of binaries and liminality; what it really means to be liminal, and understanding the liminality of a *thirunangai* in terms of her embodied realities, her sexuality and gender identities, and how she negotiates her womanhood materially, emotionally and spiritually. For instance, in her *parivaar* (usually refers to a chosen trans-family) Vidya was required to reveal her operated-upon genitals to the ocean, a black dog, and a tree in a symbolic affirmation of her womanhood. Revathi's account also tells of a ritual phase of "pollution" for forty days after the operation after which she could be accepted as a reborn woman, similar to the pollution taboo many Hindu women are expected to observe during their menstrual period. The politics and practices of *being* woman are distinctly different from the practices of elite transwomen's identities. For transwomen who can afford high-end sex reassignment surgeries, inclusive of various cosmetic procedures, they take place in expensive, premier medical facilities, complete with physiological and psychological counselling. Among traditional *thirunangai* and *hijra* communities, one hears mostly of the *nirvaanam* operation (excision of the penis and testicles). Though many never have a chance to have it performed, as it is a strict, hierarchical and nepotistic process that must be sanctioned at the *jamaat* (a meeting of *hijra* elders), it is a marker of superior status and authenticity, which bypasses seniority by age or membership. The authenticity and respect of *being* woman is bound to this corporeal transformation. These particularities, while by no means absolute, nor always positive, give us an indication of how intertwined embodied, affective and political identities are. To build a radical, dialogic solidarity, we *must* confront the messy, painful and joyous affectivity of bodies-as-personhood.

Revathi's (2010) story begins in a small town called *Namakkal* in Tamil Nadu where she describes the pain of being teased, bullied and abused because she was perceived as a young boy who enjoyed doing 'girls'' work. However, from a very young age, Revathi always harboured a secret pleasure from being identified as 'girly'. She writes, 'they would chant "Girl-boy!" "Ali!" "No.9!"' My heart would sink at these words, but I also felt faintly gratified, and even happy that these boys actually conceded that I was somehow a woman' (Revathi 2010, 5). Even this violent recognition was kinder than being misgendered. She writes of how she discovered support systems early on and therefore spent a lot of time questioning and challenging her own self, her community, sexuality and identity. This is not a luxury that many transwomen from rural and economically marginalised backgrounds often have. Revathi's discovery of others like her led to an early discovery of the *aravani* community, its system of kinship, filialness and familial bonds. Unable to endure the abuse from her elder brothers and father, Revathi ran away to Delhi, hoping to find the original *guru* who adopted her and made her part of her first trans-family, all in secret. *Thirunangai* communities have a complex and strict hierarchy of relationships, duties, obligations and expectations. Gayatri Reddy (2006) notes that living in a *parivaar* – which is the trans-family – is also a matter of prestige, as is the *guru-chela* (teacher-student) system where there is an entire complex kinship network of mothers, grandmothers, daughters, sisters and god-daughters. These kinship roles are very specific and binding, equivalent to any family structure, though of course, changes in allegiances are common, and not always kind or safe. However, for Revathi, this family was incredibly precious – it was where she was accepted as a woman. Her birth family, by contrast, was violent, and terribly abusive, and Revathi writes of how her own brothers and father beat her within inches of her life in an attempt to control her. These stories are not uncommon among *thirunangais*, and illustrate why the current law in India, which presumes the good relations between transwomen and their birth families, could actually be fatal to them.

The longing to find love and a romantic relationship is always offset by the strict rules of the *parivaar* (trans-family). The *guru*, not unlike Indian parents in a heterosexual family set-up, constantly advises new young women of the *parivaar* not to run away with a man or become trapped in their romantic messes and webs, which would ultimately end in sorrow and disrespect for the entire family. Revathi recounts what one of her *gurus* said to her: 'Beta, I don't want you ganging up with some pottais and take to drinking and seeking a husband. If you do that, you can be sure I will break your head! You be a good girl . . . and . . . I will arrange for you to have an operation' (Revathi 2010). The emphasis on honour and respect is quite clear and reflective of a patriarchal moral structure that demands absolute control of female sexuality and sexual behaviour, making femininity the bearer of moral honour and chastity. What this ultimately meant, in Revathi's case, is that she became part of a *hijra parivaar*, which was known to engage in sex work, something which her own family shunned, preferring to accept offerings, or beg. Reddy's (2006) observations about the politics of sex work within *hijra* communities help us unpack some of the moral abhorrence towards sex work, and sexual desire as a whole. She observes that while both sex work and sexual desire are highly prevalent within the community, the renunciation of desire is the highest ideal of being *hijra* for some. The ascetic or *sanyasin* aspect of being a renunciant of desire is believed to be the source of the *hijra*'s ritual power to bless or curse with respect to fertility. However, this is by no means a common, or even prescribed, path for all. As Revathi eloquently explains, 'It seemed as natural as hunger, this hankering of the flesh. I could not get married my nani would object . . . . Perhaps I could have fulfilled my wishes if I'd lived in a house for sex work' (2010). Revathi writes of heartbreaking accounts of violence, rape and abuse, and the absolute desecration of her desire for sexual happiness, companionship and love. She writes with extraordinary insight and sensitivity about the multiple layers of marginalisation and otherness on the axes of gender, sexual and class identities. She reflects on the implications of what it means to choose to live as a woman, and bear the violences that are perpetrated against her both for being woman and not being a "real" woman. Revathi's story is a powerful testimony to the complete delegitimisation of transwomen in Indian society, and the centrality of gender and sexual identities as the core of personhood and humanness. Without a thorough understanding of and engagement with embodiment, desire, emotions and right to self-determination, we cannot speak of meaningful belonging, or solidarity. Revathi's continued struggle for her right to personhood and happiness ultimately led her to *Sangama*, a nonprofit organisation dedicated to supporting *thirunangais* and other sexual minorities, and then onwards to becoming an author and renowned social and political activist.

The narratives discussed in this section are intended as (being indicative of) diverse representations of transwomen's identities, stories and personhood in contemporary Indian contexts. These representations are not meant as any kind of generalisation but rather as crucial voices that speak to us about the complexities of creating something like cosmopolitan solidarity. These narratives and representations are not intended as case studies, and I have not addressed the entirety of their personal life histories, as it were. The fact that Rose Venkatesan and Apsara Reddy are best known through their television shows, and English media interviews, while Vidya and Revathi chose autobiographies as self-representations, points to the stark difference in histories and cultural constructions of trans-identity. It is clear that transwomen like

Rose Venkatesan and Apsara Reddy play an important role in popularising a global, cosmopolitan vision of transwomen's identity formation. They are sophisticated, media-savvy articulations of identity and selfhood using a very specific, elite and liberal construction of anti-discrimination speak. These elite trans-identities clearly set themselves apart from, and sometimes contrary to, the narratives of more generally and extremely marginalised, so-called traditional transgender identities. The liberal cosmopolitan narrative of solidarity, equality and right to self-determination is, in a broad sense, supported by all four representations, but not all of them indicate the social, cultural and economic capital required to actually inhabit the kind of cosmopolitan equality which simply requires us to allow private choices to remain private, and concern ourselves with one's public capacity for success, decorum and civic contribution. As a consequence, any pain or trauma that results within the "private" realm also remains hidden. Whereas, for those without the capital, private and public realms are not at all so separate, and neither should they be. Class is clearly a deep, painful fissure, and the experience of *thirunangais* and their transitions are highly dependent on the economic variable. This is something that is echoed across queer scholarship in India, and it might be useful to understand how class and queerness intersect in other gendered spaces as well.

Alok Gupta, in his essay *"Englishpur ki Kothi"* (2005)[21] discusses the dialectics of class amidst the gay community in India. *Kothi* is posited as an indigenous identity, distinct from that of a gay man, which is seen as an elite, English-speaking category. Technically, both identities have much in common and could be used interchangeably. However, doing so would be a total erasure of the conflict and tensions that exist within the community, an important consideration in the construction of shared solidarities. Describing a scene at a Delhi-based nonprofit organisation working on sexual health and HIV/AIDS, he writes, 'So in the same physical space of the Naz India office, three completely separate groups, all dealing with homosexual men, met on different days and almost never interacted with each other' (Gupta 2005, 129). Gupta refers here to urban and nonurban gay men. This then raises the question: Does the legal/social recognition of queer desire and identity mean the same thing to queer communities across the board? Ostensibly not! As Gupta points out, the amendment of Section 377 (which has not yet taken place) could mean social access to clubs, bars and an openly queer life followed by political and civil recognition for a gay man. For a *kothi* however, the constitutional amendment means very little in light of his class position. The fact that a *kothi* cannot afford the luxury of asserting and enjoying his desire and identity automatically makes him dispossessed – the victim of a double disadvantage, that of class and that of being queer, often in that order. There is a distinct hetero-patriarchal discourse that operates within the queer community, often rendering those who refuse the mantle of a specific category, or those who identify bisexual as illegitimate in the discourse of queerness. At what point does an autonomous space transform into an exclusionary space? This is a question of critical importance, and one that the corporeal cosmopolitan framework must account for.

The dynamic of class seems to operate similarly among *aravani* communities, subjecting working-class transwomen to dangerous and cruel marginalisations. Both Revathi and Vidya describe the grim circumstances under which they had to make a living. Although from quite different familial class backgrounds, ultimately, they both lived in abject squalor, often without proper homes or nourishment, forced to either beg or threaten small shop owners for money that they had to take back to their *gurus* in exchange for kinship and protection. Being sex workers put them at risk with the law professionally (as it is illegal) on the one hand, and on the other, is often the only avenue left to many women to explore and experience sexual intimacy. Between the brutality of the police and that of their male clients, the work leaves *thirunangais* vulnerable to all kinds of abuse and terror. Vidya, in her memoir, describes how she tried very hard to make a living by "normal" means – selling little trinkets instead of begging on the local trains. 'It was tough going', she writes, 'People were not interested in buying anything from us . . . the gentlemen who exhorted us to work hard to earn a living every time we sought alms from them were suddenly strangely absent' (Vidya 2007, 114). Similarly, Revathi ponders her scanty options, and how she might fulfil her desire to work in social activism: 'I began to wonder if at the end of it all, I would be left doing sex work for the rest of my life. But as I grew older, I would not be able to do that either' (Revathi 2010).

The distinction between private and public realms, as feminists have argued for several decades now, is an enormous luxury – indeed, the distinction itself is one that benefits straight men, and those in power. The recognition, acknowledgement and acceptance of transwomen's personhood are locked within the power matrices of patriarchy, sexual morality and heteronormativity. The languages of legality, and the state, are also locked within these same matrices, and corporeal cosmopolitanism must be capable of extending itself well beyond these limited ways of speaking if it is to facilitate a larger sense of belonging. In other words, it must recognise and distinguish between the rare, elite and privileged power positions that a minority of transwomen so clearly hold and the severely marginalised positions that the majority of transwomen hold, and have held over decades. Corporeal cosmopolitanism, in my conception, is committed to fighting for a space of deep transformation, that is decolonial and radical but also dialogic. That is to say, although it must dismantle the barriers of elite and liberal cosmopolitanism, it does not have to be predicated on an oppositional politics of binarism but rather on the possibility of intersecting different experiences of marginality, through conversations action and radical compassion.

Within the power matrices and biases of knowledge and understanding, however, it changes little because we are, at best, adding another grid to the grid-box, rather than dismantling or de/constructing these grids. In other words, acknowledging the existence of fluidity in identity and ways of living does not imply an acceptance of fluidity, and this acceptance is the key to forming a better informed, more open template of acknowledging multiplicity. Unless we can ground our notional acceptance of poly-belonging in actual materiality, embodiment, affect and desire, the addition of more and more categories will only serve to reify the very things that they aim to dismantle. Without a corporeal and affective comprehension, the prospect of honest dialogue around solidarity and shared normative frameworks will remain distant, if not entirely impossible. Cosmopolitan belonging can be meaningful if, and *only* if, it speaks to the material, emotional, sexual and gendered realities of how people inhabit themselves and the world. I hope that this exploration of solidarity and experiences of community have illustrated the kind of dialogic and critical work that I envision for corporeal cosmopolitanism. Chapter four explores a different set of nuances through very different experiences of community building. Chapter four listens deeply to, and tries to recount, some stories of Indian women who immigrated to the Caribbean islands, and how they articulated their embodied multiplicities.

NOTES

1 There are a whole variety of trans-identification across different communities and parts of India. I focus on only one such identification, largely located in Tamil Nadu, India.

2 Special thanks to Srijith Sundaram, Aniruddhan Vasudevan and Priya Babu.

3 http://arableftist.blogspot.co.uk/2013/04/joseph-massad-occidentalists-other_ 21.html; https://newrepublic.com/article/62069/queer-theory; http://al-bab.com/ distorting-desire; http://ibishblog.com/2010/02/04/joseph_massad_homophobia_ gay_rights_and_categories_modernity/.

4 See Appendix B for the complete legal article.

5 For the complete Bill See: http://orinam.net/resources-for/law-and-enforcement/ trans-persons-protection-rights-bill-2016/.

6 For the complete Bill See: http://orinam.net/resources-for/law-and-enforcement/ rights-of-transgender-persons-bill-2014/.

7 For the complete Bill See: http://orinam.net/resources-for/law-and-enforcement/ msje-rights-of-transgender-persons-bill-2015/.

8 For the complete NALSA petition, See: http://orinam.net/resources-for/law-and-enforcement/nalsa-petition-tg-rights-india/.

9 See Trans-Persons Protection Rights Bill. Available at: http://orinam.net/ resources-for/law-and-enforcement/trans-persons-protection-rights-bill-2016/.

10 See also Narrain, 2012 for the complexities of sexual violence as gender neutral.

11 http://orinam.net/resources-for/law-and-enforcement/trans-persons-protec tion-rights-bill-2016/. Please see for full details of the laws and criticisms of the same.

12 Berdaches of Amerindian belief systems, Djinn in Islam, Yakshas and Kinnaras in Hinduism, and so on.

13 See Reddy (2005), Roy (2014), Nanda (1990), and Lal (1999). It is important to note that a good number of these mythological references appear in elite, often upper-caste sanctioned renderings of Hindu mythology, lending them a very particular kind of restricted legitimacy.

14 See https://www.youtube.com/watch?v=ZesYnsJiee4 for an interview with trans-activist and scholar Gee Imaan Semmalar for a critique of this issue.

15 Both Rose Venkatesan and Apsara Reddy use their surnames in the public domain, which is why I use 'Venkatesan' and 'Reddy' as per standard academic writing style.

16 For the full interview, see: http://www.dailyo.in/lifestyle/transgender-woman-apsara-reddy-gay-marriage-homosexuality-lgbt-section-377/story/1/9865.html.

17 For Apsara Reddy's description of *Natpudan Apsara*, see: https://www.youtube.com/watch?v=2btpoNYkcYA.

18 For the full interview where Reddy discusses the importance of confidence, self- esteem and success, See: https://www.youtube.com/watch?v=2btpoNYkcYA.

19 Revathi and Vidya, more in keeping with nonurban and typically Tamil names, do not take on surnames. Revathi's suffix is the initial 'A.', and Vidya takes on the title 'Living Smile'. I therefore refer to them by their first names. The absence of surnames is an important marker of political and class identity.

20 For the complete interview with Gee Iman Semmalar, See: https://www.youtube.com/watch?v=ZesYnsJiee4.

21 Roughly translated reads, 'the gay man of English-land'.

Chapter 4

Are Dispossessed Bodies Human?

Gender, Exile and Cosmopolitan Solidarities

There are many kinds of travel. Sometimes, travel can be physical movement, or it could be the movement of thought, of love and of godesses. It can be exhilarating and devastating. At still other times, it can be an eternal exile and a forgetting. Diasporic movement is often accompanied by fear. Fear of being forgotten, lost or left behind. Survival becomes a vital, sometimes deadly, goal for the dispossessed and the landless. Following the broad trajectory from chapter three, in this chapter, I explore, on a different canvas, the intersections of corporeality, emotions and cosmopolitanism, and why it is so vital to the growing academic debates on formulating global notions of community and multiplicity. I focus specifically on diasporic women's narratives of solidarity, rooted in a decolonial, black feminist understanding of cosmopolitanism that is both embodied and affective. The Caribbean islands are culturally vast and diverse, criss-crossed by different regimes of colonial violence and resonant with histories and stories of communities: African, Chinese, Carib and Latina, among others, most of them broken and beaten into slavery or indentured labour of some description. It is a land that carries tremendous depth of trauma, violence and colonial brutality, as well as a phenomenal fortitude of spirit, of resistance and of revolution. This is not to romanticise the Caribbean islands, for, like every society, it is rife with internal hegemonies of power, hierarchies of race, colourism, class and gender, all of which arise in the course of this chapter. I cannot hope to tell all those stories here, and so I have worked with narratives of Indo-Caribbean women. It was through their stories that I began to grasp the possibilities of "other" cosmopolitanisms, when I first began my research. Their songs carry the complex nuances of hybridity and layers of contradictory identities which still tell stories of home and away; of alienation and belonging; and of being Caribbean, being Indian and being women. Fighting together and building bonds of solidarity, through love, loss, trauma and music from across oceans and continents, this is a cosmopolitan belonging that is wholly composed of bodies and feelings, and so many elsewheres. My own engagement with the theatre of the Indo-Caribbean has been made possible only by encountering storytellers, and weavers of songs and words at conferences, and performances; in books, music, and film. Never having been to the Caribbean islands myself, this chapter is informed by a very different experience of corporeal cosmopolitanism. Belonging, inhabitation and solidarities can be felt just as strongly in the act of telling and sharing stories, as they might be in physical, geographic proximity. The affective and corporeal bonds of these diasporic narratives are thus often forged in the imagination, in transit and in memory. The corporeality of corporeal cosmopolitanism is therefore not bound to territory or physicality, in a literal sense.

I begin with some key ideas that inform diasporic and exilic narratives of home and strangeness, of belonging and abjection, and how they intersect with the cosmopolitan imaginary. The diasporic experience of the Indo-Caribbean community is especially complex, and I will spend some time foregrounding this experience, along with some other clarifications specific to the geographical and cultural tropes that I have chosen to deal with in the realm of Indo-Caribbean scholarship. Diasporic movement and exchange form a vital part of the cosmopolitan imaginary, and Indo-Caribbean women's diasporic experiences both strengthen and challenge the possibilities of radical cosmopolitan solidarities. Trauma and violence form an intimate core of these solidarities in this history of travel, escape and bondage. The first section thus foregrounds the connections between diaspora, travel, exile and cosmopolitan understandings of belonging. The next section sets up a brief, contextual history of the Indian entry into the Caribbean islands and the historical and colonial background of this influx, while examining the intersections of race, class, colonial violence, sexuality and gender that were such a crucial part of the Indo-Caribbean experience. I focus specifically on some Indian and African racial/cultural dynamics that form an important part of the embodied realities of both communities.

In the third section, I examine and discuss feminist scholarship on Indo-Caribbean women's experiences and significant (and often controversial) cultural and political phenomena. Much of this work deals with gender and sexual violence within the Indo-Caribbean community and the historical and cultural patterns of misogyny. I use the work of several Indo-Caribbean feminist scholars to unpack the myriad contradictions and fragmentation within the construction of femininity in Indo-Caribbean communities. Indo-Caribbean women have only recently begun to be globally heard – in writing, performance and other spaces – which makes this an incredibly rich and emergent world in which to understand how significant embodiment and affect are to the creation of a diasporic, cosmopolitan identity.

In the fourth and fifth sections, similar to chapter three, I have chosen to explore conceptual and theoretical ideas around understanding Indo-Caribbean women's identities, as well as their literary voices, through novels. Brinda Mehta (2004, 2009) uses the alternate histories represented by Caliban and Sycorax in Shakespeare's *Tempest*, to explore and narrativise Indo- and Afro-Caribbean experiences of colonial violence, slavery and abuse. Bodily trauma and pain form an important part of this chapter and highlight one of the most important elisions of corporeality within cosmopolitan thought. I use three literary narratives to demonstrate the importance of the corporeal and the emotional in the creation and performance of Indo-Caribbean women's diasporic, multiplicitous identities. The three texts I use are *Valmiki's Daughter* by Shani Mootoo (2010), *The Swinging Bridge* by Ramabai Espinet (2004) and *Coolie Woman: An Odyssey of Indenture* by Gaiutra Bahadur (2013). All three texts are distinct and unique: the first deals with queerness and sexuality in an Indo-Caribbean family; the second with double diasporic dispossession, loss and home; and the third is a nonfictional account of Bahadur's search for her own Indian ancestry. This section is not a literary examination of these books and stories. Rather, the stories are seen to be bearers of the interplays between corporeality, affect, desire and violence, all of which are central to the imagination of a cosmopolitan, diasporic identity that is always both home and away.

WINDFLOWERS: UNROOTED HOMES
AND COSMOPOLITAN BELONGINGS

Diasporic and exilic literatures are central to the conceptual and material cores of home, inclusion and belonging. Nostalgic histories and partially remembered and imagined pasts are a very important part of how we believe ourselves to be part of an "original" community tied to place and spirit. Diasporic narratives have an important relationship with notions of cosmopolitan belonging, with their challenges of what it means to be rooted and unrooted, and to belong and not belong. Among many other things, the term *diaspora* carries with it a sense of the nomadic and the ever-moving, and this idea of travel, be it geographical or sometimes purely intellectual, has been a cornerstone of cosmopolitan thought and writing. However, diasporic peoples are not caricatures of movement, and we must always resist the tendency to romanticise these ideas of nomadic freedom and hybrid homes. In my own understanding of both diasporic and cosmopolitan literatures, it is not so much the absence or denial of home that makes this constant flow of movement possible but rather the acknowledgement of the fragile, yet profound, patchwork nature of belonging. Cosmopolitan solidarity can be forged as much in pain and remembrance, and in music and art, as in political and economic realms. Movement, in this sense, as we have seen in previous chapters, does not always imply a physical dimension, and for many diasporic peoples, movement may now be centuries old, home may now be in so many different lands, but there remains the memory and the *feeling* of movement. These movements and memories contain multitudes: they tell of brutality and slavery; cooking, colonialism and songs of liberation; and poverty, death and new beginnings. The conception of cosmopolitan belonging, or any expansive sense of solidarity, needs the breadth of emotional and embodied experiences, and diasporic stories, eulogies and songs are full of these moorings and unmoorings. The Indo-Caribbean diaspora is an especially interesting site both because of its historical positioning and its ethnic and cultural relation to the Caribbean islands. The *Kālā Pāni* (literally, Black Water, so named after notions of Hindu ritual impurity associated with oceanic crossings) exodus of indentured Indians sent to the Caribbean islands as estate labourers – the real colonial response to the long overdue abolition of slavery – is a tortured and complex space within which to understand the vicissitudes of cosmopolitan belonging. The aspirational affect that is often attributed to diasporic movements is accurate, as it is deceptive and, in the Indo-Caribbean case, as we will discover, this movement was both dangerous and fraught. Neither voluntarily exilic nor entirely liberationist, this diasporic migration was the calculated result of colonialist machinations.

Indian women's experiences of migrating, community building and creating new identities in the Caribbean islands are especially powerful. This migration, for many Indian women, was a desperate bid for freedom from the shackles of cultural and religious patriarchy in India on the one hand, and, on the other, was a marker of their degeneracy and failure to be chaste, "good" Indian women. Inhabiting this new space was further complicated by clashes with the codes of existing patriarchal and religious hegemonies of White, Creole and African (in that order of hierarchy), communities, with whom they now had to share homes and lives. These women's journeys across the oceans are a vital narrative of embodied cosmopolitanism, and what it means to belong everywhere and nowhere, and what it means to leave behind worlds and still carry them all within you, in body memories – in tastes, sounds, smells, textures and emotions. The space of the island and the ship can be partially imagined as what Foucault (1984) described as a *heterotopic* space. The heterotopic space is a space of multiplicities, seemingly transparent but often with countless secret doors and rules of admittance, consisting of the chaotic difference and hybridity that are characteristic of a sense of cosmopolitan belonging, and of having no home and many homes at the same time. The writings of Indo-Caribbean women about these journeys, as sisters of the ship, suggest that deeply conflicted and complex processes lie at the heart of these heterotopic and Creole spaces. These spaces have experienced and navigated through embodied experiences of being woman and Indian, and of being widow, wife or prostitute, and a rejection of all these labels, all at once. The body, as Grosz (1994) suggests, possesses its own biography and must be recognised as a legitimate site of knowledge. The image of the phantom limb that Grosz alludes to is particularly poignant here, and in some ways, diasporic personhood is always imbued with the grief of loss – the loss of the natal, impossible home. As Anjali Prabhu (2007, 10) evocatively suggests, 'Diaspora is . . . held up by trauma. That is, it is the memory of shared trauma that assures diasporic cohesion in the present'. Moira Gatens's work (see chapter two) emphasises the importance of pain, violence and memory that is inscribed on to the body as law. She exposes the inherent sexism and misogyny of the body politic and reveals it to be a heterosexual, virile and all-powerful male body. Both Grosz and Gatens acknowledge the constitutive schizophrenia of the Cartesian sundering of mind from body and the relegation of desire, affect and embodiment to the realm of the invisible female: the absent, the irrational and the hysterical. This incapacitating of an entire mode of experiences and narratives has undoubtedly been central to the larger epistemology of the political at large, and cosmopolitan thought is no exception. It is with these broad trajectories in mind that I have chosen to explore the narratives of Indo-Caribbean women as a challenge to, and performance of, cosmopolitan identity and belonging because these narratives root and uproot themselves through the experiences of the body, desire, pain, memory and affect.

Brent Edwards, in *The Practice of Diaspora* (2003), renews the concept of *décalage*,[1] which typically indicates a discrepancy or disjointedness in both time and space. Edwards explores and opens up this embodied concept as indicative of a necessary break, or asymmetry, to facilitate a different kind of interaction with disjuncture. That is, he argues that the joint in a body, in a certain sense, signifies a break in the limbs. However, this breakage is in fact what facilitates our very capacity to move, reiterating the point that, in the body, it is this asymmetry and difference – this breakage – which allows for movement. I use Edwards's reading of *décalage* to characterise this intersection of corporeality and cosmopolitanism with the aim of engaging with these breaks, rather than adhering to a smooth spatio-temporality of modernity and colonialism while theorising and performing alternative narratives of cosmopolitanism. In other words, the relationships between embodiment, emotion and cosmopolitan practices *do* feel like fractures sometimes – a wounded brokenness – and it is my hope that Edwards's understanding of *décalage* might add the possibility of a different kind of breakage, which enables, rather than freezes, movement and dialogue. This movement and dialogue are central even to liberal cosmopolitanism, which also emphasises fluidity and constant negotiation. For instance, Appiah's notion of rooted cosmopolitanism (2006), while acknowledging patriotic allegiances and love of one's nation as important markers of identity, still argues that our modes of belonging are constantly transforming and adapting to global cultural shifts. Appiah is very aware of the nuances of multiple identities, mixed ethnicities, queer sexualities and the role of rituals and traditions within culture. However, it must also be noted that his account of these experiences are, by and large, comprehensible in economically and culturally privileged milieus, and, that kind of cosmopolitan thinking, while not totally insignificant, is inaccessible to a vast majority. Appiah's insistence on trying to fashion a larger normative, moral framework is not problematic in and of itself, and, indeed, any commitment to dialogue and solidarity is grounded in some belief around shared ground and respect for what cannot be shared. Corporeal cosmopolitanism, for me, is about questioning *how* we fashion these spaces of sharing and what we permit and stifle, that is, what is deemed legible or illegible; relevant or irrelevant; rational or irrational; and reasonable or unreasonable.

The major elision within liberal narratives of cosmopolitanism, as discussed in chapter one, is that they are unable to engage with the messy affectivity that constitutes the bases of identity, solidarity and dialogue. This inability thus precludes the entire axis of gender performativity, sexuality and embodied materiality in lived narratives of cosmopolitanism. This chapter draws on the embodied and deeply felt experiences of community, dialogue and exchange that Indo-Caribbean women forge and negotiate in order to create their identities, lives and spaces. It is not my intention to provide a thorough or linear chronology of the histories of these communities. As in chapter three, I am interested in the radical border cosmopolitanisms that are performed through the lived realities of Indo-Caribbean women. Writing about cosmopolitanism as I have has meant that some of my work, on the one hand, has involved geographical familiarity as well as holding the hands and eyes of some of the people whose stories I was told. Some of my work, on the other hand, has involved a different kind of storytelling, across continents and time scapes. This book too resides in the overlaps and interlocutions of the corporeality of bodies and texts, and I could not judge one to be less embodied than the other.

When I presented the seedlings of this chapter at a conference in southern India, a group of both Indian and African Caribbean scholars, all women, asked me if I had ever been to the places I was writing about or whether I had been to Carnival, and watched Soca or Chutney music performed live. I had not, and still have not, but hope that I can, one day. I recognise that these are such difficult spaces to tread, and that we must be both careful and honest in our writing. In the humanities and social sciences, particularly in theory, the colonial scholar, having consumed the "native", chewed her up and spat out her exotic remains, still presides over us, laying claim to a violent authenticity.

Decolonial and border scholarship is constantly finding ways, both to resist these violent authenticities, and to write with integrity, and I hope I have at least tried to do the same. My conversations with diverse spaces and stories, and my lack of physical or geographical knowledge, are part of an important question about the limits of corporeal cosmopolitanism. In my own experience – of listening to these narratives of corporeal cosmopolitanism, both spoken and written – embodiment and affect are carried into everyday performances of the political and personal in a variety of ways. We live in a world that deals increasingly in nontactile engagement, virtual resistances and solidarities, and to that extent, it must be possible to corporealise across different mediums, times and spaces to engage with corporeal heterotopias and corporeal heterochronies (Foucault 1984). My exchange with the Caribbean scholars I met identified the material and geographical lacunae in my work, through a conversation over cups of coffee, in a southern Indian city, from where both men and women travelled to Calcutta, and onwards to the Caribbean islands, in the 1800s. These migrant labourers settled in the smaller islands and were often identified differently, because their skins were of darker shades of brown and black (B.J. Mehta 2009). I learnt from that conversation and through subsequent reading and exploring that my work dealt primarily with stories from Trinidad and Tobago, and that this was an implicit subordination of voices from other islands: Suriname, Jamaica, Guyana, Mauritius, St. Helene and St. Kitts, among others. There exists an important politics of resistance against the emphasis of Trinidad as representative of the "Indian" Caribbean, and I want to emphasise that I do not in any way privilege or generalise Trinidadian narratives to either other Caribbean islands or Indo-Caribbean experiences. However, I have, for the most part, focused my work round the narratives of Indo-Caribbean women writers and scholars, many of whom are or were connected to Trinidad, perhaps owing partly to the prominent, and often domineering Indian presence there and partly to the celebration of Carnival, which takes place every year, and is a prominent feature in their stories. There is also a vast canon of Francophone literature which I do not address except by way of Brinda Mehta's (2009) work on the subject. While claiming full responsibility for the limitations and imbalances in the narratives I focus on, I hope that they will not be diminished as crucial contributions to the creation of corporeal cosmopolitan imaginaries and performances.

BLACK MASKS; BROWN MASKS: ETHNIC
CONFLICTS IN THE CARIBBEAN ISLANDS

The discourse of hybridity is a powerful presence in diasporic ontologies. In reading and writing the Caribbean islands, hybridity emerges as a primary marker of identification, both culturally and geographically. Shalini Puri's

The Caribbean Postcolonial (2004) addresses many of the issues that make the Indo-Caribbean community such a compelling presence in the cosmopolitan imaginary. Puri too makes hybridity central to the Caribbean islands, a concept much discussed and very close to cosmopolitan thought. Insisting that the nation state is very much alive and present, she challenges theories of the end of the nation state supported by scholars such as Beck (2006) and Delanty (2009) (see chapter one). She also argues that nationalism is heterogeneous and the performance of nationalism can be just as subversive as antinationalism and that in the Caribbean islands, hybridity and statehood are not always opposed. Both in the case of Haiti and Trinidad, the hybrid existed side by side with the homogenous. In fact, Trinidad, under the political leadership of Eric Williams demanded absolute national loyalty to Trinidad while simultaneously promoting the multiplicitous identity of the Creole, *callaloo*[2] nation. Implicit in this, and something I consider in the next section, is that Creole includes the gamut of "mixedness" between only black and white. South Asians and other ethnicities often do not figure in this *creoleness*. There is a constant crisis of either othering the Indo-Caribbean presence or of romanticising it, and consuming it, in an unproblematic way. Puri uses Oswald de Andrade's (1928) concept of anthropophagy (cultural cannibalism) and Martin Harris's (1977) notion of cannibalism, where the consumption of the "enemy" renders all kinds of possibilities and dislocations. It is an unsettling of the self, a constant negotiation between self and other, where the consumed always remains, sometimes as a haunting and sometimes as an absorbed essence that alters the identity of the consumer. Puri also suggests via Edouard Glissant that there is no return to an immutable or original identity but rather a 'return to the point of entanglement' (Puri 2004, 77). National identity, in this sense is always at the point of entanglement and can therefore be performative and transgressive if one so chooses. However, Puri remarks that it is 'one of the great ironies of decolonization in Trinidad that racial tensions have taken the form of lateral hostility between blacks and Indians, rather than vertical hostility directed by blacks and Indians together against the French Creole elite, the white ex-plantocracy, or transnational capital' (Puri 2004, 172).

I now explore some of the foundations of the schisms between African and Indo-Caribbean communities, and why it has been such a painful and traumatic conflict, a kind of desperate deadlock unable to articulate its own oppressor. As Puri accurately observes, it *is* one of history's tragedies that a potential subaltern solidarity was destroyed by the cruel machinations of white colonial, as well as Indian caste and colour hegemonies, for, this solidarity is the stuff of hope and revolutions. In a moment of candour, Puri explains why hybridity see also Bhabha, 1994 as a concept is still so popular, despite all its problems, biases, errors and elitism. She writes, 'The discourses of hybridity . . . themselves desire and testify to a desire for vital and harmonious community. It is the utopian desire, indeed this promise of acceptance which explains the popularity and wide circulation of cultural texts on hybridity' (Puri 2004, 83).

As I have suggested in chapter one, this hankering for an expansive peace is also what seems to drive the growing engagement with cosmopolitan imaginaries. Cosmopolitan thought is overwhelmingly ridden with conceptual obduracy, patently Western-centric discourse and colonial privilege. However, it *is* the 'desire for vital and harmonious community' (Puri 2004, 83) that brings scholars so ideologically opposed and in constant disagreement in conversation with each other.

The Indian entry into the Caribbean islands took place in the mid-1800s, following the abolition of slavery as a replacement for hitherto black slave labour. Viranjini Munasinghe (2001) argues that because this could not be openly acknowledged with classic colonial deception, British colonisers used racist discourse to vilify African population as being "morally deficient" and problematic. They insisted that a new labour infusion would "improve things" in the Caribbean islands. She writes, 'Making a case for immigrants entailed derogation of the black labouring population as dishonest, immoral, improvident and of limited mental capacity' (Munasinghe 2001, 9). This neatly fits an already deeply rooted and orientalist stereotyping of the "wild African" and the "submissive Asian", feeding the monstrous hegemony of colourism and fostering a long-standing antagonism between both communities. Between 1845 and 1917, about 144,000 Indians were brought to the sugar plantations, largely from Bihar and Uttar Pradesh in northern India and to a lesser extent, from, Bengal in eastern India and various parts of southern India. These were the *coolies*, meaning hired/wage labourers. *Coolies* were essentially bonded labourers who were either coerced into immigrating to the Caribbean islands by the British Raj or did so out of abject desperation. These Indian labourers were typically farmers whose lands were annexed by the British Raj, and they were therefore forced to borrow from the British Raj and were charged interest rates that carried over for generations, creating bonded labourers. They were a free, replacement labour force for the plantocracy and would continue the brutal work that African people had been enslaved into, until they won the bloody battle for the payment of wages for their labour. The Indian labour force essentially undermined the minimum-wage victory which black people had fought terrible battles and lost hundreds of thousands of lives for, and this made *coolies* traitors to and enemies of the struggle for liberation from slavery. This was a pseudo-enmity, encouraged by colonial masters who manipulated and abused both African and Indian peoples. Only the language changed, but the violence remained.

Indeed, the Immigration Ordinance of 1854 (Singh, 2013) was little better than slavery, indenturing Indian labourers to five years of industrial residence with virtually no rights, and ten years of labour if they wished to "earn"

a passage back to India (Khan 2005). Khan notes that the colonial obses-
sion with classifying the Caribbean islands – conflating colour, culture and
religion, and turning observations into labels – was the foundation of these
schisms. Khan (2005) and Munasinghe (2001) also argue that the discrimination and segregation were occupationally hierarchical. Indian labourers were
mostly considered rural and agricultural, while Africans occupied the urban,
artisan, teacher and lower rungs of civil service positions. In an odd inversion
of pure/mixed categorisation, to be considered "authentically" West Indian,
one had to be "mixed", for this was the mark of the *New World*. Creoleness
and the "mixing" of black and white populations marked the Caribbean colonial space. However, East Indians were not mixed, nor were they deemed
"mixable". In the Orientalist logic of colonial racism, India was a part of the
orient, and though still inferior, possessed too much cultural baggage, and
was therefore unfit for creolisation or hybridity. The same colonial violence
thus erased and delegitimised African identities cultures and ways of living to
the point where they saw the *New World* African as a tabula rasa that could be
imprinted or impregnated, with anything: 'The African . . . was seen as lacking an ancestral civilization and his or her imputed state of "cultural naked-
ness" permitted the African, through mixing, to incorporate new elements and
thereby become West Indian or Native' (Munasinghe 2001, 12).

It was the effects of this erasure that Frantz Fanon captured so terrifyingly
in his writings on 'Negrification' (Fanon 1963) and the untold psychological
violence it perpetrated against black peoples. This total erasure and denigra-
tion of African blackness created an extreme and violent self-loathing in
black ontology, causing black people to abject their blackness, and, to ampu-
tate it from their selves. The effects of this self-abnegation have travelled
through generations and across mountains and oceans, and a key part of the
healing work of corporeal cosmopolitanism lies in an deep immersion into
this abnegation. In the context of the Caribbean islands, this meant that the
Creole pyramid was three-tiered: Africans at the bottom, "mixed" or Creole
people (typically African and white; sometimes *Carib* or Chinese but hardly
ever Indian) in the middle, and white people at the top. With unerring, violent
precision, the white plantocracy manipulated the enmity between African
and Indian communities, where the "inferior" stamp given to African people
was still perceived as a stamp of recognition by East Indian labourers, who
were then resentful at being denied the status of the hated stepchild. Thus,
Creole implied hybridity and might even be considered a kind of heterotopia
(Foucault 1984). These were its secret doors of inclusion and exclusion, and
the discriminations which accompanied both. Munasinghe (2001) identifies the 1980s and 1990s as the peak time of contested national identity
amongst Indo-Caribbean communities in Trinidad against the perceived
Afro-Caribbean hegemony and exclusivity present at the time. Munasinghe

writes that Afro-Caribbeans, traditionally seen as the "original" inhabitants, inherited state control before and after independence in 1962. East
Indian representation, and Hinduism in particular, was always considered
religiously motivated and was therefore divisive. The 1980s and 1990s thus
saw an aggressive demand by the Indo-Caribbean community to be included
in the national fabric rather than be relegated to an ethnic minority, arguing
that their ethnicity was perfectly congruous with Caribbean national identity. This is an interesting development in light of the debates that liberal
cosmopolitanism has with patriotism, nationalism and global belonging. Is
ethnic particularistic identity opposed to a national one, especially when that
national identity itself claims to be an all-encompassing Creole, international
and cosmopolitan one? Incompatible or not, the Indian and Hindu demands
for inclusion only exacerbated and entrenched the differences between
African and Indian communities. Munasinghe notes that the early twentieth
century saw the formation of East Indian groups and solidarities and the
subsequent entry of East Indian elites into politics. Initially pro-colonial and
anti-African, this seems to have been a carefully cultivated response to the
fears of "African dominance", seeds planted and carefully nurtured by the
British Empire. Another important factor to consider here is India's own
complicated relationship with British colonialism, and the early Congress'
party and liberal elite's considerable support for certain aspects of British
Colonialism. Caste-, class- and colour-based hierarchies were already heavily entrenched in Indian sociocultural practice. Thus, Indo-Caribbean elites
standing with their white masters against "darker-skinned" Africans was the
extension of an already well-oiled machine, and in some ways a bid to win
the reviled-stepchild status. At the same time, Munasinghe notes that the fight
for a national identity in Trinidad caused middle-class Afro-Caribbeans to
cannibalise working-class black symbols, rendering the identity symbolically
working class but actually middle class, further complicating the dynamics of
class and race. Spurred on by India's fight for independence in the homeland,
we see the rise of a strong preservationist movement among East Indians,
causing them to articulate deep ethnic, religious and racial boundaries. Additionally, the *Aryan* discourse, yet another colonial manipulation, linking the
"proto-Aryan" to India and Europe, further estranged Indians from Africans.
This was part of a divide-and-conquer policy which European colonisers, and
the British Empire in particular, were especially skilled at. These fractures, as
would later be seen, were not dissimilar to the effects of the partition between
India, Pakistan and Bangladesh, also orchestrated by the British Raj.

Colonially constructed creoleness, with *blackness* at its centre, was West
Indian nationalism, and so it remained until the Black Power movement
began to criticise the Trinidadian government as *Afro-Saxon*, opening up
some critical space for other minority groups to speak (see Khan 2005; Puri

2004; Munasinghe 2001). Attempts at a coalition party ultimately failed, and there were increasing fears from both communities: one of brutal assimilation and another of an Indian takeover. East Indian right-wing extremism increasingly came to define Indian identity in an essentialised, glorifying way, often using dominant caste religious discourse to bolster itself. This *Aryan*-fuelled rhetoric not only alienated African communities but it also actively deepened racial differences and adopted the colonial vilification of Afro-Caribbean people as lazy, criminal and "uncivilised". It is crucial to recollect here that this time was hailed as the birth of a new nation, a *callaloo* nation of multiplicity and hybridity. From impregnation to labour, and finally, birth, we see at every stage the colonial phallus, the colonial midwife and the colonial *pater* – penetrating, delivering and disciplining. The colonial machine dictated the "mixture" of the Caribbean islands, and the resulting cosmopolitanism too was cast in the same framework. This narrative is powerful proof of Walter Mignolo's (2000a) claim that the origins of cosmopolitanism are deeply and absolutely rooted in coloniality. Coloniality cannot be erased or dialogued away – it must be borne into these new spaces we create, acknowledged and visible – at the centre of the histories we *all* must learn.

The narrative thus far has been one of state and political play, and not of people. That it is not representative of peoples embodied, material lives is a glaring example of the gaping rift between state- and empire-sponsored notions of hybridity and cosmopolitanism, and everyday performances of it. Aisha Khan (2005, 2007) draws attention to the constant slippages that occur in everyday life, regardless of state rhetoric. The divisions between black, brown and white did not, of course, play out in the same way as political parties articulated it. In large part, Indians and Africans were segregated because of geography, because most Indian labourers were segregated on plantations, and the two communities had little access to each other. In keeping with this discrepancy between political and personal narratives, Khan explores a new deployment of creolisation which emerged in intellectual and academic spaces as a fertile space of cultural transfer. However, creolisation did not include Asians in its ancestral narratives, and because the Caribbean islands gained a vast number of Asians and Indians, this exclusion was glaringly conspicuous. The backlash of orthodoxy among Indo-Caribbeans is partly the result of the fear of the loss of identity in movement from white, colonial cultural control to Afro-Caribbean cultural control, and partly the already prevalent casteist and colourist hegemonies within Indian society. Within this complex, there also existed a colonial link being drawn between *dravidian* (southern) Indians and Africans, separating them from other Indian immigrants who were from the north of India and identified with *"Aryan"* heritage, which in its turn was used to oppress "darker"-skinned south Indians (see Raghavan 2014). And finally, there was also the problem of whiteness itself, in that, white people who lived in the Caribbean islands were not considered "authentically" white. Their whiteness was rendered suspect either by birth, or worse, by their close association with so many people of colour. While the threat of syncretism, interracial marriages and dilution loomed large for Indo-Caribbeans, this did not entirely prevent their mingling with Afro-Caribbean communities, nor was it the only reason for their remaining discrete.

The notion of such an extreme sexual and social exclusion, however, is argued to have been more jingoistic stridence than actual reality. Audra Diptee (2003), discussing sexual relations between Indo-Caribbean and Afro-Caribbean communities in the nineteenth century, clearly shows that there were, in fact, several active relationships and sexual interactions between the two communities. While it is true that intimate interactions between Indo- and Afro-Caribbean communities were very low, Diptee suggests that it was not just the cultural, religious or caste prohibitions within Hinduism that were responsible for this. The severely skewed proportion of Indian women to men, with women being much diminished in number, is a big part of this complex. While the incidences of relationships between African and Indian Caribbeans were low because of the gender skew, this also gave women some amount of sexual freedom, certainly more than they would have possessed in India, which was a significant cultural shift for Indian women. The grim fallout of these changes, however, was that they were used as weapons of domestic abuse against these women, which no doubt inhibited their intimate relations with Afro-Caribbean men. The brutal conditions of plantation labour also acted as a factor in inhibiting African-Indian relations, pitting poverty and desperation against each other in capitalist competition. In addition to these factors, Diptee also notes that Afro-Caribbean women tended not to have relationships with Indian men, experiencing no shortage of men in their own community, and that the African and Chinese communities mingled far more than African and Indian communities. The point of cataloguing these observations is to draw attention to the numerous and complex elements of hybridity, cultural and corporeal exchange that took place under these colonial regimes. Cosmopolitan existences, forged in the firmament of colonial brutality, are embedded in material, embodied and affective realities, and, to that extent, the choice to engage, or dialogue, is an extremely difficult but powerful one.

Another performance of this kind of deep hybridity can be observed at the festival of *Hosay* – the commemoration of the death anniversary of Prophet *Mohammed's* grandsons. In this inter-faith and inter-race community interaction, Khan (2007) describes how this festival is celebrated by Hindu and Muslim Indo-Trinidadians and that it includes Afro-Trinidadians in its nonritual aspects: 'What the Hosay example tells us . . . is that . . . in some contexts it can . . . be a lived engagement with the ideology and politics of callaloo, a means of inscribing the presence of the muted or the absent – whether or not those means are palatable to outsiders, observers, or opponents' (Khan 2007, 65).

Similarly, during the festival of *Sipari Mai* (Khan 2005), a small black statue is worshipped as both the Virgin Mary and *Kali*, a powerful, erotic, bloody and sensual Hindu goddess. This is an instance of deep creolization and hybridity between religions and spiritual practices, highlighting the fact that an assertion of orthodoxy and "authentic" forms of knowledge by no means prevent the continuous occurrence of close interactions. It is in this milieu of interlocution that the specific narratives of Indo-Caribbean women are located, where the women have suffered multiple levels of invisibilisation and sexualisation, caught between an escape from and an imprisonment into very specific forms of violence and patriarchy, and subsequently creating and performing subversion, rebellion and celebration. It is these stories that I explore in the following sections to draw out the embodied and emotional processes that inform their practices of resistant border cosmopolitanism.

INDO-CARIBBEAN WOMEN: THE MARGINALISATIONS OF GENDER AND RACE

For many Hindus in the "upper reaches" of the caste hegemony, ocean crossing was considered taboo and impure (Mehta 2009). This travel effectively polluted the traveller, stripping them of their caste status and purity, and a long litany of purification rituals must be performed as part of this "cleansing". For Indian women crossing the ocean, however, this crossing held a dual promise, of both liberation and damnation. Many of these women who travelled to the Caribbean islands were part of severely marginalised castes, communities or classes and subject to all manner of oppression and violence. There were women escaping abusive husbands, widows who were destitute and excommunicated following the abolition of *sati* (the practice of widow immolation following the death of her husband), and also "fallen" women – those who had been "unfaithful" to their husbands or who were sex workers (Kanhai 2011; Bahadur 2013). The passage to the Caribbean islands gave them a chance to escape these particular shackles of Indian patriarchy, but the Indian men they would eventually have to cohabit with, used their so-called fall from moral chastity as instruments of torture, creating a gruesome culture of violence and abuse.[3]

The Hindu saint *Chaitanya* advocated a new practice of Hinduism in the sixteenth century, writes Gaiutra Bahadur (2013), that took root in Vrindavan, India, the celebrated birthplace of the Hindu god *Krishna*. Preaching the centrality of love, even romantic love, as pure divinity or *bhakti*, Chaitanya's *Vaishnavism* gained enormous popularity. This sect provided shelter and reprieve for destitute women: those who had been abandoned by their husbands, sex workers and widows, among others, and offered them the possibility of *moksha* (salvation) through their singular devotion to *Krishna*. These women were considered to be a combination of *gopi-kas* (women devoted to and in love with *Krishna*) and *devadasis* (ritually sanctioned, highly skilled performance artists and courtesans), who invoked sensual eroticism as a form of worship while remaining relatively outside the judgement of ordinary social norms and morals. Marriage was forbidden to these women and secrecy was a central tenet in their existence. This practice went hand in hand with high levels of exploitation and abuse, and it is Bahadur's thesis that 'a complex mix of victimization and *Vaishnavite* devotion brought them – and other estranged women – to holy sites where recruiters for indenture often found them' (Bahadur 2013, 31). The first wave of women migrants were plantation labourers, and to that extent, their status was not very different from the men. However, as previously discussed, this gave way to a selective appropriation of Indianness and Hinduism, replicating and embellishing a system of patriarchy and gender discrimination that was well established in India. As a result, Indo-Caribbean women were doubly invisibilised, both by their brownness and their gender; their voices entered the narrative of the Caribbean islands much, much later than Indo-Caribbean men and Afro-Caribbean women (B.J. Mehta 2004). The Indo-Caribbean woman, writes B.J. Mehta (2004), occupies multiple subject positions and fashions a very particular kind of fluid, postcolonial transnational feminism. The creative literature points to the centrality of the *Ramayana*, a significant religious epic in Hindu belief systems, in these women's lives, and Sherry Ann Singh (2011) explores this connection at length. The *Ramayana* tells the story of the "perfect" man and king *Rama*, who is believed to be a manifestation of *Vishnu*, one of three major gods in *Hinduism*. The epic chronicles the life and trials of *Rama* and is a moral guide of sorts, for perfect, peerless and righteous conduct. The epic is very complex and layered, eliciting love and devotion on the one hand and criticism on the other, particularly in its treatment of women and other marginalised beings. Much of the epic chronicles the exile which *Rama* undertakes with his brother *Lakshmana* and his wife *Sita*, who is abducted by an ancient and powerful king *Ravana*[4] during the course of this exile. *Sita* is also believed to be an incarnation of the goddess *Lakshmi*, *Vishnu*'s consort, and goddess of prosperity and goodness. In this manifestation, *Sita* serves as an exemplary model of chastity and purity to all women; she endures long years of captivity in perfect abstinence, although her captor is completely in love with her. For his part, *Rama*, the perfect man, husband and king, fights a great battle and rescues his beloved wife. *Sita*'s ultimate glory as a chaste wife is proved when, upon returning to their kingdom and being crowned emperor and empress, the people of the kingdom challenge *Sita*'s fidelity. *Rama*, the perfect ruler, submits to his subjects and sentences *Sita* to a trial by fire, whereupon *Agni*, the fire god himself, returns *Sita*, unharmed, declaring her absolute and divine chastity. There are many versions and nuances to the story, and the *Ramayana* is an old and complex text. In some versions, it is believed that after *Agni* returns her, *Sita* leaves her husband to live in the forest, and in still others that the earth, said to be *Sita*'s own mother, opens to receive her child back. Singh (2011) and others point out that it is Goswami Tulsidas's *Ramcharitmanas* (a poem version of the *Ramayana* from sixteenth-century northern India) that is most popular among the Indo-Caribbean community. I have provided only the barest skeleton of a summary of the *Ramayana* so that we may understand the complex nuances of the cultural archetypes[5] that influence and shape the lives of Indo-Caribbean communities. The experience of exile, suffering and otherness is a clear parallel to diasporic experiences of loss and unmooring. The vulnerability and danger that women are exposed to, both from being in foreign places and from foreign men, are combined with their superhuman capacity for resilience, moral strength and, most importantly, sexual and conjugal fidelity.

Over the years, the text has not remained static, and the oral and musical traditions that the indentured *coolie* women, the *Jahaji* (ship) sisters, brought with them transformed and morphed into new, radical and critical practices. Chief among these was the emergence of Chutney-Soca, a uniquely Indo-Caribbean musical form. Chutney-Soca adapted and blended Indian music traditions with Calypso and Soul, which are traditionally Afro-Caribbean musical genres, and absorbed tales from the *Ramayana*. The sheer irreverence of it caused all kinds of moral upset. Chutney-Soca is a hybrid expression of Indo-Caribbean femininity, its erotic and sensual appeal, its relationship with Afro-Caribbean culture, its radical critique, and its discussion of violence and trauma. Indo-Trinidadian culture, as Singh describes it, was deeply gendered and moralistic, but it was unable to practise much of its patriarchy owing to the fact that economically the women were equal contributors. There are several radically cosmopolitan moments of resistance and solidarity at work here in this mode of public and embodied performance.

The narrative of Hinduism is not in any way intended as a proxy for Indo-Caribbean identity, nor indeed, to stifle the voices of other religious identity narratives, and Christianity and Islam are an important and vibrant part of Indo-Caribbean identity. The previous narrative serves as an illustration of the complex forms of hybridity and cultural specificity, and the influences and critiques of ancestral culture, which form a cornerstone of corporeal cosmopolitan spaces. In another narrative, Halima-Sa'adia Kassim (2011), writing about Indian Muslim immigrants to the Caribbean islands, tells a somewhat different but not unrelated story. She writes that because the Islamic community was highly dependent on a small group of men for religious guidance, religious and cultural practice weighed heavily against

Muslim women. Kassim argues that this had an oppressive and detrimental impact upon Indian Muslim women's agency because 'conceptually feminism . . . did not pervade the reconstitution of Indo-Caribbean communities, in which an underlying premise of identity was religion and culture' (2011, 61). The implicit association of honour with men and shame with women emerges as another major source of discrimination in Kassim's work. The patriarchal and moral imperative, here, was to control women's sexualities and bodies, in an attempt to ensure their moral purity and protect their "chastity". One of the ways in which modern Islamic communities navigate this has been through matrimonial websites, where there is a compromise which allows for women to make their choices, while still allowing for some form of chaperoning (Kassim 2011).

What these illustrations clearly show is the significant role of religious and scriptural discourse in the production and policing of Indo-Caribbean women's identities. What Kassim's work also indicates is an absence of feminism, which is not wholly surprising considering that it is only in recent years that women of colour have fought for and claimed their places and voices in feminist discourse. Liberal cosmopolitan narratives that depend on the achievements of second-wave and liberal feminism must also contend with the racism that is endemic to those discourses. The state-supported discourse of cosmopolitanism that came to characterise Trinidad was thus able to neatly exclude Indo-Caribbean women who were policed by male arbitrators of ethnicity, gender and sexuality. As discussed earlier, the women who migrated to the Caribbean islands were also from marginalised class backgrounds. As Valerie Youssef (2011) writes, 'many women who came to Trinidad . . . were expressly seeking their freedom. Pivotal to the subsequent male attempt at Indian cultural reconstruction was the task of harnessing these women back into the perceived role of subservient wives; violence was a major plank of this process' (2011, 123).

As always, it is important to recall that this is not a blanket generalisation, but merely an indicator of the patterns that formed part of Indo-Caribbean women's identities as political and cultural actors. The brutal attempt at subjugation through violence was fiercely resisted by women, not only through education and economic equality but also through fierce and joyful performances as participants of Carnival.

Carnival, Trinidad and Tobago's annual festival, might loosely be characterised as a Bakhtinian space of revelry. Carnival opens up spaces of transgressive, erotic excess, and is a celebration of embodiment, sensuality and a Dionysian surrender. The annual festival, in many ways, is the poster child for cosmopolitan, Creole culture and the celebration of multiplicitous belonging and patriotism. However, as several feminist scholars of the Indo-Caribbean point out, this openness was decidedly conditional and had a very different response when Indian women chose to participate in the festival, performing their own versions of Chutney-Soca music and dance. Samantha Pinto (2009) provides some important insights into Indo-Caribbean women and their conflicted relationship with Carnival. Here, I discuss the implications that participation in the Carnival had for Indo-Caribbean women. (I discuss the relationship between Indo-Caribbean women, music and carnival as a subversive formation of community in chapter five in greater detail.)

Steel band and Calypso, traditionally working-class male music forms, were adopted as national symbols, while Soul Calypso (Soca) began as a form of resistance music among African men and slowly grew to include Indian percussion and Hindi music and lyrics. Chutney music, on the other hand, was a very specific form of Indian music performed by women, usually in the privacy of their homes, at *matikor* (pre-wedding gatherings exclusive to women) where women sang sexually explicit, humorous songs of desire to one another, transgressing the rules of their otherwise strictly monitored sexual and emotional lives. Chutney-Soca thus emerged as a highly controversial, morally reprehensible erotic music form that defied and threatened both Indian and African masculinities. Interestingly, it also was seen as infiltrating African Women's spaces because they had hitherto been the only women performers at the Carnival, holding both exclusivity and prestige. Still following Pinto (2009), we see that Chutney-Soca was dismissed by Caribbean society for its moral licentiousness, frivolity and vapidity, whereas Calypso music was seen as resistance music working to uplift the marginalised, that is, music with a political message. Thus, we see the way in which Chutney-Soca was dismissed and sexualised as a female form of music, frivolous and loose, with little or no substance. Chutney-Soca was also deemed unpatriotic because of the way in which it celebrated female sexuality and referred to the female body as a desiring body.

It is clear that once sexuality and gender enter the arena, a hitherto political and substantive form of music becomes frivolous and immoral, and therefore unworthy of national discourse. Because of the misogynistic eroticisation of the female body and in keeping with Gatens's (1996) comments about the nation state being definitively male, there was no way the state could sanction, let alone promote, Chutney-Soca music. This was, as Pinto (2009) notes, further complicated by the experience of sensuality, love and eroticism between women that Soca performance embodies. The pathologisation and control of sexuality and bodies, particularly women's bodies, have not been a new strategy by any means. The very articulation of Chutney-Soca is an act of resistance and subversion, and, as I see it, an iteration of corporeal cosmopolitan solidarity – creating a strong, embodied space, open to dialogue and the expression of vulnerability, power and love. These solidarities also challenged the characterisation of Carnival as inherently immoral, owing to the prominence of Afro-Caribbean female presence and celebration. Indo-Trinidadian women's performances thus challenged the yoke of both the British Empire and Hindu patriarchy, while using new and radical modes of expression and solidarity, drawing from Afro-Caribbean women's resistances and articulating new forms of community. Chutney-Soca was not only the declaration of control over their bodies and enjoyment of sexual pleasure and desire but very often also contained a double entendre, making hidden references to stories of sexual abuse, violence, injury and trauma, which were wrapped up within the erotic poetry of the music. Pinto (2009) writes about Drupatee Ramgoonai, one of Trinidad's first Chutney-Soca singers, who elicited all kinds of controversy for her music which used sexually explicit lyrics and dance moves but actually also narrated a story of domestic violence (Ramgoonai, 1992). Pinto notes that Ramgoonai faced severe authenticity-based discrimination from the African community and gender-based moral discrimination by the Indian community when she first burst on the performance scene. As an early articulation of the Indian Trinidadian women's body, Ramgoonai's presence confirmed that, thus far, Indo-Trinidadian women's bodies had not carried the public approval which, though pernicious in its own right, African Trinidadian women's bodies had been granted. To be very clear, African women's bodies were also publicly consumed in violent and misogynistic ways, but their visibility was more permissible than Indo-Trinidadian women's bodies.

Although Ramgoonai challenged and broke several shackles of gender oppression with her performances, Pinto remains cautious. She refers to one of Ramgoonai's songs, *Real Unity* (Montano and Ramgoonai, 2000), performed with an Afro-Trinidadian man, as conveying the message of political and sexual unity between the two communities. Pinto's critique is that this hybridisation and unity are made possible only in a heterosexual context with the African male subject and that too in a sexual context. This ignores all the other deep cultural wounds in both communities, and should not be so easily bypassed. Ramgoonai's work can, and should, be seen as an expression of radical, embodied cosmopolitan resistance. She rescues notions of equality, gender equality and sharing from the language of liberal cosmopolitan and places them in a robust, embodied and desirous space, while making room for more difficult kinds of solidarities and ways of belonging that are located in trauma and the experience of violence. However, these radical attempts occur within the restrictions and cultural contexts of patriarchal sexism, which elevates the heterosexual bond above all others and denigrates the significance of other kinds of expression. While this takes nothing away from the power and exuberance of Ramgoonai's work, we must be mindful of its constraints as well.

I conclude this section with a last exploration of a different kind of performance, this time as reifying "Indian" femininity through Gabrielle Hosein's

(2011) experience of *Mastana Bahar*, a televised Indian beauty pageant in Trinidad. Instituted in the 1970s, this pageant was the Indo-Caribbean community's response to the Miss Trinidad and Tobago pageant, which marginalised Indian women. Beauty pageants are an interesting space because of their popular image of being cosmopolitan Western, and modern. The *Mastana Bahar*, however, was committed to visibilising and validating Indian cultural and community presence by promoting and commodifying a very specific aesthetic. Hosein describes it as 'a performance staged to display decorative femininity, Indian iconography and the "appropriate" actions of high caste Hindu culture' (2011, 148). For participants, including herself, Hosein observes, the pageant was more about validating attractiveness and being visible to men, rather than validating an ethnic identity. Within this overt narrative of heteronormativity, ethnic validation and patriarchy though, there lived a whole host of "others" – queer designers, make-up artists, non-Indian stylists, and the like – who transformed the mandate of the pageant from the inside. That is to say, this misguided conservative resistance to an equally superficial manifestation of "modern" cosmopolitanism proved to be much more subversive than one might have predicted. While the pageant reified certain notions of hetero-patriarchy and objectification, it also acted as a counter-pageant, allowing women the space and freedom to fashion themselves. Hosein sees the pageant as a mixed, fluid and contrary space of feminist resistance. She writes of herself, after the experience of participating in the pageant: 'Not only have I stopped trying to be an "appropriate Indian girl" and to manage ethnic and gender expectations, I have stopped maintaining a claim to a racialized, sexualized, feminized self' (Hosein 2011, 155). While one must recognise that this is a privileged position to occupy, and not all women have recourse to such an articulation, the larger point I want to make is really about the nuances and complexities of what it means to fashion new identities that are hybrid and rooted, and cosmopolitan and critical. The objective of this section has been to contextualise and explore the lived space and identity experiences of Indo-Caribbean women in political and public spheres through their performances of solidarity, resistance and community building. These performances and experiences exert a profound influence on the different ways in which we might envision corporeal cosmopolitan spaces.

EXPERIENTIAL AND LITERARY TROPES IN INDO-CARIBBEAN WOMEN'S IDENTITIES

In the penultimate and final sections, I focus on the literary narratives of Indo-Caribbean women as part of this autobiographical site of knowledge, experiences, communities and politics. The previous section outlined political, societal and cultural trajectories in the shaping of Indo-Caribbean women's identities and communities; the following sections consider more individual accounts. These narratives blur the lines between fiction and autobiography, as well as literature and feminist theory. They express the tightly knit relationships between the political, cultural and the intimate. I consider these stories and modes of expression to be an important step in the direction of fostering embodied and affective dialogues and solidarities. Patricia Mohammed's (2012) paper on the symbols of Indo-Caribbean femininity provides a useful starting point while examining the way Indo-Caribbean women's narratives and writing have been shaped and produced. Given the complex mesh of Indo-Caribbean femininity that had been previously discussed, Mohammed notes that the arrival of second-wave feminism in the Caribbean islands around the 1990s largely precluded Indian women, placing them in a space of multiple exclusions, which ultimately required a new framework. The earliest reference to the Indo-Caribbean community in literature occurs in 1877 in a novel by Edward Jenkins on West Indian life. It was not until the 1950s that we see authors such as Samuel Selvon and V. S. Naipaul writing of the Indo-Trinidadian as a complete character, and Mohammed (2009) attributes some of this absence to the continuance of indenture till the 1920s, maintaining the Indian community as people in transience – never truly belonging, never truly "home". This state of limbo was used as a colonial strategy to keep the Indian community isolated and precarious. Inevitably, this tendency, no doubt, also lent itself to the exclusionary discourse of privilege that elite Indo-Caribbean men, in particular, adopted. The earliest articulation of community among Indo-Caribbean people was the kinship of the ship – the *jahaji bhai* – or *behen*, the brothers and sisters of the ship. Novels like *Coolie Woman* and *The Swinging Bridge* tell us of the brutal conditions of the Indo-Caribbean passage, some of them referring to it as another *Middle Passage* (though not as brutal *as* the first one", where many atrocities were committed upon the indentured labourers, and many lost their lives to the uninhabitable, terrible conditions on board.

In the previous section, we saw that the 1980s marked the entry of Indian women into the music scene with Chutney-Soca, but it is only in the 1990s, that we see the appearance of authors like Lakshmi Persaud, Ramabai Espinet and Shani Mootoo (Mohammed 2012). These authors presented a radical reformulation and re-narrativisation of Indo-Caribbean femininity, examining and challenging mythological stereotypes and unpacking the potency of Indo-Caribbean women's experiences. Indo-Caribbean women's writing, according to Mohammed, has not been fashioned by feminist tropes in a systematic way. Rather, it has occurred through literary, both autobiographical and semiautobiographical, works of fiction and nonfiction. In the absence of any systematic study, Mohammed, along with scholars like Kanhai and B. J. Mehta, identifies some conceptual and literary tropes or ways of explaining and understanding community that have emerged among Indo-Caribbean women in the last two decades, and they are *Jahajee, matikor* and bindi. I briefly describe these as frameworks that we may draw on in creating a vocabulary of corporeal cosmopolitanism.

The *Jahajee* sisterhood is a group of Indo-Caribbean women in Queens, New York, who originally formed as a support group for domestic violence victims, for women who crossed two black oceans: one from India to the Caribbean islands and the other from the Caribbean islands to America. Keeping the flow of the movement intact, they use narratives from both migrations. Mohammed gives us the instance of one multiauthored poem that tells of a silk cocoon from which an iron-winged butterfly emerges,[6] using the hard and soft edges of both voyages to create a larger, more globally connected sisterhood. The authors write, 'The reshaping of community is like blowing glass, moulded in the fire of violence, dipped in waters of reflection, creating priceless gifts holding the beauty of unity'.[7] This kind of community formation, very much in keeping with decolonial feminist articulations, is fuelled by an embodied, affective core, through the shared memory and experiences of trauma, pain and violence, ultimately healed and held together by love. This community building is constitutively corporeal – the memories borne by and in women's bodies are transmitted and shared through oral narratives, music and poetry. Providing a global framework of sisterhood, the *Jahajee* metaphor uses the ship as a heterotopic imaginary, a shifting, fluid canvas that stitches memories upon memories, creating a cosmopolitanism of affect, underpinned by an ethics of care and compassion (Vieten 2012). The trope of *matikor* uses the space of the pre-wedding ceremony, roughly translating into a crash course on marriage for the bride. The ceremony is all-female and rife with revelry, teasing and ribaldry that include a vast repertoire of songs and sharing of experiences about marriage and sexuality. This was the birth of Chutney music. A solidarity-building ceremony, *matikor* is a place of healing and coming together. In recent times, it is being reinvented from its traditional function as a space of sharing and strength to create new songs, stories and experiences. The last trope of *bindi* (the mark worn on the forehead, primarily, though not exclusively, by Hindu women) also based on Kanhai's work, is, once again, indicative of Indo-Caribbean women's embodied and aesthetic experiences. Used in different materials, textures and colours, the bindi signifies status and aesthetics, the vermillion signifying menstruation, fertility and childbirth, and the ash, signifying widows. Today, Kanhai observes, the *bindi* has become a visible fashion statement, rather than a conveyor of status. It has become an ethnic ornamentation used by women to visibilise themselves rather than communicate their sexual status. These tropes that have been adopted by Indo-Caribbean women writers underscore the late visibilisation of Indo-Caribbean women and their presence and draw attention to the fragmented and complex aspects of this visibility, requiring new symbols, metaphors and ways of understanding.

I now consider the ways in which Indo-Caribbean scholars and writers narrativise the experiences of violence, abuse and trauma, in their political, cultural and personal identities and communities. Brinda J. Mehta's remarkable work (2009) provides some critical and crucial lenses with which to understand Indo-Caribbean women's experiences of violence. While B. J. Mehta's book focuses on Francophone writing, I draw on her work as an affective framework, which helps to unpack literary narratives that I explore in the next section. The understanding of Caribbean diasporic experiences is rooted in the memory of violence and trauma as an extremely corporeal, material reality. The Caribbean is 'a meta archipelago with undetermined rhizomatic roots' (B. J. Mehta 2009, 2). The relationship between diasporic theorising and gender is a troubled one, and the association of colonised populations as "effeminate" often reflects a deeply rooted misogyny complicated by colonial violence and threatened masculinity. B. J. Mehta uses the term *calibanization*, borrowing deliberately from Shakespeare and other Caribbean writers, to describe the treatment of *Carib* people, the indigenous Amerindian people of the Caribbean islands, and extends this description to the Caribbean islands as a whole. Caliban, the monstrous savage, is also bereft of a female presence. His demon/witch mother Sycorax, also the black female presence in the original play, is an absent presence, and there is no partner, male or female, who is like Caliban. Thus, the savage presence of Caliban as Caribbean is distinctly stripped of any female presence, except in an evil form. Of the French Caribbean islands, she writes of the kind of oppression and rebellion which was very distinct, owing particularly to the linguistic absolutism of French dictatorship in the Caribbean islands. Consequently, we see that the Indo-Caribbean marginalisation within the French Caribbean is also very different. The migrants here were mostly from Tamil Nadu, located in the south of India, and discriminated against for their "darker" *dravidian* skin and so-called inferiority to the *aryans*. *Tamilians* were already thus bearers of colourist discrimination and marginalisation from within India, where the regional and linguistic politics are complex and sometimes violent. Thus, as doubly marginalised people, the French erasure among them was even greater than on other islands. Referring to water as an 'archive of memory and traumatic experience', she asks, 'How is trauma inscribed on the body as a corporeal text reflecting a tortured history of slavery, dictatorship, and exile?' (B. J. Mehta 2009, 11). This interplay between the constantly shifting ephemerality of water as a memory archive on the one hand, and the indelible, brutal scars, gouges and deathblows that are permanent markers of the body, on the other, is inherent to the way we frame hybridity. The constant movements, dislocations, escapes and exiles make for jagged narratives with missing pieces and scrambled chronologies. But the body remembers and speaks these memories.

Thus the histories of slavery and torture in the Caribbean islands are borne as marks, scars and wounds – both physical and psychic – by its victims. The black female body is described as the ultimate threat to colonisers owing to its capacity for productive and reproductive labour, and colonisers controlled African women's bodies with absolute brutality (B.J. Mehta 2009). The empire and the discourse of European Enlightenment distinguished itself through its "civilisation" and named everything outside itself "barbarous". Torture is thus part of dealing with this so-called barbarity, and colonialism experiences a complete inability to reconcile itself to its own barbarity, because that would admit a loss of identity of being "civilised". To cope with this irreconcilable schizophrenia, colonial regimes recast brutal torture as punishment and "necessary disciplining". The tortured body remembers itself through the marks and scars of torture. The body itself could not be destroyed, being required for labour, but it could certainly be maimed, brutalised and claimed. B.J. Mehta identifies the whip as a very particular instrument of phallic torture inflicted upon women. The executer of this torture was typically not a white man – reiterating the inability of the white West to accept its barbarity and its need to transfer anything "barbarous" to its loathed other. 'Torture represents the most abject form of non-communication between the male torturer and female victim' (B.J. Mehta 2009, 41), and the marking of the female body symbolised absolute control. Rape or corporeal colonization was the ultimate war tactic, resulting in children who were markers of that colonial rape and memories that the archives of trauma: 'The hidden limits of torture and violence also seek to disassociate mind from body in an annihilating Western binary. This splitting negates an integral African view of the body's interconnectedness with mind and spirit' (B.J. Mehta 2009, 47). Although these arguments about colonial violence are made in an extreme and brutal context, I would venture to extend this to a larger political and intellectual canvas. If we follow the discussions from chapter two, we see that colonial and imperial violence are constitutive to the creation of both Western democracy and the roots of European liberal cosmopolitanism. This constitutive violence acted as an amputation – a severing of psyche from body – articulated lucidly but not for the first time, by Descartes. Although there is a profusion of scholarship and critical theorising redressing this amputation, there is much work left to do. One of the major objectives of this book is to make some small contribution to that end. The attempt to corporealise cosmopolitanism is, in some ways, part of a larger effort to acknowledge and heal that primal wound.

B.J. Mehta (2009) discusses the possibilities of healing in the African context through ritual, dancing, music and food. (The community and healing around culinary practices are both powerful and profound. I discuss it in greater detail in chapter five.) Slave-masters, she writes, perverted the ritual healing practices of African peoples, forcing slaves to "dance" in ghastly inversions of their original forms. As a result of these perversions of healing practices, torture and trauma grafted themselves on to the bodies of its victims, alienating and abjecting their bodies from their selves, deepening the gash into an unhealable wound. The violation and desecration of indigenous rituals and practices continue to happen, albeit in less physically brutal ways. The selective appropriation and consumption of indigenous ways of living by neo-colonial capitalism is a fairly ubiquitous cultural phenomenon. The dangers of popular liberal cosmopolitan narratives are that they can sometimes be uncritical about the celebration of some of these practices, including them under that all-encompassing umbrella of diversity. This subsequently perpetuates the fiction of equality between peoples and cultures, conveniently renaming violent appropriation as cosmopolitan sharing. The Francophone version of *créolité*, as B. J. Mehta (2009) notes, was a universalising French Caribbean identity, exoticising rather than engaging with Indianness, while *Douglarization* (Puri 2007, 193), a term reclaimed by the Anglophone Caribbean, is used far more politically and clearly. The *Dougla* (mixed race) subaltern is an abject figure, and her or his abjection also contains a resistance. The reclamation of the word and the associated irreverence are also acts of resistance. For the Indo-Caribbean, the earth was important. Growing rice and spices was an umbilical act, as we will see in the literary narratives, where land is an extremely important part of the Indo-Caribbean identity. This is perhaps doubly so because of the fluidity of their passage and their identities, but there is a definite act of rooting through the land. The *Dougla* imaginary might thus be one mode of community formation, articulation and resistance for those who are subaltern on multiple levels.

When we consider how this community formation and articulation take place for women, the question becomes far more complex and loaded. Returning to the figure of Sycorax, the demon/witch woman is really a healer, a manifestation of the cosmic feminine. African spirituality contains practices of *Vodou* healing, *Mambos* and other liminal and fantastic ways of being, as do several non-Abrahamic spiritual belief systems. Sycorax, or "dangerous" femininity, is also closely associated with the serpent – a mystical, liminal creature – thus subverting the Christian dogma of woman and serpent as evil and sinful. B. J. Mehta (2009) extends what she terms *Sycoraxian historicity* to the worship of *Mariamman/Maliémin* by the Tamil diaspora in the French Caribbean. While caste did not play out in the same way as it does in India, the Caribbean islands retain the ritual and hierarchical supremacy of dominant Hindu casteism and so-called *Aryan* Brahminism. *Mariamman* is a powerful goddess worshipped primarily in Tamil Nadu, although other manifestations exist in Kerala and other Indian states. However, the uniqueness of Hindu practice in Tamil Nadu, particularly by non-brahmin communities, makes *Mariamman* a unique, subaltern and powerful feminine symbol. In the French Caribbean, the dark, black goddess destabilised brahminical hierarchy and jettisoned patriarchal control. *Mariamman* is considered too ferocious and "primitive" by brahminical Hindus and is often conflated with Mother Mary in Martinique, making *Maliémin* a complicated and hybrid figure. Both Sycorax and *Maliémin* embody trauma and violence, strength and ancient, sacred power. There is a synergetic healing and resisting potential within this trauma, which allows for many resurrections, reconstructions and re-creations, and corporeal cosmopolitanism will have need of these dark goddesses.

WRITING AS MEMORY, WRITING AS HEALING: INDO-CARIBBEAN WOMEN'S LITERATURE

The previous section explored some conceptual frameworks that are unique and particular to Indo-Caribbean women's experiences and ways of articulation. In this section, I examine specific narratives that these *Jahajee* sisters have told. The corporeal cosmopolitanism I envision is not unlike a *jahaj*, travelling in an ocean of stories. These stories we will explore are about bodies and travel, desire and violence. These stories are about new kinds of communities, crafted through ritual, performance, love, anger, food and dialogue. The three texts I have chosen are *Valmiki's Daughter* by Shani Mootoo (2010), *The Swinging Bridge* by Ramabai Espinet (2004) and *Coolie Woman: the Odyssey of Indenture* by Gaiutra Bahadur (2013). I have chosen these texts because they are all relatively contemporary and tell multiple stories of women in a way that combines current lived experiences with the full weight of the histories of trauma and violence that constitute and haunt them. Mootoo's book is categorised as fiction, dealing primarily with upper-middle-class Hindu and Indian characters and the crises of race, gender and sexuality. Espinet's book is semiautobiographical, from a Christian milieu, where the central character is doubly diasporic, weaving her trauma and life experiences with the larger history of indenture. Bahadur's book is entirely autobiographical and nonfictional, and attempts to trace a sociocultural, historical and feminist genealogy of Indo-Caribbean migration, centred round the figure of her grandmother. Through these narratives, I hope to uncover a fluid narrative of cosmopolitanism that is borne by the body and expressed through pain, love, spiritual practice and *eros*.

Valmiki's Daughter (Mootoo, 2010) is the story of an upper-middle-class Indo-Trinidadian family. The name of the father, Valmiki, the Hindu saint and author of the Ramayana, is deeply significant to Mootoo's story. Valmiki

Krishnu, his wife Devika, their daughters Viveka and Vashti and their dead child Anand form the first circle of the story, intersected by several other characters, most significantly, by Nayan, an Indo-Caribbean cacao planta- tion owner and his white French wife Anick, who are Krishnu's neighbours. Valmiki is a doctor with a successful practice, a not-so-happy marriage and something of a notorious reputation with the ladies. He is also gay. Valmiki's first experience of same-sex desire occurs in school with an older school mate, leaving him with a searing loathing, both of himself and the other boy: 'He couldn't have hated that boy more and he hated himself in equal mea- sure' (Mootoo 2010, 70). This experience turns Valmiki into a caricature of a hypermasculine, homophobic, misogynistic and heterosexual man. Valmiki's increasing desperation and loneliness are expressed in his heterosexual extra- marital affairs. In order to compensate for his queerness, he also takes up hunting with a group of Afro-Caribbean, working-class men. Valmiki also has a sexual relationship with one of these men, Saul. Valmiki is a tortured mess of masculinity, with an innate phobia of sports because it legitimised physical contact and intimacy between people of the same sex. The reason why this point becomes especially relevant is because his elder daughter, Viveka, is also queer and loves sports.

What makes Valmiki's queerness all the more unspeakable is that Saul's Afro-Caribbean wife is honest and somewhat resigned to her husband's choices, while Devika, Valmiki's wife, holds on with a strident, upper-class desperation to her increasingly disintegrating world of heteronormative, familial perfection. This is a somewhat essentialist characterisation that should be viewed through the earlier discussion about the stereotypical tropes of Afri- can and Indian women, where the African woman is already always morally suspect, sexualised and eroticised, while the Indian woman is always chaste, subservient and desexualised. Devika is also the long-suffering, "good", mid- dle-class, Indian wife, knowing but never complaining about her husband's indiscretions or "unnatural" desires, living in a cold, loveless marriage, allevi- ated only by the occasional, Mrs. Dalloway-like parties she throws.

Viveka, the elder daughter, is visibly queer and described as possessing "masculine" aesthetics and feelings of gender fluidity, which create in her a white, male alter ego, Vince. This identity crisis is further complicated by her younger sister being a model of Indian femininity: demure, "pretty" and obe- dient. Viveka experiences her queer desire for the first time when she falls in love with her physical education teacher – a white, athletic and heterosexual English woman. The full extent of Viveka's sexual and romantic longing arrives in the form of Anick, Nayan's French wife. Viveka's attraction to white women is neither straightforward nor coincidental. There are important racial- colonial and moral considerations in the dynamic of her desire. The compli- cated relationship with whiteness is also reflected in Nayan's deep inferiority in the face of the *old* "first world" that is, Europe and Britain. For instance, Nayan makes an interesting distinction between Canada, where he first met his wife, and France, where he visited her parents, describing the singular sense of inferiority that Europe evoked in him, in a way that Canada never could. We see this inferiority play out in the moment that Anick's parents offer Nayan different kinds of gourmet chocolates, never realising that a cacao plantation owner in Trinidad is *not* a chocolatier. This is an extremely important and poignant scene, the voice, perhaps, of enforced cosmopolitanism, reminding us of the spectre of empire that haunts every postcolonial subject, regardless of class and educational statuses. Indeed, Nayan's sense of self-loathing as a man with the origins of an indentured labourer constantly evokes feelings of worthlessness in the company of those who have "original" homes:

> Because in their eyes . . . we – the sugar cane and cacao Indians . . . from Trini-dad, Guyana, Fiji – we don't exist. With the Indians from India . . . even they who share our ancestors – dismiss us. As if we are poor, poor, poor copies of an original that no longer exists . . . we have nothing of our own making . . . we're groping, still shy of becoming Trinidadian. (Mootoo 2008, 376)

This is a powerful and eloquent expression of the triple crisis that besets Nayan. Unable to find home in Trinidad, plagued by his prejudices against the country of his birth and residence on the one hand, resentful and awed by colonial superiority on the other, and rejected by the land of his ancestors as inauthentic, he becomes the kind of *Indian man* he is expected to be. Hyper-masculine, misogynistic and authoritarian. His fast-failing relationship with his wife, the exoticisation of her whiteness, queerness and political radicalism soon turns bitter and untenable, and the impasse of race becomes all too evi-dent. Nayan's story is a provocative reminder of all the things that can, and do, collapse in liberal conceptions of cosmopolitan modernity. The lack of dia-logic space, both to challenge his misogyny and to express his vulnerabilities around masculinity and race, serves as powerful reminders when considering the kind of room that corporeal cosmopolitanism must be prepared to make.

Nayan's story is contrasted by Anick's own experiences of sexual and gender discrimination in Trinidad. Although she is white, her whiteness does not possess an even grip of superiority in Trinidad. Anick has a much more faltering grasp of English than the non-white inhabitants of Trinidad and is treated more or less like an exotic pet. Her passionate and consuming affair with Viveka unravels the fabric of both their heteronormative families, causing a crisis for both women but clearly direr for Viveka, a young single, nonconformist, brown, Indo-Trinidadian woman. Viveka's struggles are accompanied by a quiet, tortured solidarity from her father, with whom she shares a very close bond, but both of them are trapped, invisible and negated, both from the world and themselves, because of how they want to love and live. Anick eventually becomes pregnant with Nayan's child, and Viveka agrees to marry an Indo-Trinidadian man, though both of them seem all too aware of how short and futile their marriage will be.

The focus on sexuality and gender norms is intricately tied to the way Indo-Trinidadian Hindu communities are positioned. Valmiki, his daughter and his wife are caught in a hyper-orthodox, hetero-patriarchal chokehold, one that none of them feel able to break. Anick too is caught in her own web but with somewhat better options, primarily of leaving Trinidad and *returning* to Europe. There is no return for Valmiki and his family. Not really at home but nowhere to return *to*, either. The narrative of internationalism and cosmopolitan existence is fairly clear in Mootoo's story, and in some ways, it is a tragic conclusion, a failure of cosmopolitan openness. But if we look deeper, the embodied moments of cosmopolitan bonds appear in so many conversations, particularly between the women in the story. They happen in secret and behind closed doors, or in quiet gardens and football fields. The failure here is really the inability to dialogue with the lived experiences of race, gender, sexuality and desire. It is the absence of such a space, both physical and emotional, which causes the shutting down of lives and voices. There is a brutality in the amputation of desire, a violence in the establishment of categories, ways of living and loving, which are unable to embrace the fluidity, the fragility and the trauma of multiple belongings and identities. These are challenges that corporeal cosmopolitan dialogues must face. There will be many such seeming failures and dead ends, but every little exchange and articulation is an opening up.

Espinet's novel, also set in Trinidad, explores another important facet of the Indo-Trinidadian community – the experience of diasporic multiplicity. *The Swinging Bridge* straddles a double diasporic experience – one in Canada and one in Trinidad. The protagonist Mona Singh's story begins in Canada, with the impending death of her brother, Kello, who suffers from AIDS and reveals himself to be queer, although rather secretively. Kello's dying wish is to buy back the family's land in Trinidad, even though he abandoned Trinidad as a young man, when his relationship with his father disintegrated. The task of recovering the land ultimately falls to Mona, marking her journey into family history, trauma, violence and victories. There is a strong sense of hidden Indianness in *The Swinging Bridge* that is very class oriented, unlike Mootoo's story, where the relatively upper-class narrative, in many ways, made room for a deep exploration of queer desires and identities, despite the orthodox restraints of religious and cultural norms. In Espinet's story, it is missionary Christianity which Mona's grandfather had accepted long ago that dictates cultural and social conduct. We learn that her grandfather was married to a Hindu woman, before he converted, but the marriage was considered illegitimate and void, as non-Christian marriages could not be legally registered in the colonial Caribbean. For the doubly diasporic Mona and her family, the longing is more for Trinidad than India. The tortured relationship with India is complicated by the fact that Mona's father always considered himself a Creole man, but whose emotional ties to India were very strong. A man who wanted to study and practise law, he never achieved his dream. Mona's father resented the church's control on the estate produce and profits, and identifying as Creole was his way of rebelling against its hegemony. He revelled in his creoleness and the celebration of Carnival. Mona recalls him enjoying *J'ouvert*, the beginning of the festival: 'J'ouvert morning possessed a wonderful temporariness, a reckless space without boundaries' (Espinet 2004, 94).

The double trauma of diasporic dislocation is expressed by Mona thus: 'All it took then in Trinidad was looking Indian; all it took now in Canada was skin colour. We had not moved one inch' (Espinet 2004, 78). In ways that are quite distinct, both these exclusions are borne on the body. Land ties prove very significant in Mona's story. Although we do see the importance of land to some extent in *Valmiki's Daughter*, when, for instance, Nayan chooses to move to the family estate to revive the plantation, the land ties are much stronger in Espinet's story. Mona's family worked the land, and her entire family's umbilical cords were physically buried in the Monahambre family land in San Fernando, Trinidad. This visceral connection between body and land, where the umbilical cord, the source of life and nourishment was returned to the land, is a weighty marker of how deeply we embody physical spaces that are dear to us. It is when Mona makes her emotional and physical journey back to Trinidad, where she remembers more and more, that we experience the full extent of her psychic ties to India. Espinet superimposes the figure of Mona's great-grandmother, Gaider, as a ghostly, haunting presence throughout the narrative. Mona's search for Gaider's life and her stories braid together the trauma of the *Kālā Pāni* crossing as well as Mona's own Atlantic crossing. These oceanic journeys and experiences of new cultures bond these women to their ancestors in a deeply embodied and emotional cosmopolitan encounter of exile, loss and loneliness that scrambles both time and space.

There is a beautiful, rending description of a brief time when Mona and her family move from San Fernando to a village where she hears the grief-stricken, beautiful singing of the *Ramayana* rendered by an old woman, with her raw, strong and broken voice heaving with the wounds of exile, violence and abjection. She mourns for *Sita* and all her unfortunate daughters, who must wander and suffer with no home to claim them. Mona's connection to this dirge is instant, having been victim and witness to the violence that she, her mother, her grandmother, and all the women in her family endured. This historic labelling of the *Kālā Pāni* women as *rands* – a doublespeak for widow and prostitute – reverberates through the stories of Indo-Caribbean women. The particularly brutal nature of the *uxoricide* (wife-killing) and female-directed violence witnessed in the Indo-Caribbean community are part of this longer history of the moral degradation and dehumanisation of its first immigrant women. Mona describes the continuity in this violent history as 'new codes that would force women down on their knees, back into countless acts of self-immolation' (Espinet 2004, 292). The combinations of these embodied traumas and resistances expressed in stories and songs are a powerful testimony to the inextricable links between corporeality and community creation.

As she recounts the struggle of being an Indo-Caribbean woman and how hard it was to simply *be*, Mona's greatest fear was to be swept away into patriarchal obscurity. She was terrified of being turned into a wife, maid and mother, forced into marrying the wrong man and being enslaved 'tiptoeing through life, frightened, following rules and laws that hold down your skirt, your hair, your mind' (Espinet 2004, 133). Mona explicitly identifies some of these struggles as part of being Indian. Although she does not claim any knowledge of other communities, the fact remained that Indian girls were especially targeted when it came to sexuality. She says, 'There was talk about how Indian girls were hot hot from small – no wonder they had to marry them off as children, and no wonder wife beating and chopping was so common among those people. They were not civilized or "creolized" enough' (Espinet 2004, 133). This is a crucial articulation that connects back to the historical baggage that was discussed in previous sections, that is, the demonisation and racialisation of Indian women's sexuality and their inability to be Creole or "mixed". Victim-shaming and justifying the violence done to them was not only an internal perception but also the way non–Indo-Caribbean communities perceived its own women. Mona's own father consistently humiliates and beats Mona up, burning a dress that he considers sexually alluring and "slutty" but this was mostly stemming from his racist hatred of a relationship Mona begins with a Creole boy. He is clearly unable to reconcile his own Creole politics with his daughter's desires for the same. This is also an important reminder of how, by ignoring the realms of corporeality, desire and sexual politics, we might arrive at a cosmopolitanism that is both dishonest and dangerous. The thread of violence runs all through this tale, with one of Mona's uncles trying to assault and sexually molest Mona's mother, and Mona's own experience of unsuspectingly following a stranger, who claimed to know her mother, and nearly being raped as a result. In the annals of family history too, Mona learns that Gaider, her great-grandmother, a talented performer of high repute, married her great-grandfather Joshua, a missionary convert, without any real choice, and he banned her from ever singing or dancing in public. I read this as a mutilation and a dismemberment of Gaider's personhood and body. The misogynistic, religious and patriarchal desire to silence and break the female body and destroy the possibility of psychic and emotional expression and healing ultimately left no recourse to women who were already victims of so much abuse and horror.

There are many other such stories in Mona's discovery. The most important one occurs upon her return to Trinidad, when she finds Gaider's story scrawled in the pages of her grandmother Lil's notes and recipe books, preserved in the only private places she had. Mona discovers Gaider's songs and poetry, has them translated by another *rand*, Chandroutie, who still performed at weddings, and finally, Mona hears the songs her ancestors sung in all their visceral agony and beauty. The bawdy, funny, moving, tragic songs, adapted and refashioned from the *Ramayana* were these women's protests, desires and balms. In order to embody the understanding of contemporary cosmopolitanism, it seems to me that these stories and songs must form a core part of our understanding. These songs of exile, of deadly sea voyages, rape, resistance and the creation of new homes, new lives and new identities are songs of cosmopolitanism; of inhabiting many worlds and of dismantling, destroying and rebuilding new ways of living and new codes; and most importantly, of embodying the kind of brittle fluidity that contains infinite, rhizomatic roots that are so central to understanding cosmopolitanism.

In conclusion, I turn to Gaiutra Bahadur's *Coolie Woman*, a nonfictional narrative of the author's travails in navigating the *Kālā Pāni*. Although the (although the boundaries between fiction and non fiction are constantly shifting in my own understanding.) author hails from Guyana, and consequently there are significant differences from the other narratives, the songs and stories carry similar cadences and experiences. Bahadur's story, like Mona's, is one of double diaspora; she moved to America with her family when she was only seven years old. Bahadur writes at length about the importance of language and how it shaped her identity. Much like the bond of land and umbilical cords, despite three generations of her family never having seen India, Hindi bonded them to an umbilical Indian imaginary. Language, for Bahadur, possesses emotional resonances and provides a sense of ownership, operating on many levels. Bahadur migrated to America at a time of severe racism against Indians, something that Espinet also discusses in her novel. In Bahadur's America, the *Dot Busters* were active and violent and made no distinctions between Indians according to geography. Bahadur echoes Nayan's sentiments (from Mootoo's novel) here, when she describes how, while kinship did exist between the Indians from India and Indo-Caribbeans, it was more like a well-meaning kinship offered to stepchildren. Authenticity was *always* a glaring issue. Guyana's own fraught political history saw a zealously pro-African dominant party that drove many Indians to migrate to other countries.

Guyana experienced severe outbreaks of both economic and structural violence against women after the elections of 1997 and 2001 (Trotz 2004). While it was constitutionally very progressive, Guyana was an extremely patriarchal society, using gender and sexuality to regulate and define identities. Since women were seen as the keepers of home and tradition, they became 'pivotal in reproducing the limits of racialized groups' (Trotz 2004, 7), and women's bodies were consequently used as canvasses in the brutal inscription of identities and loyalties. This meant that the female body became the object and symbol of racial conflict because rape was the ultimate weapon of annihilation. Added to this, Trotz also writes of the frighteningly high instances of domestic violence of which the women were silent victims.

Bahadur's experiences of violence are therefore doubly traumatic. When she returned to Guyana as a young woman, she writes that, 'the deepest alienation came from the unspoken rules about what women should not and could not do' (Bahadur 2013, 12). She also spent time in India, hunting down that elusive, mercurial umbilical cord which took a different kind of toll on her identity as a woman. Her American passport was irrelevant in the face of her skin colour, which demanded that she be Indian. Her search for roots ultimately ended in ambiguity, rife with half-told tales, mistakes, memories full of holes and actual fabrication, aided by her own exotic and sometimes uncomfortable presence. Bahadur examines the absence of women's voices in Guyana, in a somewhat tangential way in that she proposes the possibility that the absence and secrecy was in fact subversion, a weapon that women deployed to keep their safety and reputations intact. Because recruiters assumed that "morally sound" women would never dream of immigrating to the Caribbean islands, they were necessarily targeting vulnerable women, already victims of multiple kinds of abuse and ostracism. The once ritually sanctioned (though not unproblematic) position of courtesans and *devadasis* degenerated completely under British rule. The futile attempts of the colonial administration to license and control sex workers (mainly for British officers and troops) ultimately resulted in a ban on sex work that left this group of women in a desperate and dangerous situation, constantly on the run from both local men and the British administrators. While it was not *only* these women who took passage on the ships to the Caribbean islands, Bahadur is very clear that recruiters frequented prostitute bazaars. It suited the British, therefore, to consider indentured labour, as far as the women were concerned, as an act of mercy – they were being 'saved' from depravity. The passage from India to the Caribbean islands, as has been previously mentioned, was a horror of basic hygiene and safety. Women were particularly vulnerable and often took husbands just for the passage. Amid starvation, sickness, child rape and other kinds of violence and abuse, theirs was a community forged in the flames of trauma. Bahadur, in fact, identifies 'coolitude' (2013, 70) as an emotional state of abjection and powerlessness for Indo-Caribbean labourers. *Coolie* women were paid less, although they worked as much as the men; they were also under threat from different groups of men, including their own. The battle against indenture from the homeland, by way of people like Gandhi, began as a plea for human rights and an end to abuse against women, but when that failed, it became a crusade against prostitution. Even then, these women were ultimately labelled the same, by men from their own communities. Bahadur's work reveals most significantly that *coolie* women inhabited a very complicated space between power and abject victimhood. Their rarity in terms of numbers meant that they did exert a certain kind of choice and preference, along with their ability to take multiple lovers. Bahadur notes that the disfigurement of a woman's face – especially her nose and ears, was a symbolic re-enactment of the *Surpanakha* story. Here, a *rakshashi* (demon) princess in the *Ramayana*, is desirous of *Rama* and his brother *Lakshmana*, and pays a terrible price for expressing her sexual desires. After toying with her emotions for a time, *Lakshmana*, on *Rama's* say-so, slices off *Surpanakha's* nose, ears, and nipples. This gory, mythological violence was adopted in living practice by men, and was sometimes perpetrated against Indian women in the Caribbean islands. This ferocious anger, Bahadur suggests, was directed against these women by Indian men as a brutal and twisted retaliation against plantation oppression, which crushed and stripped away their humanity and perceived hetero-masculinity: 'For this, too, had been a disfigurement of indenture: the complicity of women in their own fates, the tortured attachment – the tenderness – they felt and continue to feel in the cave of their hearts for their own men, who had also been disfigured by planters and the colonial state' (Bahadur 2013, 208). Bahadur's words must not be mistaken as any kind of platitude or excuse for the violence these women endured and continue to endure. What these words reveal is the twisted, painful and unendurable sorrow that goes into forming communities and kinship. Solidarity and support came from the same spaces where violence and brutality were perpetrated on a daily basis. Hatred and love, understanding and cruelty – all crammed together in a foreign, desolate space, with no power, and nothing to hold on to, these men and women forged their bonds and put down roots. This is cosmopolitanism of the grim, unrelenting, embodied realities of foreign travel and exchange. It is not always celebratory, or triumphant. It is not always bringing people together in dialogue and understanding. In a place and time where shared ethics, morals and norms were unthinkable, communities had to be created, and homes had to be built. It was mostly the women who did these things with what they carried in their spirits and psyches and bodies – wounds, scars and lashes – songs and love, children and stories. It is this deep, sometimes dark ocean of community creation that corporeal cosmopolitanism must drink from, if it wants to create safe spaces – of dialogue, as well as silence, commonality, as well as irreconcilability – in a constant state of becoming, made and unmade as we move with and through one another.

I hope that this chapter and chapter three have made a beginning in terms of illustrating the depth and complexity of corporeal cosmopolitanism as an embodied, inhabited community of practice. These chapters have considered the *performance* of corporeal cosmopolitanism. Chapter five will attempt to bring some radical and decolonial theoretical conceptions into conversations with the practices of corporeal cosmopolitanism. The idea is to create spaces for epistemological praxes which will be informed by and in turn help to inform future corporeal cosmopolitan communities.

NOTES

1 A gap, or, to be out of sync.

2 Callaloo is a kind of leaf indigenous to parts of the Caribbean islands. However, it is also described as a stew, incorporating several ingredients – a mix of hybridity on the one hand and a unique caribbeanness on the other.

3 A chronicle of the sociocultural location of these first women migrants can be found in Bahadur's (2013) work.

4 *Ravana* is the king of Lanka and an *asura* (an ancient race, generally character-ised as evil), which emerges as a symbolic discrimination against the "south", where *Rama* and his Kingdom are located in the "north" of India.

5 See Arshia Sattar, C. Rajagopalachari, Ramesh Menon, Ashok Bunker and so on, for English versions of the Ramayana.

6 *We were once caterpillars emerging from cocoons*
now butterflies with iron wings soaring to new heights.
The reshaping of community is like blowing glass
molded in the fire of violence dipped in waters of reflection
creating priceless gifts holding the beauty of unity.

7 For the full interview, and more information on the *Jahajee* Sisters, see: http://www.jahajeesisters.org/art.html.

Chapter 5

Love in the Time of Corporeal Cosmopolitanism[1]

The attempt to imagine and articulate corporeal cosmopolitanism as an active speaking, as well as performing, space has required the wholehearted acceptance of uncertainty. I do not mean the theorised, lucid uncertainty of risk societies and entangled modernities but the messy, terrifying and sometimes inevitable uncertainty of things changing or collapsing. This work demands extraordinary labour and energy: the shedding of authoritative shrouds, the absence of validation from the academy and absolute vulnerability, which is all one is left with, in the end. We are so accustomed to a given definition of how political places, and personal places, and places of joy and desire are supposed to feel, and how *separate* they are, that, unplacing these categories seems clumsy at best and dysfunctional at worst. It means that one must hold established certainties as possibilities and perhaps even potential errors, and to be open to either and neither. And yet, if we did not both accept and suspend the certainty of gravity, we would never have been able to fly.

In this final chapter on cosmopolitan inhabitation, I engage with and present corporeal possibilities in cosmopolitan scholarship, ritual, literature and performance. Some of this material may give us new ways of feeling and seeing, speaking and doing, and some of it may take things away from us. As I have reiterated throughout previous chapters, this journey has really been about what we can do to bring the political, personal and community spaces together in active, doing dialogue. This chapter examines some key foundations of cosmopolitan imagination that have been discussed in previous chapters and considers the possibilities of how these foundations might be transformed. Thus, in the first few sections, I explore the nascent theoretical possibilities of corporeal cosmopolitanism by conversing with sister articulations of decolonial theory. Finding theoretical spaces which will abide by the performances of embodied solidarities and corporeal cosmopolitanisms is crucial to the epistemic resistance in my work. These theoretical formations are embodied and decolonial: they hold coloniality and imperial violences as constitutive in the articulation of love and solidarities. This work is equally committed to resistance, vulnerability, plurilogue, love and solidarity. Decoloniality is particularly significant here because the treatment of coloniality is a conscious process of resistance and decoupling rather than just the acceptance of the complexities of the effects of colonialism. Decoloniality also declares itself as not restricted to the academy or any one space of resistance, but rather as a mode of resistance in doing, speaking and thinking.

The first part of this chapter deals with the nuances of what it means for corporeal cosmopolitanism to *be* decolonial. How do we reimagine dialogue, exchange and even liberation as decolonial? How can we continue to build solidarities and inhabit our worlds in ways that witness and address the traumas of epistemic, spiritual and corporeal violence? Corporeal cosmopolitanism is envisioned as a space for creation, performance and radical compassion – a space which does not binarise these affective belongings as separate from grief, loss or pain, but recognises them as equal and constitutive parts of embodied, emotional ways of inhabiting our worlds. The second part of this chapter focuses on feminist understandings of desire, the erotic, affect and the body as indispensable to the realm of the political and to the creation of corporeal cosmopolitanism. This section deepens, as well as challenges, some central ideas of the radical cosmopolitanisms advocated in previous sections. My understanding of corporeal cosmopolitanism is rooted in feminist, queer and subaltern understandings of and resistances to the contemporary liberal discourses of cosmopolitanism.

I conclude this final chapter in a return to the performative practices of *thirunangais* in southern India and Indian women in the Caribbean as living, growing palimpsests of cosmopolitan negotiation, community and critique.

AFFECT, EROS AND VULNERABILITY: FEELING COSMOPOLITANISM

One of the central concerns that have emerged over the course of doing this work on cosmopolitanism is about what constitutes being human. Chapters one and two discuss both narratives of contemporary liberal cosmopolitanism as well as how many of them are founded on principles of membership and exclusion. The question about the worthiness of different human lives (Butler 2004) is becoming increasingly significant, as the numbers of acutely vulnerable humans grow and grow. As chapters one and three demonstrated, the legal-constitutional dimensions of creating a *human* community are especially important to cosmopolitan thought, particularly liberal Western strains, which broadly follow Kant. One of the most popular and politicised manifestations of this internationalisation of concern for humanity is the discourse and enactment of human rights. A BBC article in 2016 ran the tragic story of the famous "Mona Lisa of the Afghan War", photographed by Steve McCurry when she was twelve years old in 1983 and rediscovered seventeen years later. She was arrested and detained by the Pakistani Government for holding fake identity documents and faced the possibility of a prison sentence and a steep fine. Mr. McCurry described it as 'an egregious violation of her human rights' (BBC News, 2016) and condemned Pakistani authorities, vowing to help his erstwhile muse Sharbat Gula. A cursory rifle through news will remind us that we have lost count, record or knowledge of the numbers and names of lives lost in Afghanistan, and in so many other parts of the world, who did not become *Mona Lisas* of war. It is difficult to say whose human rights have been recognised here, and why, or why not, without referencing elite, white, and male privilege. A highly contested and complex terrain, human rights as a political and moral discourse have been idolised, reviled and accepted as the best of bad alternatives, on different occasions. It is not my objective to examine the discourse of human rights as a discourse but to critically engage with its framework of "global humanity" as a popular articulation of the legal and constitutional dimensions of cosmopolitanism. What does it mean to refer to human rights violations, within this construct of humanity? We have explored, in some detail, the nuances of being citizen and being human, and the latter as an identity of abjection. How do we reconcile the ideological notion of humanity as equal to the abjection of bare humans who are not citizens? Douzinas's (2007) critique of the discourse of human rights is an interesting insight into this state of irreconcilability. Noting that human rights as a framework appeared first in the 1920s with reference to minorities in Europe, Douzinas argues that in recent years, human rights as a paradigm has contributed greatly to the ontology of being human and human identity as a whole.

The term *humanity*, Douzinas writes, comes to us from Hellenistic Rome, and was originally used to distinguish the Roman from the "barbarian" and to establish Roman supremacy. We also see the use of humanity in St. Paul's Christian mission to create an equal spiritual humanity (Delanty 2009), but Douzinas writes that after the eighteenth century, the notion of humanity was taken over by liberal and political philosophy, annexing it from religion in the move from the spiritual to the rational/scientific. Today, it is the 'legal personality' (Douzinas 2007, 530) that drives the understanding of humanity. Chapter three, in particular, provides some examples of how the notion of humanity is ultimately designed and identified by legality. Positivism brought the first challenge to *natural law*, and Douzinas traces the movement that brought us closer and closer to state-sanctioned violence and authority with the world wars,

Nazism and the assignment of state responsibility for crimes against humanity, a major turning point in the history of human rights. Giorgio Agamben's
(1999, 2005) work on the Holocaust, though problematic on many levels (see
chapter two), is a stark and important reminder that it was the complete and
unchallenged *dehumanisation* of Jewish peoples – as threats to the *quality*
of humanity – was what made the scale and nature of this violence possible.
Colonised peoples and slaves were considered much the same – barbarous
and a constant threat. If they could not be controlled, they would have to be
exterminated. The language of genocide is the language of extermination, in
continuance with the dehumanisation of people into vermin. This is a crucial
link to the particular ways in which non-white, marginalised, indigenous and
"foreign" people have been abused and often eradicated in various purges.
However, this state-sanctioned verdict of crimes against humanity or human
rights violations, as Douzinas argues, is used more often as a Western strategy to ensure hegemony rather than as a critical lens. For Douzinas, human
rights discourse is strategic and utilitarian, devoid of emotional and embodied
languages, and this could be traced back to the Enlightenment. He writes that
'despite the centrality of randomness in life, rationalist philosophers and social
engineers have combined in a long missionary campaign to delete contingency
and emotion in favour of reason, planning and control' (Douzinas 2007, 27).
The legalisation of affect is a big part of how constitutional and political structures deal with large-scale violence. The language of legal process, evidence
collection and proof is a language of disinterested remove, which often understands truth to be devoid of emotional capacity. It therefore allows no room to
understand the embodied, psychic and emotional facets of violence. Legalising
affect also does not allow for the joyous, compassionate or revolutionary facets
of things like liberation, or freedom. Indeed, when we consider the creation of
postcolonial nation states, they were the swan song of colonial empire screaming its final violence in the tune of law. Among several horrific examples,
Indian and Pakistani independences were secured upon the mandatory condition of partition. It is not as if this animosity was wholly manufactured by
Empire, but it was under colonial rule that it became an organising principle.
The traumas of partition are still ripping communities and peoples apart, with
militarized state violence in Kashmir killing more and more people with each
dawning day. The exaggerated levels of British involvement in the formation
of the independent Indian nation state also reveal the devastating effects of
prolonged racialised violence upon colonised peoples. The psychological and
emotional dependence that colonial rule created in its colonies is a disturbing
but familiar narrative of craving recognition from the abusive pater. Desire, or
the control of it, is thus central to law. Douzinas makes a connection between
rights and desires and sees identity as fundamentally rooted in desire. This is
also why identity is often configured in relation with, or in opposition to, the

"other". A sense of self-identity is closely tied to the need for recognition from a desirable, controlling other. A right is articulated as a demand for a need, argues Douzinas, and this need is usually combined with the need for love and recognition, for wholeness and for recognition from an "other" or the "big other" (society/state/law/language). It is a need 'to have one's whole identity recognised' (Douzinas 2007, 48). This recognition is in indefinite deferral, for if everyone wants to be recognised by the fictitious desirable other, then no one will really receive such recognition. The *legalisation* of desire, which is how Douzinas understands human rights, does not really succeed in *legitimising* identity, because the structure of legality is fundamentally about controlling and abjecting desire, not recognising it, whereas identity is deeply tied to notions of desire to claim a particular story or stories of who one is. Human rights, according to Douzinas, thus become 'expressions of the unattainable right to be loved' (2007, 49). By keeping its subjects in a constant state of deferral and denial, human rights become a 'phantasmatic supplement that arouses but never satiates the subject's desire' (49). In describing human rights as the failed articulation of need to be loved, Douzinas is placing love and emotions, at the heart of the political, something that I consider vital to the theorisation and practice of corporeal cosmopolitanism.

This elision of feelings in the framework of democratic politics – of the need to be seen, recognised and loved – is powerfully captured in Douzinas's critique of the human rights framework. It is especially relevant to the cosmopolitan imagination because human rights form an important part of the shared framework of global concerns. The refusal to address embodiment, affect, and vulnerability results in this kind of amputated acknowledgement, where desire is addressed through a framework that fundamentally abjects it. Elsewhere, Douzinas observes that 'secularised grace has been turned into the global saviour of human rights and religious transcendence into the universalism of international law' (Douzinas 2007, 95). This suggests that the need for recognition and love is not just restricted to the realms of desire and affect but to a larger conception of love as a cosmic experience. The 'secularisation of grace' is an eloquent metaphor for the far-reaching consequences of colonial oppression in the "third world". The impact of Christianity and missionary organisations has been discussed in chapter four with reference to Indo-Caribbean communities. While it is not within the scope of my work to examine the theological dimensions of human rights and liberal ideology and law, it is an important consideration. Religious doctrines (particularly Christianity in the colonial context), play a vital role in the conceptual understanding of cosmopolitan narratives and the creation of democratic, political societies in the *Enlightened*, secular West.

The liberal cosmopolitan impetus for community building and creating a global normative framework of sharing is incomplete and fractured by these elisions and violences, and within this silence is created an infinite and unacknowledged deferral of the embodied and the affective. As we distance ourselves from the articulation of affect, the desire for it is relegated to the realm of the unspeakable, the unattainable. It allows us to construct an entire epistemology of identity and political belonging that is wounded and binarised, and haunted by desire and loathing, all at once. The constitutional right to personal choices and freedom to choose a sexual partner that were discussed in chapter three suggest that the human rights framework ultimately elides and eludes the conversation about desire and emotions that remains sundered from the language of legality, citizenship and rights. Douzinas observes that 'the right to same-sex marriage . . . exposes the artificiality of the ego by increasingly colonising its intimate parts' (49–50). That is to say, by appropriating the important dimensions of desire, love and sexual wanting into the heteropatriarchal legality of marriage, the right to same-sex marriage does nothing to actually ensure the safety, acceptance or recognition of queerness. Feminist and queer resistances have clearly articulated their objections to framing queer desire as legitimate, through the institution of marriage. The law, as a heteropatriarchal institution, is fundamentally antidesire. While, on the one hand, these constitutional victories are very important to make the lives of queer people safer, it is vital to critique the modes by which that safety is achieved. There is a deep sense of invalidation when queer desire can only be legitimised in civil society by rite of marriage, an institution with a stunningly heteropatriarchal and exploitative history. I want to be careful with this particular observation in that these deeply institutionalised and acculturated practices of love are complicated. Simply put, I neither object to nor disapprove of queer marriages – I have been part of many beautiful ones. People's relationships to institutionalised cultural practices are complex and nuanced, and many of us reinterpret these practices in radical and resistant ways. Sometimes, we may simply acknowledge a deeply held attachment to these institutionalised practices as deeply problematic but still significant, and that is entirely acceptable. The critique here is not of individuals' relationships to the question of marriage but the state's use of the institution of marriage to validate one's right to love freely. There is no room in legality for the love that we so fundamentally need and want. By wrenching away the fleshly, desiring and affective dimensions of sexual, reproductive and bodily rights, we close off an entire dimension of experience while knowing full well that it is central to these rights. As the self becomes more and more disjointed, the demand for rights increases exponentially, creating even more wounded selves and fractured communities.

The struggle for identity recognition cannot be mitigated by liberal multiculturalism because people 'start demanding the world and not just a corner in brick lane' (Douzinas 2007, 44). This, in many ways, encapsulates the failure of liberal multiculturalism in much of the "developed north" in the last few decades and also, perhaps, explains the increased interest in cosmopolitan dialogue and scholarship across states and global/local borders, particularly in Europe. The liberal discourse of rights comes to stand in a proxy for something far richer and deeper. By framing rights as individual and based on "private" or "personal" choices which only need to be tolerated, liberal discourses shut down the possibilities of deeper emotional relationalities. The language of toleration closes off the paths to engaging in loving and compassionate ways. In fact, the practice of tolerance, in some ways, maintains the "otherness" of the other in "manageable " terms but always articulating the self in adversarial terms. The capitalistic formulation of the individualistic, neoliberal self requires the silencing of emotional and corporeal modes of experience. This kind of right-bearing self is incapable of recognising these "other" elements as related to itself. It cannot truly accept foreigners, marginalised peoples and communities within an equal rights framework because such a framework has been produced by imperial-colonial ideologies of superiority and inferiority in the first place.

The colonial, white-Western framing of its racialised "others" as the negative opposite of itself only permitted less-than-human interpretation of their personhood. While we have made many positive strides away from that form of violent categorisation, it would be naïve to suggest that it no longer exists in any form. The characterisation of the less-developed "others" continues in largely orientalised paternalistic modes or in dangerous, threatening modes. The non-white body is still caricatured in several media contexts either as immigrant/refugee or as terrorist – one deserving of pity/loathing, and, the other, of extermination. Douzinas too, in his work, analyses this narrative and identifies 'three masks of the human: the suffering victim, the atrocious evil doer and the moral rescuer' (2007, 69). The victim is always collectively decimated, powerless and helpless but always innocent and feminised. The victim is an indistinct mass, bare life, faceless and nameless, abandoned by politics and never a bearer of rights. The second mask, Douzinas elaborates, is the diabolical "savage", the second face of the "other" – the monstrous, the grotesque who torture their own, and the victim "other" who must be rescued from their own. Either way, both emerge as lacking in basic dignity and self-reflection. That is to say, Western or "civilized" action against the "barbarous natives" does not count as crime because "natives" were not considered fully human. These violences were construed as necessary, benevolent and paternal. The truly 'horrible, atrocious acts are only committed by the evil inhuman other' (Douzinas 2007, 176), never by the coloniser. This is one of the main reasons why the Holocaust was identified as the first *real* crime against humanity 'because only the West is endowed with full humanity and can become a proper victim of atrocity' (Douzinas 2007, 79). The absolute horror of the Holocaust is indisputable but also not so far removed from the crimes of colonialism and slavery, which were less condemnable because the victims were not considered completely human by the colonial West. The narrative of considering Jews as "fully human" is certainly not a consistent one, and appears more as an afterthought in the Allied narrative. It is here that one gets the complete sense of how the colonial-capitalist matrix recognised the humanity of "others" in systematic, and strategic ways. Similar to the treatment of the Irish, these lines between whiteness and non-whiteness have been drawn and continue to be redrawn in arbitrary acts of brute violence. However, the visual markers of difference, in terms of obviously discernible skin colour, make it far easier to profile non-white "others". In either case though, we can easily recognise the saviour narrative at the heart of liberal conceptions of both humanitarianism and cosmopolitanism. It is thus easy to understand how the third face of humanity – that of the "moral rescuer" – can only be a "modern", Euromerican, western face. This saviour face of humanity is a combination of pity, superiority and extreme othering. Indeed, this saving is only made possible by difference. The popular understanding of pity, as a discursive strategy, requires the inferiority of the pitied and as such, is markedly different from the discourse of compassion. Compassion, which is something I envision as part of corporeal cosmopolitan affect, requires both equality and relationality, along with an acute understanding of interconnectedness. Pity, however, is an affective dimension of colonialism and capitalist developmental discourses, and Douzinas offers the visual politics of humanitarianism as an example of this. He concludes that the eroticisation of suffering and pain, especially of the "third world" and the collective recognition of the South as victims of suffering have become its standard representation, while the response of the North is inevitably that of pity. Humanitarianism thus became a replacement for the 'civilizing mission', a response that lacks any real depth and is actually a kind of 'antipolitics' (Douzinas 2007, 84).

There is much to be said for the problems in Douzinas's approach and his alarmist tendencies in critiquing the concept of human rights as a monolithic entity. However, Douzinas's work is highly relevant to the theoretical and intellectual formations of corporeal cosmopolitanism, because it is an important warning about the dangers of de-politicisation. Placing the history of imperial and colonial violence at the heart of cosmopolitan thinking reminds us that corporeal cosmopolitanism must always be resisting this. Similarly, identifying contemporary universal legalistic discourse like human rights and humanitarianism as antiaffect and antiembodiment reminds us of the need to insist on dismantling such political and discursive spaces.

COSMOPOLITANISM/COLONIALISM: THE JANUS-FACED NEXUS

The importance of European, British and American colonialisms has been a central theme throughout my work on cosmopolitanism. Cosmopolitan solidarity, exchange and commonality are not a wholly benevolent story about travel and sharing, although there are surely many instances of these too. However, it is important to recognise that many of these so-called commonalities come from violent and bloody histories of subjugation. Colonial conquest plays a crucial role in the deployment of modernity as a discourse of desirable progress, and this too is an important part of how we understand cosmopolitanism as a global imaginary. Part of addressing colonial difference and violence lies in constant articulation, remembrance and resistance. It requires revisiting the known stories. The control of stories and narratives is part of the legacy of colonialism and European and American-centric orientations. Liberal cosmopolitanism is a bearer of this legacy.

In *Local Histories/Global Designs* (Mignolo 2000a), Mignolo sets out his vision of an alternative epistemology: one that places 'colonial difference', which has transformed 'differences into values' (2000a, 13), at the heart of its experience. Part of imagining a new cosmopolitanism is that it requires different stories, new ways of thinking and speaking, a new syntax and a new cosmology, even. Mignolo's conceptualisation of 'border epistemology' as a 'fractured enunciation' (2000a, x) is a move towards creating a new approach, a new understanding of knowledge. He uses the term *border gnoseology*, arguing that gnosis embraces a wider conception of knowledge than epistemology. 'Border gnoseology', in Mignolo's work, is a critique of knowledge production both from interior and exterior borders, replacing the original aim of salvation inherent in gnosis with that of decoloniality. The reimagination of salvation as liberation is an important challenge to colonial regimes of religious control. For corporeal cosmopolitanism, this process of constructing a 'border gnoseology' is a powerful means of bringing the body back into the notion of knowing as an embodied act. This is a layered space, considering the biblical connections between knowledge, flesh and pleasure, and as such, it also bears the memory of these theological and historical narratives. The idea here is to challenge the very bases of knowledge and its conditions of naming. Freeing knowledge from its overwhelmingly epistemic constraints means that a 'border gnoseology' might be a strong starting point to reclaim knowledge as corporeal, experiential and sensual, rather than empirical. The act of knowing thus becomes an embodied performance of dialogue and sharing, instead of becoming an accumulative and possessive action. Knowledge might then be liberated from the shackles of capital. It transforms itself into an engaged relationship between peoples and worlds, unmaking the privileging of the cerebral as a seat of authority.

The specificities and variations of colonial difference and experience are complex and many. Although it is harder to imagine hierarchy within the resistances of colonised sufferers, here too, the spectre of marginalisation is clear and present. After the eighteenth century, it was Orientalism (the "eastern" imaginary) that became synonymous with Europe's "other". Mignolo (2000a) argues that 'the Occident (Latin America) was never Europe's other but the difference within sameness; Indias Occidentales . . . and later America . . . was the extreme West, not its alterity' (2000a, 58). The logic of binarisation demonstrates its capacity to invisibilise, once again. The dynamic of alterity means that difference must necessarily be singular, and any difference that does not fit the narrative of the big Other is simply silenced or co-opted. The understanding of this nonbinary conception of othering and of the ways in which exclusion can happen both through deliberate differentiation and through deliberate mimesis, is critical to understanding the various harms that othering causes. With respect to cosmopolitan constructions of solidarity, this understanding of sameness and otherness as different facets of exclusion is particularly significant, because the processes of sharing and openness are difficult and complex. Sharing our stories and changing existing ones are likely to be a painful, uncomfortable and time-consuming experience. The nuanced understandings of colonialisms are important to corporeal cosmopolitanism because it must position itself as a space of multiple retellings and fluid historicity. If we ossify the space of history, then we freeze the understanding of cosmopolitan belonging. The conception of cosmopolitan solidarity is impossible with mere acknowledgement of colonial violence, which most liberal narratives are happy to do. There must be an ongoing acceptance and engagement with subaltern critiques, anger, pain and sorrow as responses to the violence and damage. The current response of liberal multiculturalism and the tendency to enforce political colour-blindness, while simultaneously waging war against non-white lives, is antithetical to corporeal cosmopolitanism. The demand to *move on* is a state of amnesia, and violence; it not at all the same as the path of healing. Memory is central to healing, as is openness, repetition and the disruption of linear time and space. Trauma is a spiral, and, sometimes explosive, and corporeal articulations of cosmopolitan solidarity cannot operate in linear frameworks of progress, or moving forward. The movement can only be towards places of less fear, pain and fracture – it cannot be a movement of forgetting.

One of the ways in which we might construct these spaces of decolonial knowledge is in actually using non-Euromerican scholarship as the legitimating bases in equal participation and conversation with Euromerican scholarship. Consider, for example, the way Mignolo uses the Moroccan theorist Abdehebir Khatibi's ideas of 'double critique', 'dialectical synthesis' and 'an other thinking' (Mignolo 2000a, 52) as a theoretical centre in a particular section of his book. Khatibi's work is located at the interstice of Arabic and European scholarship and politics, particularly to do with the Maghrebian region. A 'double critique . . . releases knowledges which have been subalternized' (Mignolo 2000a, 67). Khatibi deploys double critique as a constant disruption of binary thinking and as a way to resist any monolithic oppression. Double critique moves in and out of many different spaces, voices and languages, resisting the call of critique itself to be unified into a singular narrative. Mignolo describes Khatibi's formulation of an 'other thinking' as 'universally marginal and fragmentary' (2000a, 68). The acceptance of this constant destabilisation and interstitial movement is one of the key formulations of corporeal cosmopolitanism. Solidarity that is built on affective, compassionate bases of shared experiences and embodied, felt practices makes for a very different kind of bond between people. Solidarities are not based on authenticity and a single "truth" but a plurality of experiences that allows us to create a relationship of experiences that can be accessed through different dialogic practices. 'Macronarratives from the perspective of coloniality are precisely the places in which "an other thinking" could be implemented, not in order to tell truth over lies, but to think otherwise, to move forward toward "an other logic' – in sum, to change the terms, not just the content of the conversation' (Mignolo 2000a, 69–70). The fact is that in order to create new spaces and change the terms, forms and content of conversations, we need many more stories, histories and experiences to draw from. If all our imaginations are fuelled by more-or-less similar knowledge schemas, then we are unlikely to produce anything radically different from them. This affects the production of knowledge as a resource, and this is, of course, controlled by strict hierarchies of power and discourses of superiority. Corporeal cosmopolitanism must encounter and resist such power imbalances between silenced and silencing societies. These imbalances play out in visceral, often violent, ways, and the resulting subalternization of knowledge and voices is so complete that they are entirely invisiblised in knowledge discourse. Over the years, I have had so many conversations with friends and colleagues – academics of colour who teach a variety of subjects in different parts of the world. The dynamics of teaching in the "global north" are markedly different from teaching in the "global south", but the dominant discourses we struggle against, collectively, are many. In the "global north", the constant and exhausting emotional labour of pointing out the violences of knowledge production, while still having to claim the space of the "objective" teacher, takes a severe toll on many. The struggle to practise decoloniality in the classroom is a very real one, and it needs the support and grounding of decolonial scholarship and knowledge-making. This is one way to ensure that individuals do not take on the task of validators or justifiers and that we do not find ourselves in a situation where our already exhausted bodies are called again and again, to be Black Atlas this time, instead of Caliban. In the "global south", the colonial schoolmasters have left different kinds of caretakers and heirs, or else, certain forms of violent, casteist nationalism have picked up the baton that colonialism left behind. The particular ways in which colonial rule manipulated and legalised or systematised existing local hierarchies have created hybrid structures of violence and oppression which pose a slightly different set of challenges. In this situation, we see colonial violence and racialized discourses passing in the guise of mimesis, on the one hand, and hybrid, new oppressions, on the other. As a consequence, the strategies of resistance respond a little differently. It is, therefore, important to understand the multiplicity of subaltern positions here. The stories will be many, and multiple tales from various peoples and communities with affective and material bonds and differences. However, the new imaginaries can only be made possible through sharing, through a rhizomatic exchange which will allow the grafting of resistances, knowledges and practices. As Mignolo notes, 'Scholarship, travelling theories, wandering and sedentary scholars, in the First or the Third World, cannot avoid the marks in their bodies imprinted by the coloniality of power' (2000a, 186). These varied imprints of violence also have corresponding imprints of courage, compassion and knowledges, and it is these imprints that will contribute to solidarity that is also a profusion. In building something like a border gnoseology for corporeal cosmopolitanism, it will therefore also be important to consider different conceptions of cosmopolitanism across different cultural, historical and spiritual spaces. The call for decolonial action and thought in relation to corporeal cosmopolitanism will require consistent and constant dismantling and rebuilding. The need for interdisciplinarity to challenge the basis of knowledge boundaries will become increasingly necessary, if we are to counter hegemonic knowledge structures, but it will also resist the urge to build an "other", single-counter knowledge form, as Radhakrishnan's (1996, 2007) work reminds us in chapter two. The task is enormous, but, we are many.

Decolonial spaces are thus those 'that can bring the diversity of local histories into a universal project displacing the abstract universalism of ONE local history' (Mignolo 2000a, 92). The universal project thus becomes *pluriversal*. The understanding of local histories as pluralistic, diverse and sometimes even conflicting must be at the heart of any genuinely dialogic space. The colonial act of describing, exoticising and categorising non-European knowledges relegates them to a position of inferiority and exclusion. In keeping with this, Mignolo argues that we require the 'discursive formation [of a] subaltern rationality' on a 'set of theoretical practices emerging *from* and responding to colonial legacies at the intersection of Euro/American modern history' (2000a, 94–95). I find the notion of the decolonial *pluriversal* as a productive way of thinking about how to speak to the large and small elements of solidarities and belonging. The interplays between these spatial and spiritual imaginaries are where identity lives and where the political plays itself out in so many different ways. In corporeal cosmopolitan terms, colonial difference, gender, class, sexuality and corporeality will all need to be constitutive elements in articulating this pluriversality. The logic of colonial-modernity, rationalism and progress involved a systematic devaluation of

Blackness, emotion, queer and femme articulations, as well as economically and culturally marginal voices. The large elements of corporeal cosmopolitan solidarities will be about bringing these conversations together.

Although corporeal cosmopolitanism is about corporealising and embodying cosmopolitanism, I have struggled with *how* to make this explicit. When the language and vocabulary of colonial modernity do not admit or acknowledge embodiment and affect, how does one invoke them? There is no clear line in the sand between the ways in which coloniality and decoloniality imbue colonised people's identities and subjectivities. However, I believe that the frameworks of decolonial pluriversality and border gnoseology provide valuable roadmaps to help make these journeys. The strong commitment to interstitiality, the consistent refusal to narrate a single story and the openness to multiple forms of critique, excavation and reflection are surely the first steps towards trying to build the knowledge space of corporeal cosmopolitanism.

LOVE AND THEORY IN CORPOREAL COSMOPOLITANISM

This section explores the characteristics and potentials of another dimension of theorising critical and radical cosmopolitanism. The task of theory, in decolonial and subaltern scholarship, is to imagine and produce new horizons of futures and possibilities, while reclaiming and reinscribing history. Cosmopolitan thinking, as we know, is quite old and its scope is enormous. Corporeal cosmopolitanism is, first and foremost, a decolonial, pluriversal and compassionate space of subaltern solidarities. It is, by its constitution, also an important critical response to contemporary liberal narratives of cosmopolitanism. In order to create a theoretical scope or indicative framework, we must draw from various sources and consider different approaches to what constitutes theory and theorising. Affective and embodied ways of knowing and understanding require that theory not remain in its purely epistemic, elite-Western framing. Decolonial and subaltern theory, as we saw in chapters three and four, involves literature, performance and oral histories as part of its work of theorising. In both chapters, theories are reconceptualised as stories, modes of resistance and reclamation. Corporeal cosmopolitanism is founded on the premises of love, healing and radical compassion. Because these words have been flattened out into empty, capitalist memes or ghastly caricatures of themselves, I can feel my nervousness rising as I write this. In some ways, the emotional realms of trauma, pain and violence demand a certain moral response and anger. That is not to say they always elicit such responses, far from it, in fact. But there is a certain gravitas that allows one to speak of pain in particular ways – ways that have been closed to speaking about love.

In my own practice of the political, the intellectual, the personal and the spiritual, I have always identified love as a web that holds everything together and makes living possible. In her compelling meditation on love, bell hooks describes love as 'action and participatory emotion – it is a practice' (2001, 165). For hooks, the demotion of love as *just a feeling* is a grave injustice to it, since it also comprises action. There is an interesting dynamic that presents itself here between feeling, action and emotion, and I have tended to use the word *emotion* over feeling, precisely because it conveys the sense of movement, or action, that must accompany a feeling. For hooks, presenting love as something devoid of pain, sorrow, grief and solitude empties it out. She firmly believes that if love is presented as a superficially positive, or happy thing, it is no longer love. Many parts of hooks's writing are profoundly moving and startlingly insightful. For my own work, along with all these insights, love is also always both queer and decolonial. The political practice of love and to use love as a life choice, a way in which one inhabits the world, means that it must be pluriversal and always moving in and out of myriad spaces, connecting, listening and healing. Love is a deeply embodied, spiritual and political practice, and in its fully realised capacity, it is the complete dismantling of violence. The capitalist-colonial mode has, through its particular strategies of simulation and mimesis, made the discourses and appearances of love impossible to distinguish from violence. Deep love, as hooks notes, is firmly embedded in justice. The destructively mimetic, violence-as-love, however, has no interest in justice. It is perfectly contiguous with the discourses of individualism, nuclear living and "personal" choices. It passes off tolerance as understanding, and under the guise of preserving individual autonomy, allows no real connections nor vulnerabilities to flourish. In such a world, love does, in fact, become *just a feeling*, a sentimental description, an unreliable emotion which impedes judgement and "rational" action. Such a love needs controlling and taming – it requires a system of order and of "reasonable" decision. However, if we look to the much deeper understanding of love as practice and world inhabitation, we see an entirely different set of possibilities for living. Acting and making choices from a place of love is neither selfish nor unreasonable – it is imbued with the ethics of compassion and care for larger community well-being. It is this sense of deep, radical love, love as community, solidarity and resistance, that animates corporeal cosmopolitanism. The sense of isolation and alienation that neo-liberal imperialism produces is a very important part of why solidarities are so difficult to produce and maintain in the inhabitation of the everyday.

Boaventura deSousa Santoas characterises the contemporary era as one of 'societal fascism [which is] pluralistic, coexists easily with the democratic state and its privileged time-space, rather than being national, is both local and global' and excludes 'large bodies of populations [from] any kind of social contract' (Santos 2001, 186). This description of 'societal fascism' sounds uncomfortably similar to the characterisation of global "risk societies" of uncertainty and fear, where we are compelled to live and interact in particular ways by capitalist and other authoritarian structures. Indeed, Santos describes 'societal fascism' as that which keeps society in a constant state of instability, swinging wildly from the trivial to the dramatic, with random, unprovoked acts of violence, with no perceived or real rationale. This 'societal fascism', for Santos, is closely tied to the neo-liberal promotion of globalisation and global capitalism. For him, under Western capitalism, there is no genuinely global condition, and all globalisations become the victory of some localism, which he sees as hegemonic and oppressive. This is an important point that corporeal cosmopolitanism must reflect upon. The nexus between conditions of globality and global interconnectedness are closely connected to the structural oppressions of neo-capitalist regimes. Corporeal cosmopolitanism must be rooted in subaltern and working-class politics, and the focus on emotions and embodiment will go a long way in helping us distinguish between global solidarity that has been manufactured by neo-capital relations and solidarities that are rooted in dialogue, openness and resistance. Once such solidarities have been identified, we are then faced with the question of how these solidarities can operate and articulate decolonial practices and knowledges. One interesting illustration of such an articulation can be found in Santos's theorisation of the radical potential of counter-hegemonic globalisations. The first practice that he proposes is that of the 'sociology of absences' (Santos 2001, 191), which is a process of unveiling the suppressed, absent and incomplete components of hegemonic globalisation. Because the dominant classes live in a state of wilful oblivion to oppression and torture, the oppressed *must* include this constitutive exclusion of their experience by the elite classes into their own narratives. That is to say, decolonial communities and solidarities must openly declare and make known these violences as constitutive of their selfhood and life experiences. For such openness, though, Santos advocates the second way of understanding – that is, the 'theory of translation' (Santos 2001, 193). Mutual intelligibility of struggles is essential, and this is possible only through self-reflexivity within every struggle. Whether the struggle is rooted in equality or difference, Santos argues that translation between groups maintains autonomy and creates common ground. Once this has been achieved, his next step – the third way – is to create manifesto practices that codify alliances and mobilization. While I am uncertain about the third practice of manifesto building as *the* appropriate theoretical articulation for corporeal cosmopolitanism, Santos's first two ideas are important steps in building sustainable solidarities. Urging the telling of absent, untold or otherwise suppressed stories, bringing constitutive exclusion to the fore, is a big part of the corporeal cosmopolitan journey. This reclamation, along with the translation and mutual sharing of various subaltern and invisibilised struggles between marginalised peoples all over the world, is also a vision that corporeal cosmopolitanism shares. For instance, the experiences of transwomen in southern India and Indo-Caribbean women (along with several other communities), as articulated in songs and stories, must form the theoretical and practical bases of corporeal cosmopolitanism. The corpus, as it were, must be both embodied and affective, and we must be constantly willing to experiment and try new things in order to nurture such a corpus. The idea of translation is also an important and productive one, in relation to corporeal cosmopolitanism. Translation requires a very particular form of emotional labour and ethical commitment to understanding each other and to communicating the nuances and contexts of words, which precludes imitation. There is a kind of immersion in translation, and if it is based on a fundamental commitment to love, then its potential can be truly transformative. For dialogue to really work, it is the emotional, embodied dimensions of experiences and knowledge that must be understood and shared. For the words to be carried across languages, territories and cultures, they must become a part of the translator; she or he must imbue the words and embody them first, before she or he can translate them. The stories have to be borne and lived in our bodies, in ways that we understand them to *be* us, and once that has happened, then the bonds will form between bodies, words and minds, without linearity or hegemonic order.

The decidedly disruptive quality of Santos's theorisation of resistance lends an infectious urgency to his cause. His vision of *Nuestra* America is that of an America that is 'at the antipodes of European America' (Santos 2001, 193). *Nuestra* America must be rooted in knowledge of the margins; it is Caliban's America, not Prospero's, and its political thought must be internationalistic, anticolonial and anti-imperial. Santos's *Nuestra* America lives 'permanently in transit and transitoriness, crossing borders, creating borderland spaces' (2001, 197). Resisting the discourse of Western modernity forms an important cornerstone in much of the theorising around postcoloniality and decoloniality. There are different approaches to dealing with the omnipresence of modernity. Modernity has been characterised as fluid or liquid, as scattered, and without centre, as multiplicitous and discontinuous, and sometimes, as a purely European, colonial hegemonic tool. A popular one is to decouple the idea of the "modern" from the cartographic imaginary of the Euromerican west. In my own work, I refrain from becoming too entangled within the semantics of modernity, largely because in formulating oppositions to it, there is a real risk of producing a single counter-hegemonic antimodernity. I am also wary of using the discourse of multiple modernities, that is, the idea that modernity existed in all cultures, because here, the risk of violent naming is quite high. The narrative of cosmopolitanism itself does not have a comfortable relationship with modernity, as even its European articulations predate discourses of the modern. It is only post-Kantian, liberal articulations of cosmopolitanism which subscribe to particular Euromerican understandings of modernity. As a critical response to liberal cosmopolitan narratives, I see corporeal cosmopolitanism as a constant resistance to any totalising discourse of modernity. Because it moves in and out of spaces and works as much in marginal "northern" spaces, as it does in the "global south", it dismantles the authority of a modern narrative, In Santos's work, though, there is a tendency to actively counter the hegemonic discourse through disruptive marginal challenges. In this particular case, he offers 'baroque modernity' as eccentric modernity, 'open ended and unfinished' (2001, 198) and always challenging conformity. Santos identifies seventeenth-century baroque in Latin America as 'centrifugal, subversive and blasphemous imagination' (2001, 198), similar to the Bakhtinian grotesque. This emerging vocabulary of subalternity and subversiveness opens up and challenges the selective mainstream knowledges we have come to accept as truth, allowing long-silenced voices to speak. Baroque subjectivity is a mode of fluidity and instability, and Santos claims it as a subaltern mode, a 'temporality of inter-ruption' (Santos 2001, 199) and ever-suspended resolution, rather than as restricted to a particular historical time. While I am not particularly drawn to the idea of offering *a* counter-narrative to modernity, the idea of inter-rupted temporality is a trope that I find most insightful. Subaltern theorising is deeply tied to reclaiming history and dismantling existing timelines of those in power. The body too is interrupted by time – desire, violence, mor-tality, reproduction and healing, all take place over different cycles of time, and nothing is ever complete in the body. Rather, all things are processual and in a constant state of becoming. Interruption, writes Santos, 'provokes wonder and novelty, and impedes closure and completion' (2001, 199). This metaphor of interruption is also relevant to the understanding of affect and embodiment as epistemologies, particularly if we envision it in conjunction with Edwards's (2003) notion of *décalage* or breaks/fractures. The temporal and experiential space of corporeality is constantly interrupted and broken up by waves of loving and wounding, healing and scarring. This fluidity of time, space and experience is an element of baroque modernity which has a strong affinity with corporeal cosmopolitanism.

Baroque subjectivity is extreme, both in its capacity to produce and to devour or destroy. It is the extremities of baroque subjectivity that lend it the explosive capacity for revolution, flexibility and change. Santos uses the imagery of the baroque feast to give us a sense of this largeness. Dis-proportion is key to the baroque feast, and so is laughter, as a subversive force. Santos points out that 'capitalist modernity declared war on mirth' (2001, 202), turning labour union meetings, for instance, which used to be filled with laughter, play and festivities, into something 'deadly serious and deeply anti-erotic' (Santos 2001, 202). The chokehold of a certain version of liberal-capitalist modernity over these corporeal practices of desire, joy and the erotic has been made apparent through multiple non-Western narratives. The use of laughter as resistance is also something that is important to the framing of cosmopolitan solidarity. Just as Butler (2004) describes grief and mourning as important bonds of solidarity, mirth, laughter and joy are equally important bonds between us, and, corporeal cosmopolitanism must also be capable of joyous corporeal practices. I am acutely aware that laughter is a difficult practice to write about amidst so many accounts of violence and pain, but it is certainly one that is most visible in everyday practices of resistance. The ways in which laughter combines pain, irony, anger and love are unique to it, and it is probably one of few emotional performances that so readily spreads by contagion. There is a certain irreverence and power in spontaneous laughter that has both the power to intimidate and disarm. The sheer lightness and sense of cleansing that accompany laughter are necessary experiences in healing.

The process of reading Santos's work was an important one for me in my forays to find decolonial modes of theorising. Santos's writing exudes energy and charisma – it is angry, passionate, polemical and utopic. I found his resolute defiance of existing theoretical tropes productive and inspiring in relation to my own work. Dialoguing with his work and the work of so many decolonial resisters gives me nourishment and courage and makes my own writing possible. Ultimately, the thing that was missing the most, for me, is that baroque subjectivity is incredibly subversive and dissenting but oddly heteronormative. Its speech, while evocative and mesmerising, is still reminiscent of a hetero-masculine kind of aggression. Its largeness and loudness and its excess and explosiveness indicate the risk of swallowing marginalities that are softer, gentler or quieter. My understanding of corporeal cosmopolitanism is that it will be a space of listening fully and deeply before speaking and that it will make room for those without speech and for voices that speak in different tongues. I do not want it to be so large and so ferocious in its desire to resist that it consumes those it cannot hear. The elements of translation and interrupted time in particular are frameworks that I found enormously helpful in articulating the ways in which solidarities could be constructed. In the next part of this chapter, I want to focus my entire attention on feminist and queer articulations of solidarity, love and resistance. It is not that I see some essentialising or irreconcilable differences between the decolonial scholarship of men but more that I see some wonderful and unique ways in which queer women and trans-feminists reconfigure these tropes that I have discussed in this section. The ways in which they articulate love as a political, lived practice have been the strongest influences in my own work, and they have appeared throughout this book. Here however, I would like to dedicate some undivided space to unpack those influences more fully, and illustrate how they shape the imaginary of corporeal cosmopolitanism.

DESIRING COSMOPOLITANISMS: AFFECTIVE AND EMBODIED SOLIDARITIES

This segment of the chapter is particularly important to my conceptualising of corporeal cosmopolitanism as a dialogic space of love and decoloniality. Although the entirety of my work – theoretical, literary, political and performative narratives – is rooted in decolonial feminist and queer epistemology and ontology, there are some specific formulations of emotional and corporeal practice that need to be elaborated and placed at the centre of the corporeal cosmopolitan imaginary. Black, decolonial and queer feminisms have always insisted on the necessary commitment to community building and intersectional understandings. Love as a political practice makes room for the expression and understanding of rage, grief and trauma. It makes possible the practice of tending to multiplicity, in a way that doesn't affect depth and focus. This is what Audre Lorde (1984) explicated so beautifully in her piece *There is no Hierarchy of Oppressions*. It is easy to respond to this articulation in a flat way – and understand it as simply to mean all oppressions are equal. But it is important to remind ourselves that Lorde is not indicating similitude here – she is signposting the need for an affective practice that allows us to connect with the *trauma* of all oppressions equally, which is quite different from saying that all oppressions are equal. The political practice of love nurtures such connections and the space to listen and feel, rather than understand, in an explanatory sense. In other words, it allows us – even in a situation of imminent necessity – when a single issue *must* be addressed or responded to, to hold other issues within a matrix of radical compassion.

The silences that surround women of colour, queerness, desiring bodies, traumatised bodies and spirits are often deafening. One of the ways that decolonial, queer feminisms break these silences is by telling their own stories in the ways that they want to be heard. The narrative mode of autobiography as theory is an important marker of decolonising theory and challenging the exclusion of those *outside* theory. Thus, in *Sister Outsider* (1984) Lorde writes and speaks her stories in several of her essays and speeches. In an extraordinary piece about being a black lesbian mother to a boy of mixed-ethnic parentage, Lorde asks profoundly painful and complex questions about how to engage with masculinity when you are part of a lesbian parental kinship unit. Practices of decolonial and queer resistance are fundamentally about an opening up, not a shutting down. The permissibility of a discourse is gauged by the ethics of compassion, rather than of "correctness".

Placing the focus on the emotional effects that conversations might have on people helps us understand both the motivations for and the consequence of dialogue. Lorde uses her personal experiences extensively as part of her work, and the nuances of race that run through her work are closely tied to her familial relationships. In another poignant essay, Lorde writes of the hypervisiblisation of black women owing to their physical appearances and the simultaneous invisiblisation that surrounds them due to the 'depersonalization of race' (1984, 42). She writes, 'it is not difference which immobilises us, but silence. And there are so many silences to be broken' (1984, 44). The enormous weight of silence that presses down upon colonised and marginalised people as well as their ideas and narratives is something that I constantly grapple with in this book as well. The impasse of inarticulability or being placed outside the limits of language and comprehension is central to corporeal cosmopolitanism. This deafening silence, which is as oppressive as it is formidable, makes speech both frightening and shameful. Bringing *the* body back also involves bringing *my* body back, and in that context, the invisibility that Euromerican colonial epistemologies impose on us is also a bizarre shield.

The biggest struggle lies in trying to say the unsayable, in breaking the endless silences that Lorde speaks of. It is also a commitment to making ourselves visible and heard. It is very *hard*, both as effort and as texture, to write about the affective, vulnerable epistemology that subaltern/coloured feminisms and queer studies present. As Mignolo (2000a) argues, here literary narratives *become* theory, and I constantly experience my own intense discomfort at breaching the lines between theoretical/academic and cultural production. Writing against violence is simultaneously a lament. The academic practice of critique is also an indictment against injustice. My discomfort when I engage with Euromerican feminists is less pronounced, even though the articulations and theorising are not always opposed to and can even be strong allies of decolonial feminism. The authority that white privilege bestows on white feminism somehow transforms the timbre of the way white feminism takes on the violences of white hetero-patriarchy. In my days as a young postgraduate student, I often experienced myself as a child, listening at the door to what grown-ups were saying. It is a feeling that I know is shared by many, many non-white students, though we always reminded ourselves that our experiences of marginality were much more privileged than others'. The only way to resist and challenge this experience of self as lack is to keep speaking our stories, through our bodies, in spaces of community and safety. I have been forced to encounter my own fears of being an imposter within the spaces of Western academic writing and scholarship. It is hard to balance the conscious practice of decolonising one's own scholarship with the constant fear of being perceived as unscholarly. There is a real fear that engaging with canonical Euromerican scholarship in decolonial modes will result in some kind of intellectual ostracism. Mignolo's point about the centrality of colonial difference within writing on cosmopolitanism is a crucial one. It has not been easy to dialogue with such formidable proponents of liberal cosmopolitanism who are so multifarious and sometimes strongly grounded in liberal and Cartesian rationality, and before that, a Greco-Roman patriarchy, both of which excluded women, people of colour and other subaltern peoples in different ways. As narratives that have been deeply and variously excluded, they articulate themselves as subjugated knowledges. These resisting knowledges push my own subject positions to their farthest limits, demanding that I engage in an active dismantling of Euromerican patriarchal and epistemological hegemonies. However, the dismantling has to be held together with the requirement to speak in a valence and a language that will be recognised as legitimate.

> I find I am constantly being encouraged to pluck out some one aspect of myself and present this as the meaningful whole eclipsing or denying the other parts of self. But this is a destructive . . . way to live. My fullest concentration of energy is available to me only when I integrate all the parts of who I am, openly . . . without the restrictions of externally imposed definition. (Lorde 1984, 121)

The move towards corporealisation is a move to reclaim an integrated sense of power. It is the steadfast rejection of the organism as an organising principle. Corporealisation recognises the centrality of love and a desirous politics of life. The importance of passion and *eros* has even found its way into more mainstream articulations of cosmopolitan belonging. The recognition of the erotic as a source of immense creative and political energy played a significant role in my desire to articulate corporeal cosmopolitanism as an idea and practice. I have no desire to essentialise or romanticise any notion of the erotic as a cis-"feminine", monolithic understanding. However, I do think it important to articulate certain aspects of feminist scholarship and the excluded realms that women inhabit in order to create an embodied understanding of cosmopolitanism. Lorde, in *The Uses of the Erotic* (1984), argues that the erotic has always been vilified as an element constitutive of women and their "dangerous" sexuality. The erotic here is understood as a source of power, and its loss, particularly for women, is a loss of their own power and autonomy. The patriarchal demonisation of the erotic and the misguided notion that its suppression is symbolic of moral strength and goodness is, for Lorde, one of patriarchy's most effective weapons. Drawing on indigenous feminist narratives, from Africa and elsewhere, she condemns the equation of the erotic to mere sensation. Relegating the corporeal to the "base" level of tactility has made it a morally suspicious space, thereby denying its rightful place in meaning-making and identity creation. hooks (2001), as discussed in an earlier section, also suggests something similar when she discusses the demotion of love to a mere feeling. For myself, I am not sure if the descriptions of the erotic and of love as feelings or as tactility should be characterised as demotions in and of themselves. It seems to be that the dismissal of feelings and tactility as modes of experiencing and knowing is part of the larger strategy of Enlightenment-led discursive regimes. Rather than characterise feelings and tactility as superficial, we might reimagine them as significant affective and embodied practices which should be included in the corporeal cosmopolitan imaginary. What I find most powerful about Lorde's articulation of the erotic is that she considers it the nurturer of deep knowledge that is beyond language, learning or any so-called objective knowledge. This understanding of the erotic as knowledge must be inscribed into corporeal cosmopolitanism, where it will form part of a new 'border gnoseology'. To deny the erotic is 'an abuse of feeling' (Lorde 1984, 59), and such a constitutive violence to the self cannot be overlooked in any search for common ground. Corporeal cosmopolitanism should therefore be founded on experiencing and practicing love, and the power of the erotic. If corporeal cosmopolitanism wants to engage in a large-scale creation of solidarity, these are the frameworks on which it must draw.

I want to return briefly to an aspect of creating this 'border gnoseology' (Mignolo 2000a, 2002) that was discussed in the first half of this chapter, and it is to do with the political and methodological modalities of articulating decoloniality. Gloria Anzaldúa (1987, 2009) attempts this monumental task by writing from and in different languages, where she negotiates her alienation and abjection as a *Chicana* woman with Amerindian, Latin, and white heritage, as a lesbian feminist and an academic and poet. There is a particularly poignant moment when Anzaldúa narrates her experience as a teacher, trying to speak with two of her lesbian students, and one of them says to Anzaldúa that she (the student) always thought homophobia meant a fear of returning home. Anzaldúa thoughtfully examines this profound (mis)understanding, connecting it to the fear of rejection that so many queer peoples face from their homes, their mothers and their cultures. This explicit tension between the association of home with safety and acceptance for most mainstream folks and home as danger and expulsion for many queer people, refugees and other diasporic peoples is important to the understanding of cosmopolitanism as a manner of inhabiting the world. These tensions must inform the elaboration of what we *mean* by solidarity and belonging – that is, the associations with home must be carefully navigated and unpacked. In the case of Anzaldúa's students, the multiple marginalisation of the *Chicana* woman bound by Indian, Mexican and white patriarchies, combined with the devaluation of Indian and black heritages, poses an enormous challenge of identity negotiation and community imagination vis-à-vis cosmopolitan narratives. One of the biggest challenges of articulation is the act of speech itself. When the lilt of your speech, the shape of your tongue and words doubly out you as "foreign", it is not always possible to speak. Language, in this sense, is carried in and by the body, both as speech and shackle, self and invisibilisation. For Cherríe Moraga (1993), the body is akin to land, replete with strength, grain, pain and violence, a weight that colonised people carry in them all the time. The connection between colonial slavery and land is particularly visceral, and the absolute domination of body and land were closely tied together. The *language* of corporeal cosmopolitanism is thus carried by and within the body. There is no way to create a vocabulary of corporeal cosmopolitanism that is not tactile and embodied. The words must be embodied and the body must be worded, because how corporeal cosmopolitanism speaks will be reflective of who it includes and excludes.

An example of this can be found in Anzaldúa's work, where she refers to the ways in which multiplicitous heritages of Spanish in Europe are further complicated in South America. Among diasporic Mexicans/Latinas in the United States, *chicano* Spanish is perceived as a bastard language as it combines Spanish with English, the language of betrayal. Anzaldúa laments the fear and mistrust within *chicana* communities, where speaking English will be considered traitorous, but speaking *chicana* Spanish carries with it the label of shame and inauthenticity. She also identifies the acts of listening to *chicana* music and eating *chicana* food as central to identifying as *chicana* but that listening to border music – *corridos*, songs about valiant Mexican heroes struggling against Anglo oppressors – was considered shameful. 'Cradled in one culture, sandwiched between two cultures and their value systems, *la mestiza* undergoes a struggle of flesh, a struggle of borders, an inner war' (Anzaldúa 1987, 100). It would be a grave mistake to think that the resistance of corporeal cosmopolitanism can be spoken in one tongue or language. There are ways in which languages combine, and recombine, resist, revolt and exclude, and we must be able to make room for these processes as we try to speak to each other.

Another dimension of articulating decoloniality, particularly within non-white and indigenous feminisms, is that of spirituality and spiritual identity. Global narratives of pre-Kantian cosmopolitanism are often found in spiritual texts and scriptures. Large religious communities like the Islamic Ummah or the Christian Brotherhood articulate the idea of a universal community of God. Still other practices like Buddhism and Hinduism articulate a slightly less formalised but equally universal sense of love and spiritual oneness. In feminist scholarship, however, the spiritual references are far more personal and specific to identity articulations. Colonised and diasporic cultures often experience religion and spiritual practice as both complex and hybrid. On the one hand, there is the purist nostalgia of origins, and on the other, the contingent, hybrid formations, of new gods, goddesses and ritual communities. For instance, the spiritual importance of the goddess's presence holds particular relevance in Anzaldúa's work, and should be understood and explored as a bearer of community identity and belonging, particularly in light of the ways in which Abrahamic religions colonised and consumed indigenous spiritual practices. The Spanish/Christian de-sexing of the Amerindian mother Goddess and her transformation into the Virgin of Guadalupe hold a very significant place in *chicana* identity. Although they are quite different historical-cultural contexts, Anzaldúa's illustration of the Virgin of Guadalupe has many resonances with the Mother Mary/*Mariamman* hybrid *Maliémin* (B. J. Mehta 2009) that was discussed in chapter four. The significance of goddesses and cosmic female energies is important to indigenous feminisms because it provides a specificity of space and context when discussing the erasure of their female and queer identities. The ways in which colonial Western patriarchies interacted with these cultures involved both a real and symbolic destruction of female agency, or what Paula Gunn Allen (1986) referred to as *gynocide* in Amerindian societies (see chapter two). In a potent demonstration of how spiritual beliefs and symbols combine with the fleshly, affective memories of her community, Anzaldúa identifies three maternal images within *chicana* imaginaries that she contends have been subverted by patriarchal hegemony: the Virgin of Guadalupe, the steadfast mother who has not abandoned her children; *Chingada*, the raped mother who has been abandoned, a particularly powerful image of the Amerindian woman; and finally, *la Llorona*, the mother searching for her lost children. Anzaldúa describes the patriarchal subversion of the three mother figures in these words: 'Guadalupe to make us docile and enduring, *la chingada* to make us ashamed of our Indian side, and *la llorona* to make us long suffering people. This obscuring has encouraged the *vigen/puta* (whore) dichotomy' (Anzaldúa 1987, 31). The exoticisation and eroticisation of the subaltern woman is a well-established elite, as well as colonial, form of misogyny. The images of the devoted mother and the devious, lascivious "whore" are part of South Asian, African, Caribbean and Latin American narratives. For Anzaldúa, the western Cartesian severance of rationality from spirit and body is the 'root of all violence': 'We are taught that the body is an ignorant animal; intelligence dwells only in the head. But the body is smart. It does not discern between external stimuli and stimuli from the imagination. It reacts equally viscerally to events from the imagination as it does to "real" events' (Anzaldúa 1987, 37). Like Lorde's understanding of the erotic, Anzaldúa too writes of *la facultad*, a psychic, *chthonic*, deep intuitive sense that is latent in all of us. Often unlocked by deep traumas, many marginalised people have this sense, a sensitivity beyond the strictly empirical. The connections between trauma, violence and the body among marginalised and abjected people are very significant. The body is the space of both violence and resistance, and both these can take very extreme forms. For example, B.J. Mehta explains that death was the ultimate redemption for many slaves, because they had no recourse left to any kind of healing. Midwives used their knowledge to perform abortions as protests against rape and the creation of more slaves. Abortion was seen as protection against the 'corporeal colonization' of African peoples (B.J. Mehta 2009, 56). Sometimes, slave women would barter with slavers and bear their children in exchange for the child's future liberty. The horrific accounts of rape and violence in the narratives of the *thirunangais* in chapter three also tell a similar story of bodily domination. The issues of rape and violence within the *thirunangai* community are very much part of the narrative of rape as a symbol of ultimate misogynistic control. Rape is one of the most brutal weapons of the male coloniser, always used to maximum effect. Because it is institutionalised colonial violence (B.J. Mehta 2009; Anzaldúa 1987; Lorde 1984), it is part of nearly every subaltern narrative. Corporeal cosmopolitanism must engage with visceral experiences of the body, which are part of the cultural psyche of entire nations and continents. This shared and frighteningly ubiquitous narrative of sustained violence and abuse forms part of the ways in which corporeal cosmopolitanism understands solidarity and sharing experiences between communities across times and spaces. Addressing rape as a violent criminal offence within the legal realm is simply not sufficient because rape has been a systematic method of exercising absolute domination among several colonised communities and subjugated peoples. Many liberal cosmopolitan narratives remain closed to these kinds of vulnerable experiences of trauma that are enormously significant to fostering or damaging dialogic processes. Because it is a closed space – for many victims of trauma and inheritors of violent histories – it is also a deeply unsafe space.

I envision corporeal cosmopolitanism, above all else, to be a place of safety and healing, something that can make and hold space for those who are struggling to speak or raging, those who are distraught and in pain. The kind of resistance I associate with corporeal cosmopolitanism is not a simple binaristic challenge to status quos or an antistance. As Anzaldúa argues, a counter-stance is a step towards liberation but not a way of life. It is still locked in the discourse of lack and abundance of authority. As an act of defiance, counter-stance is essential. Audre Lorde (1984) sums it up eloquently:

> Anger is useful to help clarify our differences, but in the long run, strength that is bred by anger alone is a blind force which cannot create the future. It can only demolish the past. Such strength does not focus on what lies ahead, but upon what lies behind, upon what created it – hatred. And hatred is a death wish for the hated, not a life wish for anything else. (Lorde 1984, 152)

I do not want to suggest that corporeal cosmopolitanism is intended to perform some standardised version of pacifism. The perpetration of so much violence – of colonial domination, xenophobia, misogyny and queerphobia, many of which are unspeakable and irreconcilable in some senses – *must* produce responses of anger. As I have stated before, I am *not* suggesting that dialogue will always be possible or necessary. It may be completely impossible. Equally, it does not mean that any and every dialogic approach is futile. Corporeal cosmopolitanism is imagined as a space not only for those of us who are able to engage in such an exchange but also for those of us who cannot or are too exhausted or angry. Corporeal cosmopolitanism is envisioned as a possible way through the impasse that is often created through the rhetoric of irreducible difference. The potential of cosmopolitan dialogue resides precisely in its capacity to negotiate the terrains of irreducible difference should it open itself up to a pluriversal articulation. These theoretical tropes that I have discussed in some detail are examples of spaces and imaginaries in which these dialogic navigations take place in one form or another. A large part of resistance and the reclamation of stories happens through the formation of communities. Anzaldúa's new *mestiza* – her vision for healing – is an inhabitor of everywhere and nowhere; she is a priestess of the crossroads, and Anzaldúa likens this new revolutionary woman to an ear of corn: hybrid, tenacious and kind. As Lorde reminds us:

> To grow up metabolizing hatred like daily bread means that eventually every human interaction becomes tainted with the negative passion and intensity of its by-products – anger and cruelty. (Lorde 1984, 142)

We need spaces that help us to metabolise love and compassion and that we may be able to generate them out of ourselves, our bodies and spirits. We need places that will allow us to practice deep speech as well as deep listening and give us room for understanding, without fear and in our own time. We need sanctuaries to rest and be tired or hopeless, if that is how we feel, but trusting that the space and communities of love will heal us and bring us back to the resistance and the new creations.

CORPOREAL COMMUNITIES: RITUALS OF BELONGING

In this final section of the chapter, I want to focus on some examples of embodied rituals of community and belonging (see also Turner, 1969). Over the course of formulating these ideas and practises, people have asked me what this *corporeal cosmopolitanism* would actually *look like*, and the honest truth is, I do not know, because I am still learning about it. I know that it already exists in many communities and groups. It has also been expressed in larger solidarities in bursts of strong convictions. All I have tried to do is articulate and imagine a narrative and performative decolonial space, in the practice and scholarship of cosmopolitanism. My main motivation here has been to create an embodied, affective and dialogic narrative, which jettisons the liberal, individualistic monopoly on cosmopolitan solidarities. The gaping distances and silences within liberal narratives of cosmopolitanism, for reasons that I hope have become clear by now, is really why the idea of corporeal cosmopolitanism was born. In time, it may become something altogether different, and I am eager to grow and change with it. In my travels with corporeal cosmopolitanism, and what comprises embodied community practices, I learnt from all sorts of likely and unlikely places. I want to revisit some of these practices and lives and imbibe a sense of what corporeal cosmopolitanism will look like and how it resists popular liberal notions of cosmopolitanism. One of the recurring images, throughout accounts of decolonial community building was that of food: a special space of corporeal and erotic performance. We see this in Anzaldúa with her *mestiza* as both the producer and creator of nourishment framed in the imagery of an ear of corn. Other writers including Niranjana (2006), Allen (1986) and Ramona Perez (2004) have reflected on these connections. This is not to be mistaken for a simplified or essentialist connection between woman and food as a patriarchal weapon but as practices of identity and community formation. Indigenous and subaltern feminist scholarship reappropriates these connections in the context of feminist autonomy, performance and love, as well as community creation, and it is this position that I am writing from.

The Caribbean islands have been described as rhizomatic: a strongly rooted space which still resists the idea of a major or singular root, very much in keeping with previous discussions of subaltern fluidity. B.J. Mehta (2009) extends this image of the rhizome into the epicurean realm, noting that Caribbean food, like its culture, is full of both literal and metaphorical roots. Food is a powerful force, travelling between the corporeal, intellectual, emotional and spiritual facets of identity and belonging. The ways in which communities are built and dismantled around food and culinary cultures are a powerful example of how corporeal cosmopolitanism might approach the notion of solidarity and sharing. B.J. Mehta describes food as a healer of diasporic wounds. She also writes of how African cooks used food as a symbol of resistance by feeding the slave masters (and sometimes entire slave communities including themselves) poisoned food. They were thought to be the wielders of a great power. Because it is connected to such a basic condition of survival, food touches multiple levels of simplicity and complexity when it comes to community belonging. B.J. Mehta describes the sharing of food as an act of 'cultural repossession' (2009, 98). This sharing of food is combined with the sharing of stories and is, therefore, symbolic of multiple inclusions.

Where men traditionally articulate verbal stories, she suggests that women often *cook* their stories, which may be too difficult or painful to be turned into speech acts.

There is a poignant scene in *The Swinging Bridge* (Espinet 2004) when Mona finds the story of her ancestral great-grandmother, Gaider, scrawled in the pages of her grandmother Lil's recipe book. Stories of trauma, bravery, violence and fierce joy hidden are woven into recipes for food and form an imagined homeland and recipes for new hybrid foods. Similarly, in *Valmiki's Daughter* (Mootoo 2010), we see Valmiki's wife, Devika, obsessing about food in times of her deepest crises. The connections between subaltern women's suppression and their relationship with food are no accident. There is a very conscious and deliberate attempt to use food as script, perhaps because of its immediate connections with the body and with affect, and the particular forms of labour, caretaking and the forging of affective bonds that accompany its production.

Among diasporic communities, food has immediate connections to the memory of home. Nonvisual senses – the smells of ancestral lands and spices, the sound of a pressure cooker or the way mixing foods together feels under one's fingertips – are powerful ways in which communities forge and retain identities and solidarities. The use of coconut milk in Caribbean cooking, for instance, is an obvious influence of South Indian (Kerala and Tamil Nadu) cuisine, and coconut milk can become 'liquid memory' (B.J. Mehta 2009, 100). In this case, coconut milk carries a very particular set of inscriptions and memories of a people who were doubly marginalised culturally and linguistically, both by Afro-Caribbean culture and by Indo-Caribbeans, who hailed largely from Northern India. She writes, 'Food fills the void of exile and homelessness in acts of culinary belonging that delineate recognizable mappings of home' (B.J. Mehta 2009, 102). This longing and yearning, and the affective nostalgia that food as a living cultural artefact produces can span continents and connect people in all kind of different ways. Corporeal cosmopolitanism must be able to speak to and account for these kinds of solidarities and bonds. Food production and consumption can both reinforce and challenge gender performances, as well as allowing for new practices of resistance, hybridity and sharing to evolve in communities. New rituals and shared practices of cooking, eating and remembering can make way for new forms of community building which challenge old oppressions without abandoning the space altogether. Tejaswini Niranjana (2006) also draws attention to the strong connections between food and eroticism and sexuality. These connections are often misogynistic or racist in their content. The comparisons of women's bodies to particular kinds of meat, herbs or spices are important articulations of misogyny that can become shared in diasporic contexts. For example, the image of the "spicy", "exotic" Indian woman and the connection to her voracious sexual appetite (see Espinet in chapter five), or ranking women of colour by the shades of their skin colour. These kinds of misogynistic practices also have ways of creating patriarchal, sexist solidarities, and these must be challenged and dismantled by corporeal cosmopolitanism.

Another element that is important to the ways in which food communities are disrupted and undone has to do with class and the influence of global capitalism. B.J. Mehta (2009) makes particular note of the problems and isolation caused by modern food and minute meals and the resulting alienation among various ethnic and cultural communities. The corporatising and engineering of food and turning food into a class marker have demonised and damaged local food cultures and communities in the Caribbean, as in many parts of the world. The long arm of colonialism did not spare food cultures, and as an example of what B.J. Mehta termed *culinary vampirism* (2009, 109); she points out that turkey, touted as classic French cuisine, was actually discovered in the West Indies, which, as we know, Christopher Columbus mistook for India and therefore misnamed d'inde (from India). Scholars like Appiah (2006) might describe this as 'cultural contamination' (see chapter one), as a space of exchange and hybridity and as a cosmopolitan moment. However, my conception of corporeal cosmopolitanism would describe this as colonial violence, which must be addressed and treated as such. I do not want to confuse the hybridisation and travel of food with the colonial appropriation of it. It is true that these lines are far from clear and that we cannot possibly draw absolute distinctions. However, as Santos says of the 'society of absences' (2001), formerly colonised societies must articulate the difference, for the violence of cultural and culinary appropriation distorted and damaged their sense of identity and belonging. Similarly, B.J. Mehta (2009) also argues that the colonial introduction of pork into the Caribbean diet was an act of culinary colonisation, an act that destroyed the digestive health of indigenous *Carib* populations. Europe consumed the best produce, leaving the low-quality meat for its colonised slaves and subjects. The narrative of conquest and colonial violence must be acknowledged and accounted for. We must not mistake violent erasure for hybridity.

The Western capitalist hold over so-called beauty standards has also aided the demonisation of indigenous foods and cuisines, causing considerable detriment to the natural nutrition balances, as well as the affordability of healthy food in different parts of the world. A vast swathe of Caribbean and South Asian foods have been labelled unhealthy, fattening or simply unfashionable. There is also, as Anzaldúa (1987) points out, a deep sense of shame associated with eating home cuisine and all that it entails. I can remember a time, when I was a young girl of maybe thirteen or fourteen and was abroad for the first time with my parents. We were at a restaurant, where my parents discovered that the chef was from South India. In the rush of joyful excitement

that is so characteristic of diasporic interactions abroad, my mother managed, at a restaurant which only served *haute*, non-Indian cuisine, to bring
us South Indian food. I remember being utterly horrified and ashamed as
I watched my parents eat with the abandonment that is characteristic of food
eaten by hand, of *home*, of being South Indian, Tamil, and "other". I can still
remember people's eyes boring into the back of my head – I had never seen
so many White people before. I cringed at every swish, crunch and slurp,
wishing that I wasn't with *them* (my parents), or that I was *someone else*.
These oppressions of colonial, British eating-etiquette did not appear to me
out of a vacuum. They belong to the refrain of subaltern and colonial rupture
that must be addressed and discussed at multiple levels of community building within cosmopolitan imaginaries, something I hope that we can entrust to
corporeal cosmopolitan thought and practice.

   In a related narrative of food and community building, I want to examine
Perez's (2004) work on the Mesoamerican *fiesta*. This departs from the previous discussion in some important ways, primarily because it is not diasporic,
and also because Perez's work speaks to the grim, sometimes blatantly dangerous, ways in which embodied community practices are negotiated and
performed to maintain solidarities. This illustrates the complex and difficult
work that corporeal cosmopolitanism will have to do, in order to create communities of healing around traumatic experiences. A religious festival of
ritual drinking and feasting, the *fiesta* is used, according to Perez, as a cultural, artistic, political and conflict resolution space. A *fiesta* is usually held
to commemorate saints or important life passages of Jesus and Mary. It is a
deeply significant social event, and attending the *fiesta* is a sign of strength
and networking as well as being heavily male-centric. Because drinking is so
central to the festival, there are several health risks to both men and women,
added to which women also emerge as victims of severe domestic violence.
Unmarried daughters typically care for the men during the *fiesta*. Here too,
Perez indicates the importance of cooking as a communal ritual for women.
Fiesta cooking is traditional and does not use any modern appliances. The use
of modern cooking technology may ease the labour pressures on the women,
but Perez insists that it will also break their ritual bonding – 'the maintenance
of this communal bond is considered far more important than the quick prepa-
ration of food' (Perez 2004, 273). The public display of violence is unique to
the *fiesta*, and the violence is accepted and to a certain extent sanctioned as a
price to be paid for modernity and for the shifting gender roles that are placing women at the economic centre. This is also a story about fragile and vulnerable masculinities, and unemployment and poverty, stripping men of their
traditional economic roles. The sanction of violence is a price that is paid in
aid of maintaining community solidarity, because the loss of community solidarity is unthinkable. Perez writes at length on the way violence is performed

and enacted, usually by the man towards his wife or by men towards other men. There is absolutely no condoning of violence in this narrative, either by Perez or myself. I want to draw attention only to the complicated relationship that indigenous and colonised communities have to modernity, and the price they pay for unmediated, enforced change. It is crucial that we resist the typecasting of this as a simplistic situation of a "backward" community that is misogynistic and in need of a certain kind of modern, liberal cosmopolitanisation. Indeed, it is worth reiterating that the conditions of deterioration within the community are directly connected to the structural mechanics of neo-liberal, capitalist development. Perez's narrative is a deeply complex one, of a community that has been existing at the crack of ages, where it not only resists being consumed by imperial globalisation but also rejects the deeply ingrained misogyny that oppresses the women of the community. The women here possess and exercise agency, and in some sense they sacrifice their bodily integrity and safety for that of the community. They also form groups to protect each other against male violence and often fight the men back. Perez's work was an important reminder of how fragile the notion of solidarity is and how easily it can be bent to other, more violent wills. The challenge for corporeal cosmopolitanism is really about how it will respond to narratives and practices like these. Can it create a safe space for this community to speak, and more importantly, can it actively listen to what is being said? These will form the difficult passages, and how we process these stories and these acts of violence and resistance will ultimately reveal the dialogic limits and possibilities of corporeal cosmopolitanism.

The next illustration of embodied and affective practice that I want to discuss is situated around the emotional bonds of grief and mourning. I briefly alluded to the *Koovagam* festival of the *thirunangai* community in chapter three. I return to it now in more detail to elicit the possibilities of grief as a community bond. Judith Butler (2004, 2014) argues that mourning is an irreversible transformation that completely jettisons the distinctions between self and other. The space of grief creates a very unique kind of solidarity that is affective, embodied and common to all those in mourning. The community-creating power of grief thus challenges the liberal cosmopolitan understanding of universalism. Jeff Roy's (2013) short films on the *Koovagam* festival (*Koovagam, Meet Gopi, The Importance of Being Miss Koovagam* 2013) are a detailed and beautiful narrative. Roy himself is a conscious and dialogic "other" in the filming and telling of these stories, particularly because he frames *Koovagam* as a powerful, performative space of articulation and self-determination. The optics and Roy's own subject position as a non-local are part of the performative nature of the ritual celebrations and mourning, making this encounter even more layered and complex. The interviewer/narrator in the film is Taejha Singh Susheela, a dancer and queer activist from

Chennai, India. He narrates many of the *thirunangai* stories and the religious mythology through dance *mudras* (motifs). At the *Koovagam* festival, as Susheela explains, the *aravanis* are all *Mohinis*, symbolic of the female form that *Krishna* took to be the bride of *Aravan* (see chapter three for the story of *Aravan)*. The brides of *Aravan* are all enveloped in the ecstatic, collective experience of love and sexual desire. The festival is not restricted to *Koovagam* alone. There are about forty-eight temples dedicated to *Aravan* in Tamil Nadu, and each temple claims him for their own. While the *Koovagam* festival is certainly the most popular and attracts much media attention, these other festivals bring together nonidentified *thirunangais*, most of whom live the lives of cisgender, straight family men (Babu and Sundaram 2014, personal interview). They dress in women's clothing but wear all the symbols of masculinity such as facial hair and body hair and have a "male" physique, unaltered by hormones, making it very distinct from many *thirunangai* participants of the *Koovagam* festival, which sees a very different aesthetic altogether.

Transwomen from all over the country come here, and bedeck themselves as brides (See Mitra, 2010). Many of them spend months and years to save money in order to be *Aravan*'s brides. The local priests perform a symbolic marriage ritual, after which a procession and enactment of the war in the *Mahabharata* take place. An effigy or statue of *Aravan* is ritually beheaded and killed, simultaneously widowing all the brides at the festival. The ritual mourning that follows the death of *Aravan* is deeply significant. Wailing and beating their breasts, devastated at the death of their husband, *thirunangai* women are ritually widowed (a practice with deeply patriarchal implications), their bangles are broken, their *pottus* (the vermillion mark worn on the forehead that identifies a married woman) are rubbed away and their *thaalis* (necklace worn by women signifying their marital status) are cut from their necks. As one, the widows perform the *oppari*: the traditional mourning dirge for the deceased in Tamil traditions of death and mourning (there are different versions of it all over India and other cultures). As their voices rise in a keening lament, there is an expression of grief that takes place at multiple levels: personal, political and cosmic. The *oppari* is a testimony to personal sorrows, losses, trauma and pain to political and societal ostracism and invisibilisation, as well as the ritual, transcendent grief of cosmic mourning. The ritual enactment of mourning is at once a spectacle and an identifier. It provides a cultural heteronormative legitimacy to *thirunangai* identity, while still othering them. It is also important to recall that the *Koovagam* festival is rife with reports of violence, rape and sexual abuse against transwomen who are attacked by men year after year (Tejonmayam 2015). What I want to highlight, once again, are the dense complexities that inform embodied practices of identity and community building. The affective ritual practice of mourning is not merely a celebration of religious tradition but speaks to the living trauma of contemporary abuse and violence. Constitutional measures and legal reform cannot hope to reach these places of vulnerability, and it is my hope that corporeal cosmopolitanism will be able to do so.

The *Koovagam* festival is a significant cultural space for transwomen in India, and articulates many different iterations of identity and community belonging. Perhaps as an intentional counter-narrative to the "traditional" ritual celebration of *thirunangai* identity, the festival also hosts the *Ms. Koovagam* beauty pageant, which is also the subject of one of Roy's films. The embodied politics of this performance are very different from the other one. Another interesting feature of this event is that it has two judges, who personify seemingly irreconcilable politics, and yet work together. Revathi, whose story I discussed in chapter three, was one of the judges and is openly critical of the media coverage this pageant receives. She described the whole process of *judging* women by external beauty as highly unproductive and problematic. The other judge who organised the pageant, Malika, a trans-activist and model and was completely in agreement with mainstream fashion and the beauty pageant format. Although Revathi and Malika are very different women (Roy 2013), with what one might say are oppositional politics, they have managed to create a space of conversation and sharing, and work together to organise this pageant as part of the festival year after year. The creation of community through an expression of grief is central to the way the festival takes place: 'A loss might seem utterly personal, private, isolating, furnishes an unexpected concept of political community' (Butler 2014).[3] At the same festival, however, we also see the expression and performance of the body as a beautiful, desirous, erotic site, by way of the beauty pageant. The seamless movement between oppositional positions, disagreements and the coexistence of orthodoxy and resistance are a good indication of how I theorise and explain the politics of corporeal cosmopolitanism.

As I bring this section to a close I hope that these accounts and illustrations of embodied performances and practices have painted the blueprints of a beginning. In this final section, I have drawn on different experiences of corporeality and emotional inhabitation; I considered food cultures, feast and festival rituals, as well as beauty pageants. The idea was to look at embodied practices of identity and community building that are both distinct from one another but are constituted by the relationship to body, emotion and spirituality. I have not been wholly celebratory about these experiences, because corporeal cosmopolitanism is not made of a simplistic emotional matrix. Much of the work it must do is rooted in trauma, violence and pain but equally in the practice of love, speech and radical compassion. The illustrations of embodied solidarities from within these communities are intended as an illumination and to help us imagine some possibilities should we open ourselves to such an attempt. Corporeal cosmopolitanism, to me, is an intellectual, emotional and practical space of compassion, dialogue and healing; but in order for it to realise that potential, we must first recognise and acknowledge wounding. There will be anger and suspicion, absence of faith, pain, and, apathy, first. But if we do the work we must and are able to sit with all of those responses and feelings, we will find room for love, space and healing, both for ourselves and each other.

NOTE

1 Inspired by Gabriel Garcia Marquez's work *Love in the Time of Cholera* (1988).

Bookends

Incanting the Political into the Body

It is early 2017 as I attempt to gather fragments of both myself and this book, together. For many of us, across the world, this last year has been one of devastation, death and a terrifying increase in racist, misogynistic, queerphobic and xenophobic violences. For many of us, it has been a time of loss and mourning. Like several friends, family members and colleagues, I have spent many days in tears, trapped in the horror images of our perilous futures. Revisiting this material and these decolonial, feminist hopes has been no easy task. On many days, it has felt so futile and childish to wish for such things as I have here. On many days, I have only metabolised hatred, to borrow from Audre Lorde, and fury has been the only offering I have been able to make to the world. I have written over and over again in this book that corporeal cosmopolitanism is rooted in the practice and politics of love and that such a practice of love has room for grief, fear and anger. In my own small and privileged capacity, I have been supported and grounded by an exuberance of such love. For every act of violence and for every expression of grief, fear and trauma, there have been overwhelming responses of courage and solidarity. People of colour have come together in swelling numbers, rising and speaking out against racism, white supremacy and xenophobia, while still raising important, valuable questions around structural privileges and the absence of solidarity from within their own communities. Women have come out in the hundreds of thousands, but we have also heard the powerful voices of women of colour, transpeople and genderqueer people speaking against the systemic, deracinated oppressions within feminist articulations of solidarity. When I speak to friends in India, I hear more and more voices speaking up against hegemonic caste violences and the crushing of intellectual autonomies, even as the country experiences a surge in vitriolic violence against marginalised caste and class communities, and women and queer peoples. In Trinidad, the

Leave She Alone campaign, demanding the safety and autonomy of women's bodies during Carnival, has gained extraordinary momentum. Trinidadian designer Anya Ayoung Chee asks poignantly: 'Coming out in the streets in the tens of thousands, owning your space, owning your freedom, what is that besides activism?' (Powers, 2017). As the crush of violence intensifies, so too does the resistance. Except that now, the resistances are being owned and performed by those whose voices and bodies were stolen, silenced or broken. The refusal to accept hegemonic chains of authority and the rejection of privileged proxy narrators demonstrate the strength of decolonial protests. The injustices of neo-imperial, racist and capitalist systems are being recognised and called to account in ways that they were not before. In my own cocoon of relative safety, for every single time I have been unable to keep myself together from grief; somebody has written something in a novel, or spoken a poem, made a film, or just picked up the phone, a continent away to speak, or listen, or just be silent, and hold that space for those in pain. In my own experiences and in those of people I meet, and speak with, and read about, I have witnessed the animating forces of corporeal cosmopolitanism at work. I have seen what radical love and compassion can achieve. Even on days when I cannot believe in these things, I know they wait with me, until I can again.

At the risk of being repetitive, I want to remind us – both you and myself – that I am not advocating a universal blanket of dialogicity. I am all too aware that many spaces have become too embittered, or too steeped in pain, and harm, and death, that it is not possible to have speech. But I also think that these spaces are not as many as we might fear. There is always a danger, I think, in writing about love, or hope, or sweetness. If one is not careful enough to reflect on where one is speaking from, then it is easy to mistake privilege and elite security for love. That is, it is possible to speak of love, only when it is safe enough to do so. I fully acknowledge both the risk and my own relative safety, though it is by no means absolutely safe to be writing as a South Asian woman of colour, an immigrant and a citizen of the "global south", while living in a time-space continuum of dangerous and violent xenophobia (across multiple axes). In my own experiences, observations and readings, the embodied and affective performances of solidarity of corporeal cosmopolitanism are rooted in a very different practice of love. The love that I have tried to describe, practise and write about is one that rises from histories, cartographies and anatomies of suffering, violence and brutality. It is also a love that embodies a fierce and profound joy that both understands the need for moral justice and the dangers of moral absolutism. A love that is as much political and intellectual practice as it is an unencumbered and tactile vulnerability. Decolonial love is resistance, freedom and strength – its languages are fluid, and its performances, multiple. It recognises the need for silence and refusal, as much as it makes room to listen and learn.

One of the most important lessons that I have learnt in these innumerable interlocutions with decolonial, feminist, queer and spiritual cosmopolitanisms is that if and when dialogue is possible, we must always be prepared to recognise and be witness to pain. The practice of radical compassion in corporeal cosmopolitan spaces must be large enough to hold one's own pain and witness another's without feeling overcrowded or invalidated. For corporeal cosmopolitanism to be meaningful, there must be a willingness to have conversations with all our myriad selves, our wounds, traumas, anger and joys. It requires a constant unmaking of the self, a complete vulnerability and a constant questioning of hegemonic violences everywhere. Part of decolonial resistance is to dismantle the structure that flattens us into the "oppressed" – I do not mean that in the postmodern sense of individualistic, ubiquitous fluidity but in the sense that we must dismantle the homogeneity of our oppressions. *La Prieta* (Anzaldúa 2009) is perhaps the first time that I seriously considered the personal extents of these conversations we must have with and about ourselves. She writes, 'I was terrified because in this writing I must be hard on people of color who are the oppressed victims. I am still afraid because I will have to call us on a lot of shit like our own racism, our fear of women, and sexuality' (2009, 39). One of the hardest things about imagining large solidarities has to do with the kinds of commitments and binding loyalties they demand. In a committed solidarity, the lines between reflexive critique and betrayal can be very blurry sometimes, something Anzaldúa expressed in many powerful pieces. In my own descriptions and imaginings of corporeal cosmopolitanism, these remain important issues. We must constantly think about how to frame conversations between unequal power-holders in ways that validate and stand by those inequalities, without always ossifying them into impasses (while still remembering that sometimes they can be, and are). We must also look for ways to articulate critique that are not purely adversarial. Here again, I find the practice of love particularly helpful. If critique is rooted in places of love and compassion, then, first, the focus of the critique ceases to be narcissistic aggrandizement, and second, it becomes possible to hold space for the pain that is likely to result from such critique. This is also one of the reasons why I chose to continue working in the suspect space of cosmopolitanism. 'What does it mean when the tools of a racist patriarchy are used to examine the fruits of that same patriarchy? It means that only the narrowest perimeters of change are possible and allowable' (Lorde 1984, 110–113). The possibility that I have in fact tried to use 'the masters tools' to 'dismantle the master's house' has been a recurrent cause for anxiety. It has not escaped me that for all my toil and effort, it may feel to you, reading these words, that I am simply trapped in some simulacral fantasy of the master's tools. The attempt is an ambitious one, but the intention has been to dismantle the master's appropriation of these large conceptions of solidarities. Building on existing decolonial writing about cosmopolitanism has been a conscious effort to break the unspoken ownership of liberal narratives over cosmopolitan imaginaries. There are many historical and spiritual cosmopolitanisms that are decidedly and geographically not of the "global north", of course. However, one of the reasons I avoided speaking about them in those terms is precisely because that orientalised discourse is part of the master narrative of irreducible difference.

Although my engagement with liberal cosmopolitanism is largely critical, as I have said at the beginning of this book, I had the opportunity to learn about many of its key ideas from contemporary scholars of contemporary liberal cosmopolitanism. I watched and listened to scholars of liberal cosmopolitan literature navigate and explain their positions in academic spaces of the "global south" and participate in the dialogues that they wrote about and were so invested in. I learnt very quickly about the ways in which structural elisions of privilege could be completely compartmentalised and cordoned off from individual behaviours. In time, I also learnt that challenging and dismantling those compartments tended to provide extremely fruitful grounds for an actual conversation about the iterations of privilege and marginalisation, rather than abstracted versions of the same. That is to say, these scholarly/personal interactions altered the nature of my exchanges with the literature of liberal cosmopolitanism, because I had a chance to watch it being performed by its authors. Without this primary engagement, I am not sure that I would have really understood what dismantling the master's narrative using decoloniality really meant. My personal relationship with what I had thus far identified as intellectually and politically oppositional to my own beliefs and work began to transform into something much more mutable and dialogic. I came to understand many of the core principles that liberal cosmopolitanism drew from. I learnt to recognise the tremulous hope that some of these liberal cosmopolitan ideas held out for humanity, while I still held them accountable and responsible for their egregious exclusions and oppressions. I was able to discern the nuances within the liberal cosmopolitan framing of dialogue and disagree with the specificities of its understanding and practice of what dialogue constitutes. One might argue that, ultimately, this kind of deep understanding does not meaningfully alter the political endgame, but I strongly believe that it does. Deep understanding and radical compassion are antithetical to binaristic, categorical action – and this, to me, is a crucial step in the decolonial dismantling of the master's house. Ultimately, the only way to bring the body *back* is to actually bring it up, persistently and unapologetically. We are so frightened of speaking because the silence is perfectly smooth in its oppression. There are no cracks or tears through which we might wiggle our way in. This kind of exclusion is not meant for wiggling. It is too total and too well practised to misstep in that way. The only way to build corporeal cosmopolitanism is to do just that, by making it visible, by questioning its absence and declaring its presence, over, and over again.

As an urban-raised child of a postcolony, my own subject/object crises lie within a deeply Western-colonial, English-language–dominated academic background, as is the case with many (though by no means all) academics from the "global south". This desire that I harboured for corporeal cosmopolitanism demanded a genuine epistemological metamorphosis, a questioning of the constitution of categories and what it would mean to no longer inhabit them in the old ways. I was forced to engage with my interiorised others and my exteriorised Others in ways that I would never have considered necessary.

To build a dialogic space like corporeal cosmopolitanism that was founded on the radical practice of love and compassion meant that I had to really examine what I understood by practices of resistance and whether I would be willing to resist parts of my own cultural constructions of self. As hooks (2001) argues, the deep practice of love is fundamentally entwined with the concept of justice. Thus, being able to read an Other text from a place of love does not mean that the reading will be in any way devoid of justice. It simply means that we might spot spaces of conversation and productive critique that we might not have ordinarily done. The communities of resistance and solidarity that I have written about are all immersed in this complexity of belonging and exile, love and alienation. But they are always living: singing and dancing, screaming and revelling. Corporeal cosmopolitanism is not a space of resolution. I do not offer it as an ending but as one possibility among many beginnings. It has taken several different kinds of growths, detachments and recognitions to find my way here. I hope, if you have managed to travel with me this far, that you now have another place to inhabit and build from. The emotional, intellectual and physical wounds that so many of us have endured and continue to endure need different kinds of healing. My spirit-prayer is that we will find ways to practise queer love, decolonial solidarity and radical compassion. Towards corporeal cosmopolitanism is a coin at the bottom of a fountain, a note in the crevice of a wall, a *trisoolam* (trident) pierced through my skin. It is my offering, at the altar that chose to have me.

References

Adams, David, and Galin Tihanov, eds. 2011. *Enlightenment Cosmopolitanism.* Leeds: Legenda.
———. 1998. *Homo Sacer: Sovereign Power and Bare Life.* Stanford, California: Stanford University.
———. 1999. *Remnants of Auschwitz: The Witness and the Archive.* New York: Zone Books.
———. 2005. *State of Exception.* Translated by Kevin Attell. Chicago: University of Chicago Press.
Ahmed, Sara. 2014. *Cultural Politics of Emotion.* Edinburgh: Edinburgh University Press.
Allen, Paula Gunn. 1986. *The Sacred Hoop: Recovering the Feminine in American Indian Traditions.* Boston: Beacon.
Andrade, Oswald de. 1928. "Anthropophagite Manifesto". Date Last Accessed: 1/06/2017. http://www.391.org/manifestos/1928-anthropophagite-manifesto-oswald-de-andrade.html
Anzaldúa, Gloria. 1987. *Borderlands: La Frontera.* San Francisco: Spinsters/Aunt Lute.
Anzaldúa, Gloria. 2009. *The Gloria Anzaldúa Reader.* Edited by AnaLouise Keating. Durham: Duke University Press.
Appadurai, Arjun. 2002. "Spectral Housing and urban Cleansing: Notes on Millenial Mumbai." In *Cosmopolitanism.* Edited by Carol Breckenridge, Sheldon Pollock, Homi Bhabha and Dipesh Chakrabarty, 54–81. Durham: Duke University Press.
Appiah, Kwame Anthony. 2002. "Cosmopolitan Patriots." In *For Love of Country? Debating the Limits of Patriotism.* Edited by Joshua Cohen, 21–29. Boston: Beacon Press.
———. 2005. *The Ethics of Identity.* Princeton, New Jersey: Princeton University Press.
———. 2006. *Cosmopolitanism: Ethics in a World of Strangers.* New York: Norton.
Arendt, Hannah. 2006. "What is Authority." In *Between Past and Future: Eight Exercises in Political Thought (1950).* London: Penguin.

Bahadur, Gaiutra. 2013. *Coolie Woman: The Odyssey of Indenture*. London: C. Hurst.
Bakhtin, Mikhail. 1981. *The Dialogic Imagination: Four Essays*. Edited by Michael Holquist. Austin: University of Texas.
———. 1984. *Rabelais and His World*. Translated by H. Iswolsky. Bloomington: Indiana University Press.
Balibar, Etienne. 2002. *Politics and the Other Scene*. London: Verso.
———. 2005. "Difference, Otherness, Exclusion." *Parallax* 11(1): 19–34. http://dx.doi.org/10.1080/1353464052000321074.
BBC News. 2016. "Afghan Girl: National Geographic photographer vows to help". Retrieved From: http://www.bbc.co.uk/news/world-asia-37782580
Beck, Ulrich. 1992. *Risk Society: Towards a New Modernity*. London: Sage Publications.
———. 2006. *The Cosmopolitan Vision*. Cambridge, United Kingdom: Polity.
———. 2007. "The Cosmopolitan Condition: Why Methodological Nationalism Fails." *Theory, Culture and Society* 24(7–8): 286–290. http://journals.sagepub.com/doi/abs/10.1177/02632764070240072505.
———. 2009. "Critical Theory of World Risk Society: A Cosmopolitan Vision." *Constellations* 16(1): 3–22. doi:10.1111/j.1467–8675.2009.00534.x.
Benhabib, Seyla. 2006. *Another Cosmopolitanism*. Oxford: Oxford University Press.
Benjamin, Walter. 1979. "On Language as Such and on Language of Man." In *One-Way Street and Other Writings*. Translated by Edmund Jephcott and Kingsley Shorter. London: NLB.
Bhabha, Homi. 1994. *The Location of Culture*. London: Routledge.
———. 2001. "Unsatisfied: Notes on Vernacular Cosmopolitanism." In *Postcolonial Discourses: An Anthology*. Edited by Gregory Castle. Oxford: Blackwell Publishers.
Bhan, Gautam. 2005. "Challenging the Limits of Law: Queer Politics and Legal Reform in India." In *Because I Have a Voice: Queer Politics in India*. Edited by Arvind Narrain and Gautam Bhan, 40–48. New Delhi: Yoda Press.
Bose, Sugata, and Kris Manjapra, eds. 2010. *Cosmopolitan Thought Zones: South Asia and the Global Circulation of Ideas*. Hampshire: Palgrave Macmillan.
Breckenridge, Carol, Sheldon Pollock, Homi Bhabha and Dipesh Chakrabarty, eds. 2002. *Cosmopolitanism*. Durham: Duke University Press.
Brock, Gillian, and Harry Brighouse, eds. 2005. *The Political Philosophy of Cosmopolitanism*. Cambridge: Cambridge University Press.
Butler, Judith. 2002. "Universality in Culture." In *For Love of Country? Debating the Limits of Patriotism*. Edited by Joshua Cohen, 45–52. Boston: Beacon Press.
———. 2004. *Precarious Life: The Powers of Mourning and Violence*. London: Verso.
Butler, Judith, and Gayatri Chakravorty Spivak. 2007. *Who Sings the Nation-state?: Language, Politics, Belonging*. London: Seagull.
———. 2014. "On the Edge: Grief". Last modified 27 February 2014. https://pen.org/on-the-edge-grief/.
Butler, Judith, Ernesto Laclau and Slavoj Žižek. 2000. *Contingency, Hegemony, Universality: Contemporary Dialogues on the Left*. London: Verso.
Chamberlain, J. Edward. 2003. *If This Is Your Land, Where Are Your Stories?:Finding Common Ground*. Toronto: A.A. Knopf.
Chatterjee, Partha. 2004. *The Politics of the Governed: Reflections on Popular Politics in Most of the World*. New Delhi: Permanent Black.

Cixous, Helene. 1976. "The Laugh of the Medusa." Translated Keith Cohen and Paula Cohen. *Signs: Journal of Women in Culture and Society* 1(4): 875–893.

Dekker, Rudolf, and Lotte Van de Pol. 1989. *The Tradition of Female Transvestism in Early Modern Europe*. New York: St. Martin's.

Delanty, Gerard. 2009. *The Cosmopolitan Imagination: The Renewal of Critical Social Theory*. Cambridge: Cambridge University Press.

———, ed. 2012. *Routledge Handbook of Cosmopolitanism Studies*. Abingdon, Oxon: Routledge.

Deleuze, Gilles, and Félix Guattari. 1986. *Kafka: Toward a Minor Literature*. Translated by D. Polan. Minneapolis: University of Minnesota Press.

———. 2004. *Anti-Oedipus: Capitalism and Schizophrenia*. London: The Continuum Publishing Company.

Derrida, Jacques. 1993. "The Politics of Friendship." *American Imago* 50(3): 353–391.

———. 2005. *Rogues: Two Essays on Reason*. Stanford: Stanford University Press.

Descartes, René, Haldane, Elizabeth Sanderson & Ross, G. R. T. 1911. *The Philosophical Works of Descartes*. London: Dover Publications.

Diouf, Mamadou. 2002. "The Senegalese Murid Trade Diaspora and the Making of a Vernacular Cosmopolitanism." In *Cosmopolitanism*. Edited by Carol Breckenridge, Sheldon Pollock, Homi Bhabha and Dipesh Chakrabarty, 113–137. Durham: Duke University Press.

Diptee, Audra. 2003. "Cultural Transfer and Transformation: Revisiting Indo-Afro Sexual Relationships in Trinidad and British Guiana in the Late Nineteenth Century." In The Society for Caribbean Studies annual conference papers, Vol. 4.

Douzinas, Costas. 2007. *Human Rights and Empire: The Political Philosophy of Cosmopolitanism*. London: Routledge-Cavendish.

Edwards, Brent. 2003. *The Practice of Diaspora: Literature, Translation, and the Rise of Black Internationalism*. Cambridge, Massachusetts : Harvard University Press.

Espinet, Ramabai. 2004. *The Swinging Bridge*. Toronto: Harper Perennial Canada.

Fanon, Frantz. 1963. *The Wretched of the Earth*. New York: Grove Press.

———. 2008. *Black Skin, White Masks*. New York: Grove Press.

Fire. 1996. Directed by Deepa Mehta. Mumbai, India: Trial by Fire Films Inc. 1996, DVD.

Foucault, Michel. 1972. *The Archaeology of Knowledge*. Translated by A. M. Sheridan Smith. New York: Pantheon Books.

———. 1978. *The History of Sexuality, Volume 1: An Introduction*. Translated by Robert Hurley. New York: Pantheon.

———. 1980. *Power-Knowledge: Selected Interviews and Other Writings, 1972–1977*. Edited by Colin Gordon. New York: Random House.

———. 1984. *Of Other Spaces: Utopias and Heterotopias*. www.web.mit.edu/allanmc/www/foucault1.pdf.

———. 1985. *The Use of Pleasure: The History of Sexuality, Vol. 2*. Translated by Robert Hurley. New York: Pantheon.

———. 1986. *The Care of the Self: The History of Sexuality, Vol. 3*. Translated by Robert Hurley. New York: Pantheon.

———. 1988. *Madness and Civilization: A History of Insanity in the Age of Reason*. Translated by Richard Howard. New York: Vintage Books.

Gatens, Moira. 1996. *Imaginary Bodies: Ethics, Power and Corporeality*. London: Routledge.

Giddens, Anthony. 1991. *Modernity and Self Identity*. Cambridge: Polity Press.

———. 1994. *Beyond Left and Right: The Future of Radical Politics*. Cambridge: Polity Press.

———. 1998. *The Third Way*. Cambridge: Polity Press.

Grosz, Elizabeth. 1994. *Volatile Bodies: Toward a Corporeal Feminism*. Indiana: Indiana University Press.

———. 2002. "A Politics of Imperceptibility: A Response to 'Anti-racism, Multiculturalism and the Ethics of Identification." *Philosophy & Social Criticism* 28(4): 463–472.

Gupta, Alok. 2005. "Englishpur ki Kothi: Class Dynamics in the Queer Movement in India." In *Because I Have a Voice: Queer Politics in India*. Edited by Arvind Narrain and Gautam Bhan, 123–142. New Delhi: Yoda Press.

Harcourt, Wendy. 2004. "Body Politics: Revisiting the Population Question." In *Feminist Post-development Thought: Rethinking Modernity, Post-colonialism & Representation*. Edited by Kriemild Saunders, 283–297. New Delhi: Zubaan.

Harris, Martin. 1977. *Cannibals and Kings*. NY: Random House.

Harvey, David. 2009. *Cosmopolitanism and the Geographies of Freedom*. New York: Columbia University Press.

Held, David. 2005. "Principles of Cosmopolitan Order." In *The Political Philosophy of Cosmopolitanism*. Edited by Gillian Brock and Harry Brighouse, 10–27. Cambridge: Cambridge University Press.

Hirschfield, Magnus. 1991. *Transvestites: The Erotic Drive to Cross Dress*. Translated by Michael A. Lombardi-Nash. New York: Prometheus.

Ho, Engseng. 2006. *The Graves of Tarim: Genealogy and Mobility across the Indian Ocean*. California: University of California Press.

Holliday, Ruth, and John Hassard eds. 2001. *Contested Bodies*. London: Routledge.

Honig, Bonnie. 2006. "Another Cosmopolitanism? Law and Politics in the New Europe." In *Another Cosmopolitanism*. Edited by Robert Post, 102–127. Oxford: Oxford University Press.

hooks, bell. 2001. *All about Love: New Visions*. New York: Harper-Perennial.

Hosein, Gabrielle Jamela. 2011. "No Pure Place of Resistance: Reflections on Being Ms. Mastana Bahar 2000." In *Bindi: The Multifaceted Lives of Indo-Caribbean Women*. Edited by Rosanne Kanhai, 141–164. Jamaica: The University of the West Indies Press.

Howson, Alexandra. 2005. *Embodying Gender*. London: Sage Publications.

The Importance of "Miss Koovagam." 2013. Directed by Jeff Roy. https://fulbright.mtvu.com/2013/06/25/the-importance-of-miss-koovagam/.

Ippadikku Rose. 2008a. First broadcast December 19 by Star Vijay. Directed by Anthony Thirunelveli.

———. 2008b. First Broadcast January 10 by Star Vijay. Directed by Anthony Thirunelveli.

———. 2008c. First Broadcast April 3 by Star Vijay. Directed by Anthony Thirunelveli.

Irigaray, Luce. 1985. *This Sex Which Is Not One*. New York: Cornell University Press.

———. 2001. "The Fecundity of the Caress: A Reading of Levinas, Totality and Infinity." In *Feminist Interpretations of Emmanuel Levinas*. Edited by Tina Chanter, 119–144. Pennsylvania: Pennsylvania State University Press.

Judovitz, Dalia. 2001. *The Culture of the Body: Genealogies of Modernity*. Michigan: The University of Michigan Press.

Kanhai, Rosanne, ed. 2011. *Bindi: The Multifaceted Lives of Indo-Caribbean Women*. Jamaica: The University of the West Indies Press.

Kant, Immanuel. 1917. *Towards Perpetual Peace*. Translated by M. Campbell Smith. London: George Allen and Unwin.

Kant, Immanuel, Pauline Kleingeld, Jeremy Waldron, Michael W. Doyle, and Allen W. Wood. 2006. Toward Perpetual Peace and Other Writings on Politics, Peace, and History. Yale: Yale University Press.

Kassim, Halima-Sa'adia. 2011. "Rings, Gifts and Shekels: Marriage and Dowry within the Indo-Muslim Community in Trinidad: 1930 to the Globalized Present." In *Bindi: The Multifaceted Lives of Indo-Caribbean Women*. Edited by Rosanne Kanhai, 52–100. Jamaica: The University of the West Indies Press.

Khan, Aisha. 2005. *Callaloo Nation: Metaphors of Race and Religious Identity among South Asians in Trinidad*. Durham: Duke University Press.

———. 2007. "Mixing Matters: Callaloo Nation Revisited." *Callaloo* 30(1): 51–67.

Khanna, Akshay. 2005. "Beyond 'Sexuality' (?)." In *Because I Have a Voice: Queer Politics in India*. Edited by Arvind Narrain and Gautam Bhan, 89–104. New Delhi: Yoda Press.

Koovagam (Part 1). 2013. Directed by Jeff Roy. https://fulbright.mtvu.com/2013/05/15/koovagam-part-1/.

Kristeva, Julia. 1982. *Powers of Horror: An Essay on Abjection*. Translated by Leon S. Roudiez. New York: Columbia University Press.

———. 1991. *Strangers to Ourselves*. New York: Columbia University Press.

———. 1993. *Nations without Nationalism*. New York: Columbia University Press.

Lal, Vinay. 1999. "Not This, Not That: The Hijras of India and the Cultural Politics of Sexuality.". *Social Text* 61: 119–140. Durham: Duke University Press.

Lorde, Audre. 1984. *Sister Outsider: Essays and Speeches*. Trumansburg, New York: Crossing.

Manjapra, Kris. 2010. *M. N. Roy: Marxism and Colonial Cosmopolitanism*. Delhi: Routledge.

Marcos, Sylvia. 2004. "Gender, Bodies and Cosmos in Mesoamerica." In *Feminist Post-development Thought: Rethinking Modernity, Post-colonialism & Representation*. Edited by Kriemild Saunders, 313–330. New Delhi: Zubaan.

Massad, Joseph Adoni. 2002). "Re-Orienting Desire: The Gay International and the Arab World". *Public Culture* 14(2), 361–385.

Meet Gopi (Koovagam Part 2). 2013. Directed by Jeff Roy. https://player.vimeo.com/video/67143992.

Mehta, Brinda J. 2004. *Diasporic (Dis)locations: Indo-Caribbean Women Writers Negotiate the Kala Pani*. Kingston, Jamaica: University of the West Indies.

———. 2009. *Notions of Identity, Diaspora, and Gender in Caribbean Women's Writing*. New York: Palgrave Macmillan.

Mehta, Pratap Bhanu. 2000. "Cosmopolitanism and the Circle of Reason." *Political Theory*. 28(5): 619–639.

Menon, Nivedita. 2005. "How Natural Is Normal? Feminism and Compulsory Heterosexuality." In *Because I Have a Voice: Queer Politics in India*. Edited by Arvind Narrain and Gautam Bhan, 33–39. New Delhi: Yoda Press.

———. 2012. *Seeing Like a Feminist*. New Delhi: Zuban and Penguin.

Menon, Ramesh. 2006a. *The Mahabharata: A Modern Rendering. Vol. 1*. Lincoln: iUniverse Books.

———. 2006b. *The Mahabharata: A Modern Rendering. Vol. 2*. Lincoln: iUniverse Books.

Merleau-Ponty, Maurice. 2002. *Phenomenology of Perception*. London: Routledge.

Mignolo, Walter. 2000a. *Local Histories/Global Designs: Coloniality, Subaltern Knowledges, and Border Thinking*. Princeton, New Jersey: Princeton University Press.

———. 2000b. "The Many Faces of Cosmo-polis: Border Thinking and Critical Cosmopolitanism." *Public Culture* 12(3): 721–748.

———. 2002. "The Geopolitics of Knowledge and the Colonial Difference." *The South Atlantic Quarterly* 101(1): 57–96.

———. 2011. *The Darker Side of Western Modernity: Global Futures, Decolonial Options*. Durham: Duke University Press.

Mitra, Maureen, 2010. "The Brides of Aravan." Last modified 10 April 2010. http://www.caravanmagazine.in/reportage/brides-aravan.

Mohammed, Patricia. 2009. "The Asian Other in the Caribbean." *Small Axe* 13(2): 57–71.

———. 2012. "Changing Symbols of Indo-Caribbean Femininity." *Caribbean Review of Gender Studies: A Journal of Caribbean Perspectives on Gender and Feminism* 6: 1–16.

Montano, Machel, and Drupatee Ramgoonai. 2000. *Real Unity*. Machel Montano. Ruf Rex Records/Xtatik Ltd. https://www.youtube.com/watch?v=_81pSzuHRog.

Mootoo, Shani. 2010. *Valmiki's Daughter*. Toronto: House of Anansi Press.

Moraga, Cherríe. 1993. *The Last Generation*. Boston: South End Press.

Morson, Gary Saul, and Caryl Emerson, eds. 1990. *Mikhail Bakhtin: Creation of a Prosaics*. Stanford, California: Stanford University Press.

Mouffe, Chantal. 2005. *On the Political*. Oxford: Routledge.

Munasinghe, Viranjini. 2001. "Redefining the Nation: The East Indian Struggle for Inclusion in Trinidad." *Journal of Asian American Studies* 4(1): 1–34.

Mundkur, Aarti, and Arvind Narrain. 2013. "Betraying the Third Way." Last modified 13 June 2016. http://www.thehindu.com/opinion/op-ed/betraying-the-third- way/article4630899.ece.

Nagar, Richa. 2014. *Muddying the Waters: Coauthoring Feminisms across Scholarship and Activism*. Champaign: University of Illinois Press.

Nanda, Serena. 1990. *Neither Man Nor Woman: The Hijras of India*. New York: Wandsworth.

Narrain, Arvind. 2012. "The Criminal Law Amendment) Bill 2012: Sexual Assault as a Gender Neutral Offence." Last modified 12 September 2012. http://www.epw.in/journal/2012/35/web-exclusives/criminal-law-amendment-bill- 2012-sexual-assault-gender-neutral.

Narrain, Arvind, and Gautam Bhan, eds. 2005. *Because I Have a Voice: Queer Politics in India*, New Delhi: Yoda Press.

Narrain, Siddharth. 2003. "Being a Eunuch." Last modified 14 October 2003. http://www.countercurrents.org/gen-narrain141003.htm.

Natpudan Apsara. 2013a. Episode 3 First Broadcast August 24 on Thanthi TV. Director n.a. http://www.tamilserials.tv/category/tv-shows/natpudan-apsara-than thi-tv/.

———. 2013b. Episode 7 First Broadcast August 24 on Thanthi TV. Director n.a. http://www.tamilserials.tv/category/tv-shows/natpudan-apsara-thanthi-tv/.

Nietzsche, Friedrich. 1968. *The Will to Power*. Edited by Walter Kauffman. New York: Random House.

———.1995. *The Birth of Tragedy*. New York: Dover Publications.

Niranjana, Tejaswini. 2006. *Mobilizing India: Women, Music, and Migration between India and Trinidad*. Durham: Duke University Press.

Nussbaum, Martha C. 2002. "Patriotism and Cosmopolitanism." In *For Love of Country? Debating the Limits of Patriotism*. Edited by Joshua Cohen, 3–20. Boston: Beacon Press.

Nyers, Peter. 2003. "Abject Cosmopolitanism: The Politics of Protection in the Anti-Deportation Movement." *Third World Quarterly* 24(6): 1069–1093.

Pamment, Claire. 2010. "Hijraism: Jostling for a Third Space in Pakistani Politics." *The Drama Review* 54(2): 29–50.

Paul, Diana Y. 1981. "Buddhist Attitudes toward Women's Bodies." *Buddhist-Christian Studies* (1) 63–71. doi:10.2307/1390100.

Perez, Ramona. 2004. "Practicing Theory through Women's Bodies: Public Violence and Women's Strategies of Power and Place." *Feminist Post-development Thought: Rethinking Modernity, Post-colonialism & Representation*. Edited by Kriemild Saunders, 263–280. New Delhi: Zubaan.

Pin-Fat, Véronique. 2013. "Cosmopolitanism and the End of Humanity: A Grammatical Reading of Posthumanism." *International Political Sociology* 7(3): 241–257.

Pinsky, Robert. 2002. "Eros against Esperanto." In *For Love of Country? Debating the Limits of Patriotism*. Edited by Joshua Cohen, 85–90. Boston: Beacon Press.

Pinto, Samantha. 2009. "Why Must All Girls Want to Be Flag Women?: Postcolonial Sexualities, National Reception, and Caribbean Soca Performance." *Meridians: Feminism, Race, Transnationalism* 10(1): 137–163.

Piu, Sreemoi Kundu. 2016. "How society made Apsara regret wanting to be transgender". *Daily O*. Last Modified 3/04/2016. http://www.dailyo.in/lifestyle/transgender-woman-apsara-reddy-gay-marriage-homosexuality-lgbt-section-377/story/1/9865.html

Powers, Martine. 2017. 'Leave Me Alone': Trinidad's women find a rallying cry for this year's Carnival. Retrieved from: https://www.washingtonpost.com/world/the_americas/leave-me-alone-trinidads-women-find-a-rallying-cry-for-this-years-carnival/2017/02/26/3888f116-f9e6-11e6-aa1e-5f735ee31334_story.html?utm_term=.fc16fe20fed2

Prabhu, Anjali. 2007. *Hybridity: Limits, Transformations, Prospects*. Albany: State University of New York.

Puri, Shalini. 2004. *The Caribbean Postcolonial: Social Equality, Post-nationalism, and Cultural Hybridity*. New York: Palgrave Macmillan.

Radhakrishnan, R. 1996. *Diasporic Mediations: Between Home and Location.* Minneapolis: University of Minnesota.

———. 2007. *Between Identity and Location: The Cultural Politics of Theory.* New Delhi: Orient Longman Private Limited.

Raghavan, Anjana. 2014. "The Fragmented Minor: Tamil Identity and the Politics of Authenticity." *Becoming Minority: How Discourses and Policies Produce Minorities in Europe and India.* Edited by Jyotirmaya Tripathy and Sudarsan Padmanabhan. New Delhi: Sage.

Ram, Kalpana. 2008. "'A New Consciousness Must Come': Affectivity and Movement in Tamil Dalit Women's Activist Engagement with Cosmopolitan Modernity." In *Anthropology and the New Cosmopolitanism: Rooted, Feminist and Vernacular Perspectives.* Edited by Pnina Werbner, 135–158. Oxford: Berg.

Ramgoonai, Drupatee. 1992. *Lick Down Me Nani (Careless Driver).* Spice Island Records.

Reddy, Apsara. 2012. "Being a Transexual." Last modified 11 June 2012. http://ori nam.net/being- a-transexual/.

Reddy, Gayathri. 2006. *With Respect to Sex: Negotiating Hijra Identity in South India.* New Delhi: Yoda Press.

Reed, T. J. 2011. "Germany: The Straggler as Leader." In *Enlightenment Cosmopolitanism.* Edited by David Adams and Galin Tihanov, 2–11. Leeds: Legenda.

Revathi, A. 2010. *The Truth about Me: A Hijra Life Story.* Translated by V. Geetha. New Delhi: Penguin Books.

Reyna, Stephen. 2011. "Heaven on Earth: The Rise and Fall and Rise and Fall and Rise Again of the Concept of Progress in Anglo-American Anthropology." In *Enlightenment Cosmopolitanism.* Edited by David Adams and Galin Tihanov, 110–132. Leeds: Legenda.

Ringrose, Kathryn M. 2003. *The Perfect Servant: Eunuchs and the Social Construction of Gender in Byzantium.* Chicago: University of Chicago,.

Robertson, Ritchie. 2011. "Cosmopolitanism, Patriotism and Nationalism in the German and Austrian Enlightenment." In *Enlightenment Cosmopolitanism.* Edited by David Adams and Galin Tihanov, 12–30. Leeds: Legenda.

Roy, Jeff. 2014. "A Photo Exclusive: Unveiling Koovagam." Last modified 30 July 2014. http://www.worldpolicy.org/blog/2014/07/30/photo-exclusive-unveil ing-koovagam.

Santos, B. De Sousa. 2001. "Nuestra America: Reinventing a Subaltern Paradigm of Recognition and Redistribution." *Theory, Culture & Society* 18(2–3): 185–217.

Singh, Sherry Ann. 2011. "Women in the Ramayana Tradition in Trinidad." In *Bindi: The Multifaceted Lives of Indo-Caribbean Women.* Edited by Rosanne Kanhai 21–51. Jamaica: The University of the West Indies Press.

Singh, Sherry Ann. 2013. "The Experience of Indian Indenture in Trinidad: Arrival and Settlement" in Cruse & Rhiney (Eds.), Caribbean Atlas. http://www.caribbean-atlas.com/en/themes/waves-of-colonization-and-control-in-the-caribbean/waves-of-colonization/the-experience-of-indian-indenture-in-trinidad-arrival-and-settle ment.html.

Sinnott, Megan. 2004. *Toms and Dees: Transgender Identity and Female Same-Sex Relationships in Thailand.* Honolulu: University of Hawaii.

Spivak, Gayatri Chakravorty. "Can the Subaltern Speak?" In Marxism and the Interpretation of Culture. Edited by Cary Nelson and Lawrence Grossberg, 271–313. Urbana: University of Illinois Press.

———. 1999. *A Critique of Postcolonial Reason: Toward a History of the Vanishing Present*. Cambridge, Massachusetts: Harvard University Press.

Srinivasan, Geeta. 1993. "The landscape of a body." *In Our Feet Walk the Sky: Women of the South Asian Diaspora*. Edited by Dharini Rasiah, Sheela Bhatt, Preety Kalra, Aarti Kohli, and Latika Malkani, 287–288. San Francisco: Aunt Lute.

Tejonmayam, U. 2015. "Fear of Sexual Assault Keeps Transgenders away from Koovagam." Last modified 4 May 2015. http://timesofindia.indiatimes.com/city/ chennai/Fear-of-sexual-assault-keeps-transgenders-away-from-Koovagam/article show/47143811.cms.

Tihanov, Galin. 2011. "Cosmopolitanism in the Discursive Landscape of Modernity: Two Enlightenment Articulations." In *Enlightenment Cosmopolitanism*. Edited by David Adams and Galin Tihanov, 133–152. Leeds: Legenda.

Towle, E.B., and Lynn M. Morgan. 2002. "Romancing the Transgender Native: Rethinking the Use of the 'Third Gender' Concept." *GLQ: A Journal of Lesbian and Gay Studies* 8(4): 469–497.

Tripathy, Jyotirmaya. 2014. "Biopolitics, Torture, and the Making of the Terrorist: An Essay on Un-moderning." *Social Semiotics* 24(2): 1–16.

Trotz, Alicia D. 2004. "Between Despair and Hope: Women and Violence in Contemporary Guyana." *Small Axe* 1st ser. 8(15): 1–20.

Turner, Victor. 1969. *The Ritual Process: Structure and Anti-Structure*. Chicago: Aldine Transaction.

Ung Loh, Jennifer. 2014. "Narrating Identity: the Employment of Mythological and Literary Narratives in Identity Formation among the Hijras of India." *Religion and Gender* 4(1): 21–39.

Vālmiki. 2000. *The Ramayana*. Translated by Arshia Sattar. New Delhi: Penguin.

Vasudevan, Aniruddhan, and Padma Govindan. 2010. "The Razor's Edge of Oppositionality: Exploring the Politics of Rights-Based Activism by Transgender Women in TamilNadu." In *Law Like Love: Queer Perspectives on the Law*. Edited by Arvind Narrain and Alok Gupta. New Delhi: Yoda Press.

Venkat, V. 2008. "From the Shadows." Last modified 16 February 2008. http://www. frontline.in/navigation/?type=static&page=flonnet&rdurl=fl2504/stories/ 20080229607610000.htm.

Vidya, Living Smile. 2007. *I am Vidya*. Translated by V. Ramnarayan. Chennai: Oxygen Books.

Vieten, Ulrike. 2012. *Gender and Cosmopolitanism in Europe: A Feminist Perspective*. Farnham: Ashgate.

Werbner, Pnina, ed. 2008. *Anthropology and the New Cosmopolitanism: Rooted, Feminist and Vernacular Perspectives*. Oxford: Berg.

Youssef, Valerie. 2011. "Finding Self in the Transition from East to West: Indo-Trinidadian Perspectives." In *Bindi: The Multifaceted Lives of Indo-Caribbean Women*. Edited by Rosanne Kanhai, 121–140. Jamaica: The University of the West Indies Press.

Appendices

APPENDIX A

Excerpt of the Supreme Court Judgement on Transgender Rights (*NALSA vs Union of India*) ruled by Justice K. S. Radhakrishnan and Justice A. K. Sikri in 2014.

(1) Hijras, Eunuchs, apart from binary gender, are required to be treated as 'third gender' for the purpose of safeguarding their rights. (2) Transgender persons' right to decide their self-identified gender is also upheld and the Centre and State Governments are directed to grant legal recognition of their gender identity such as male, female or as third gender. (3) We direct the Centre and the State Governments to take steps to treat them as socially and educationally backward classes of citizens and extend all kinds of reservation in cases of admission in educational institutions and for public appointments. (4) Centre and State Governments are directed to operate separate HIV Sero-surveillance Centres since Hijras/Transgenders face several sexual health issues.

(5) Centre and State Governments should seriously address the problems being faced by Hijras/Transgenders such as fear, shame, gender dysphoria, social pressure, depression, suicidal tendencies, social stigma, etc. and any insistence for SRS for declaring one's gender is immoral and illegal. (6) Centre and State Governments should take proper measures to provide medical care to TGs in the hospitals and also provide them separate public toilets and other facilities. (7) Centre and State Governments should also take steps for framing various social welfare schemes for their betterment.

(8) Centre and State Governments should take steps to create public awareness so that TGs will feel that they are also part and parcel of the social

life and be not treated as untouchables. (9) Centre and the State Governments should also take measures to regain their respect and place in the society which once they enjoyed in our cultural and social life.

Source: http://supremecourtofindia.nic.in/outtoday/wc40012.pdf

APPENDIX B

Section 377, IPC reads as follows:

"377. Unnatural offences. – Whoever voluntarily has carnal intercourse against the order of nature with any man, woman or animal, shall be punished with imprisonment for life, or with imprisonment of either description for a term which may extend to ten years, and shall also be liable to fine.

Explanation. – Penetration is sufficient to constitute the carnal intercourse necessary to the offence described in this section.

Source: http://www.lawyerscollective.org/vulnerable-communities/
lgbt/section-377

Index

Adeni, 80, 112
Affectionately, Apsara (TV programme), 106–7, 109–10, 116–17, 120n14
African communities, 122, 124, 129–33, 138–39, 144–45, 147, 152, 177, 180
Afro-Caribbean. *See* Caribbean communities
Agamben, Giorgio, 57–59, 62, 67, 160
Ahmed, Sarah, 16, 52
Amerindian culture, 69, 120n11, 143, 178, 180
anticolonialism, 41, 47–49, 59, 61, 172
anti-semitism, 57, 160, 164. *See also* Holocaust
Anzaldúa, Gloria, 178–83, 185, 193
Appiah, Kwame Anthony, 2, 28–36, 45, 99, 106, 109, 126, 185
Arjuna, 102–3

Bahadur, Gaiutra, 123, 134–35, 146, 152–54, 155n3
Bakhtin, Mikhail, 60–61, 137, 173
Beck, Ulrich, 35–38, 39, 44, 80, 106, 109, 128
Benhabib, Seyla, 2, 41
black communities, 22, 37, 59, 62, 77, 82, 87, 127–34, 143, 144, 146, 167, 169, 175–76, 178

blackness, 130–31, 169
Black Water. See *Kālā Pāni*
bodyscapes, 4, 9, 67
border cosmopolitamisms, 44–45, 47–48, 126, 134
border gnoseology, 165, 168–69, 178
British Raj. *See* India: colonial
Buddhism, 101, 179
Butler, Judith, 33, 38, 44–45, 77, 94, 97

Caliban, 49, 123, 143, 167, 172. *See also* Shakespeare
Calypso (musical sub-genre), 136, 138. *See also* Caribbean communities: Chutney-Soca
Caribbean communities, 11, 49, 119, 121–24, 127–46, 150–54, 155n2, 158, 161, 172, 180, 183–5; Chutney-Soca (musical sub-genre), 126, 136, 138–39, 141–42; Trinidad, 127–28, 130–31, 133, 136–37, 139–41, 146, 148–50, 152, 191–92
Carnival, 60–61, 92, 126–27, 137–38, 150, 192. *See also* Caribbean communities
Cartesianism, 7–8, 52, 63–64, 66–69, 72–74, 125, 177, 180. *See also* Descartes, Rene

About the Author

Dr. Anjana Raghavan is Senior Lecturer in Sociology in the Department of Psychology, Sociology and Politics at Sheffield Hallam University. Her teaching and research interests include decolonial feminisms, and socio-political formations and performances of love. She is also interested in the production and decolonization of social and cultural theory. Her enduring research and teaching hopes are to create radical, compassionate spaces of conversation and action, in decolonial and free knowledge communities.

Lightning Source UK Ltd.
Milton Keynes UK
UKOW04n1439230118

316696UK00001B/79/P